DIARIES
OF A
YOUNG
POET

RAINER MARIA RILKE

In translations by M. D. HERTER NORTON
Letters to a Young Poet
Sonnets to Orpheus
Wartime Letters of Rainer Maria Rilke
Translations from the Poetry of Rainer Maria Rilke
The Lay of the Love and Death of Cornet Christopher Rilke
The Notebooks of Malte Laurids Brigge
Stories of God

Translated by JANE BANNARD GREENE and M. D. HERTER NORTON
Letters of Rainer Maria Rilke
Volume One, 1892–1910   Volume Two, 1910–1926

Translated by DAVID YOUNG
Duino Elegies

In Various Translations
Rilke on Love and Other Difficulties
Translations and Considerations of Rainer Maria Rilke
Compiled by JOHN J. L. MOOD

RAINER MARIA RILKE

DIARIES OF A YOUNG POET

TRANSLATED AND ANNOTATED BY
EDWARD SNOW AND MICHAEL WINKLER

■ ■ ■

W. W. Norton & Company   New York   London

For information about permission to reproduce selections from this book, write to Permissions, W. W. Norton & Company, Inc., 500 Fifth Avenue, New York, NY 10110.

The text of this book is composed in Garamond
with the display set in Thermo
Composition and manufacturing by the Haddon Craftsmen, Inc.
Book design by Guenet Abraham

Library of Congress Cataloging-in-Publication Data

Rilke, Rainer Maria, 1875–1926.
  [Tagebücher aus der Frühzeit. English]
  Diaries of the young poet / Rainer Maria Rilke ; translated by
Edward Snow and Michael Winkler.
      p.   cm.
  Includes bibliographical references and index.
  ISBN 0-393-04553-6
  1. Rilke, Rainer Maria, 1875–1926—Diaries.   2. Authors,
German—20th century—Diaries.   I. Snow, Edward A.   II. Winkler,
Michael, 1937–   .   III. Title.
PT2635.I65Z47513   1997
838' .91203—dc21
  [B]   97-10132
                                                        CIP

ISBN 0-393-31850-8 pbk.

W. W. Norton & Company, Inc., 500 Fifth Avenue, New York, N.Y. 10110
http://www.wwnorton.com

W. W. Norton & Company Ltd., 10 Coptic Street, London WC1A 1PU

  3 4 5 6 7 8 9 0

⫼ CONTENTS ⫼

The illustrations will be found following page 138.

‖ INTRODUCTION ‖

Between 15 april 1898 and 22 december 1900 Rainer Maria Rilke wrote three diaries that span a crucial period in his artistic growth. At the beginning of this phase the young poet had perfected, if not yet exhausted, the rhetorical techniques and mannerisms of his early, impressionistic style. His verse was still prone to the gossamer and was given more to a flirtation than a sustained artistic engagement with the exquisite and the delicate. Thus it often enough veiled its extraordinary sensitivity to nuances of mood and perception in an ethereality that could easily slide into preciosity and tended to sacrifice simplicity and clarity of purpose to this very perfection of a method. But Rilke had come to realize only too well that he needed to constrain his busy games of make-believe and learn how to control his ingenious lyricism. This made it necessary, most of all, to free himself from the rapturous self-indulgence that could spin mellifluous lines and intricate rhymes with prolific ease. He had to submit himself to the kind of self-discipline that comes with the ascetic solitude of regular, arduous work.

Rilke's three early diaries reflect this search for a language that might capture the specificity of things natural and crafted and at the same time convey their intrinsic spirituality. They chronicle, in other words, the emergence of the "sachliche Sagen," the objective and visually precise language that will come to characterize his "poetry of things." At the same time they are very different books. Each has a distinct rhetorical style and a persuasive purpose of its own. Yet they complement each other, even as they confound our expectation that they might reveal intimate details from the poet's daily affairs. Rilke's diaries do maintain a certain chronological flow, albeit one with breaks and longer interruptions, but they are not directly the immediate account of a specific time; it is not their intent to record the minutiae of day-to-day life. For this reason, they have not become identified by their chronology. Rather, they are usually titled after three places where Rilke lived and, at least for a time, felt at home: Florence (and the Tuscan countryside), the village of Schmargendorf just outside of Berlin, and Worpswede, an artists' colony in the moors near Bremen.

Yet each of these places also marks a significant turning point, one that may be identified by a personal crisis to which Rilke responded, as he was wont to do throughout his life, with a sudden flight. These precipitous departures (in two instances immediately preceded by rapturous expressions of at-homeness) are impossible to reduce to a single cause. This is especially true of his sudden decision to leave Florence for Viareggio. The justification he gives for this unsettling retreat—his disgust with riotous youths throwing stones into the Loggia dei Lanzi—surely hides more than it explains and leaves unarticulated (in a diary of all places) what must have been a painful blow to his sense of self-worth as a poet.[1] His abrupt departure for Worpswede (halfway through the Schmargendorf Diary) was no doubt motivated in part by tensions in his relationship with Lou Andreas-Salomé that had intensified toward the end of their trip to Russia, and his equally headlong return to Schmargendorf (halfway through the Worpswede Diary) must have had something to do with the news of Paula Becker's secret engagement to her teacher and their mutual friend, Otto Modersohn. These spontaneous moves signal reversals and ruptures in Rilke's private affairs that have shaped the particular character of these three diaries. But the precise manner in which the concatenation of impulses and reasons worked as a motivating force remains elusive and perhaps was not clear even to the diarist himself.

That we should have "diaries" from Rilke in any form is on first consideration surprising. Rilke was as averse to publishing anything autobiographical as he was to exposing the fragility of his mental constitution in a confessional *poésie du coeur*. He was more likely to seek a sense of calm maturity, which he considered the disposition necessary for beginning a diary, by honing his talent for precise observation and visually vivid depiction. He also had become aware of how strongly his writing needed to reach a responsive companion. This dialogic urge makes its presence felt more as an animating, compulsive energy than as an argumentative voice with fixed convictions. It is a significant and underappreciated aspect of his art. Perhaps even more openly than in his letters, its prevalence is evident in the rhetorical structure of these other-oriented diaries.

The person to stimulate this kind of discursive sociability in Rilke was a woman nearly fifteen years his senior, Lou Andreas-Salomé. When Rilke met her she was already an accomplished writer with a considerable reputation that derived from perceptive books on Ibsen and Nietzsche, from a variety of essays on contemporary issues, and from her fictional work, much of it an "autobiographical" exploration of female psychology.[2] Rilke approached her with subtle determination, first by sending her poems anonymously, then with an epistolary masterpiece of seductive insinuation (dated 13 March 1897) that speaks of their shared interest in the workings of religious creativity. When they met, on 12 May 1897, she was thirty-six, he, twenty-two. They were attracted to each other at first sight, discreetly became lovers, and remained close companions for nearly three years. Their attachment survived Rilke's marriage to Clara Westhoff and endured as an ever deepening friendship for the rest of their lives. It was a liaison that also yielded what is perhaps Rilke's single most important correspondence.

It was under Lou's tutelage that René became the poet Rainer Maria Rilke. She made him shed the eccentricities of the young genius, and curtail his propensity for turning everything about and around his own person into quickly improvised verse. Her own mental regimen included keeping a diary, as an incentive to formulate impressions and remembrances accurately and as a way of communicating with a soul mate during and after a temporary separation. She had recorded, for example, her conversations with Nietzsche in

1882 in a journal written specifically for her friend Paul Rée, and unlike Rilke, she wrote a diary of their travels through Russia during July 1900.

When she sent Rilke off to Florence in April 1898—ostensibly so that he might experience on his own, directly and differently, what his assiduous studies of Italian art had prepared him to see—it was with the understanding that he would bring her back a diary. It is impossible to say, however, exactly what kind of a diary she encouraged, or perhaps even commissioned, Rilke to write. Was it to be a specific, coherently inclusive description of how the city's historical ambience and its prominent as well as ubiquitous works of art affected him? A refined travelogue that would show Rilke's control over a bewildering variety of impressions? Did she also expect a penetrating account of his social experiences, especially those with connoisseurs of art, that might challenge and sharpen his own perceptions? Was it to be a self-analytical record, a probing of his responses to conflicting stimuli and unique encounters for the purpose of clarifying the complex interaction of his senses and psyche with an objective reality that is constantly in flux? We are left with little more than speculations. But it is very likely that Rilke had to overcome, at least initially, strong misgivings about the (conventional) diary as a literary genre, that he had doubts, at least, about the apparent randomness of its material and about the unpolished spontaneity of its style.[3]

It is certain, however, that Rilke arrived in Florence both with a burden of learned ballast and with the need to find his own ambitions for contemporary poetry, and indeed for culture, confirmed in the art of the early Renaissance. He felt so closely akin to its "festiveness" and to its "springtime" splendor, to the promise of its exuberant beauty, that he soon dropped the protective guise of the shy initiate and gave in to his desire to absorb as much aesthetic pleasure as he could. In his diaristic ruminations and musings on art he radiates enthusiastic convictions or speculations, some with the self-evident falsity of aphoristic generalizations, a few with the oracular overbearingness and convolution of prophetic or vatic pronouncements, and not a small number of them taken from current discussions and sharpened with his own nuances.

But it is less instructive to trace the provenance of these notions than to observe how skillful Rilke can already be in his shaping of an authentic voice, one that does not become so private and egotistically esoteric (or sublime) as to lose its ability to persuade. It is equally revealing to notice how much spontaneous delight Rilke took in visual impressions, in paintings and sculpture and unusual places, how intensely he pays attention to gesture and intonation, how flashes of characterization build up a general atmosphere, how precisely he captures an instance and seizes its emotional tenor. His imagination was not sparked by what he might learn from retracing the processes of history. Great personages fascinated him, but he found little of interest in the evolution and passing of time, which he saw only as decline and loss.

But it comes as a surprise nonetheless that (modern) Florence soon overwhelmed Rilke and even turned into a labyrinthine threat from which he had to escape before he could fully enjoy and take in anew what he had come to savor with such avid intensity. Whatever may have been his reasons, Rilke departed much earlier than he had planned. And if he did not flee in a panic, then certainly it was at least with the need to regain his composure. Viareggio, an elegant resort up the coast a short distance from Florence but virtually deserted in May, offered him the respite of solitude and of communion with a tranquil nature.

Rilke must have anticipated a joyful reunion with Lou Andreas-Salomé. Yet their meeting, in the Baltic sea resort of Zoppot, turned into a disappointment. At least so the ambivalent apologia suggests that Rilke added to his Tuscan reflections on 6 July 1898. It is a jarringly saddened—and powerfully written—coda to so confident a profession of his accomplishment and maturity, which he had hoped would find appreciative acceptance. There is no clear indication why and how Lou failed to satisfy his expectations for her as the single intimate reader of his book. But her reaction, whatever the justification or misunderstanding behind it, must have been so profoundly disturbing that Rilke could only respond with a lamentful self-vindication that leaves much unsaid and the cause for his unhappiness obscure.

We also have no external information that would explain Rilke's motivation to start a second diary once he was back in Schmargendorf. Did Lou encourage him to continue, with new emphases and in a different style? Even though she is addressed at the second diary's outset, she is no longer the center of its attention and the personal confidant of its concerns; and thus she fades more and more as its addressee. It may well be that Rilke also wrote his second diary specifically for Lou. But this new book, which contains material written in Schmargendorf and in Worpswede, has a different purpose than the Tuscan apothegms and impressions. The Schmargendorf Diary reflects Rilke's attempt to transform his experiences and feelings, both new themes or sensations and recurring obsessions, into stories, to change the inward news of emotions and imaginings into sustained narratives. After a transitional introduction, we have, then, first a sequence of novellas and tales, some fully developed and poignant, one brilliantly shocking, others little more than fleeting episodes. With the shift to Worpswede, this series of independent single works gives way to the personal stories he writes down as the communal remembrances that his new friends have told him about each other. These stories, in turn, blend in with Rilke's own encounters, conversations, infatuations, and intensely visual "Worpswedean" impressions. Recollections of things done, descriptions of new experiences, and the evocation of a remarkably variegated nature alternate and work together to create an interplay of voices and a sociable atmosphere that imbues the words said and the things told with an abiding intensity of presence. This immediacy of experience had to have been felt as life, perhaps daily life, before its core could be chiseled further into the order of poems.

The Worpswede Diary captures this refinement of communal narration into lyrical verse, its predominant mode of expression. It has a slower, more private, and self-absorbed momentum, a stronger involvement with the writer's inner life. There is also a relaxation both of narrative and of reflective intensity, at times almost a casual attitude with its disregard of firm structure. The first impression is one of fragmentary, even disjointed arbitrariness. But there is also an underlying assurance—or need to believe—that everyday occurrences and things may yield a meaningful purpose, that they can embody a significance within and beyond their outward presence. A waterwand that fails in its practical purpose (p. 201) becomes a thing with its "potential" still inside it, and thus can be saved up for some future Rilkean expedition. At present, though, these "hours when I am full of images" (p. 241) are his most satisfying time. It is only to be expected, therefore, that many of the Worpswede poems are "occasional" pieces actuated by something personal and grounded in particular incidents.

Rilke acknowledged that he had learned how to observe the phenomena of nature, the "things" all around him, much more perspicaciously when he followed the guidance of two young artists especially, who had become his favorite companions and the twin objects of his infatuation in Worpswede: the sculptor Clara Westhoff and the painter Paula Becker. They taught him to recognize, even in apparently so simple, stark, and almost primitive a landscape as that of the moors, the ubiquity of specific images, of *Bilder* as the stuff from which paintings and sculpture are made. They also made him aware that he should no longer treat nature as little more than an extension of or setting for his own feelings. It is true that Rilke was not untouched by the neoromantic passion for nature as an élan vital, even though he never wrote what may conventionally be called "nature poems." Yet in Worpswede he came to appreciate a "selfless" participation in nature, one that heightened the daily alertness and attentiveness of his senses turned outward. He was amazed at his own increasing ability both to look unsparingly into his own self and to "look away from himself" and not to fear that he was constantly being watched by his own or someone else's observing eyes.

It is a quality of self-understanding and of objective perception, keen in its attention to details and alert to their symbolical relevance for wider contexts, that had earlier attracted Rilke to the works of Jens Peter Jacobsen. What impressed him especially was the elegant precision with which this Danish writer evoked a finely nuanced complexity in human behavior and in a social environment. When he himself was beginning to trust in his ability to perceive "things" the way a painter and a sculptor does, he was able to see in Rodin's work an altogether new way of structuring space and arranging the images of human interaction. Rilke's reflections in the last two diaries on Rodin's sculpture legitimate his claim—far more convincingly than his concluding admiration for Gerhart Hauptmann's rather mediocre play about the painter Michael Kramer—that his stay in Worpswede had developed from a diverting episode into an important apprenticeship time—a time that prepared him for Paris and made possible the *New Poems* as well as *The Notebooks of Malte Laurids Brigge.*

Rilke wrote these diaries of his early years in dialogue with a beloved mentor. They were not intended for publication, but they are clearly a part of his poetic oeuvre. He must have valued especially the Florence diary, since he had it bound—we do not know exactly when—in white patent leather embossed with the city's heraldic lily. His daughter Ruth and her husband Carl Sieber first edited and published the three diaries in 1942 as *Tagebücher aus der Frühzeit* (Diaries from the early years). This 1942 edition, reprinted without textual emendations in 1973, makes no claims to being a work of philological scholarship. But it is at present the only accessible text.[4] We have followed it even where, on occasion, there is reason to doubt its accuracy. Misprints and obvious errors have been corrected without comment, along with Rilke's faulty spelling of non-German names. For greater ease and clarity we have placed all dates at the beginning of the respective entry. And "*Diaries of a Young Poet,*" it should be emphasized, is an editorial invention, our own title for this English translation of Rilke's three untitled books.

Our translation of the diaries seeks to stay as close to the stylistic individuality of the original as the different structure and rhetorical traditions of English will accomodate. We have tried to present a "congenial" version. Thus we interfere as little as possible with Rilke's language, i.e., with a personal literary idiom that can seem obtuse, portentously vague, or fussy and pretentious, and then a moment later achieve a delicateness, clarity, and imaginative vigor, a focused precision, a subtle variability of expressive strategies, and a richness of suggestive nuances that often enough defy attempts to find a complementary equivalent in English. During his early years, the poet Rilke never felt the attractions of experimental or radically innovative writing of the kind the Expressionist generation practiced. In that sense he was conservative. But he expanded the compass of poetic German to its very limits by turning the cadences and semantic possibilities of a highly refined conversational mode of writing into art.

The *Diaries* provides more than early glimpses of this style. To find equivalents for his unobtrusive neologisms, for his tight as well as dense abstractions, for his shifts in rhythm, timing, and emphasis, for the wide range of his sound effects, for the synaesthetic coloring of his vocabulary—all this presents a constant challenge to the translator, and can easily turn into a provocation to reinvent English in Rilkean terms.

This is especially true of Rilke's verse. The prosodic ease and agility of his poems slip away from any attempt to force them into matching forms in English. His formal dexterity, the fluid weave of his images, and his unmistakable tone—languid and yet fully alert to its own tensions—at times display their ingenuity too freely, to the detriment of his poetry as art rather than skillful show. But they do entice the translator to enter into their carefully choreographed dance with the confidence of fascinated innocence, until he falters with clumsy turns and distracting flourishes, once and again, and soon finds himself out of step altogether. We have found it advisable, therefore, to let the exact cast of Rilke's meanings, variable as they are with each new context, guide the translation, inevitably at the expense of his rich sound and rhymes. Rilke was, after all, the only one of his readers resourceful enough to reproduce Rilke's style successfully.

We would like to thank Jill Bialosky for her encouragement, support, and above all for her patience with this project. Our thanks also to Ernst Stahl and Ralph Freedman for their generous advice. Our greatest debt is to Terry Munisteri, who shepherded this manuscript through every phase of its production with insight and care.

NOTES

1. The diary does not mention a chance meeting in the Boboli Gardens with the severely self-disciplined poet Stefan George (1868–1933),

the mentor of a carefully chosen circle of artists and, since 1892, the editor of a privately printed journal, *Blätter für die Kunst,* to which Rilke had offered contributions. But in a letter to Friedrich Oppeln-Bronikowski, dated 29 May 1907, Rilke recalls, still with obvious discomfort, how George reproached him for having published too much poetry prematurely, without discriminating between his good and his bad verse, and how he (Rilke) could only meekly assent to the older poet's criticism. The occasion must have been a traumatic one for the insecure young poet.

2. For a more elaborate account of Lou Andreas-Salomé's life and accomplishments, see the biographical sketch (pp. 277–79) that prefaces the notes to the Florence Diary. Following this introduction there is also a detailed chronology of Lou's relationship with Rilke during the period the diaries span.

3. As late as 1913, in a conversation with Stefan Zweig, Rilke mentions how difficult he still finds it, even in a letter, to write with a visual objectivity ("gegenständlich") equal to his perception of things. He goes on to say that he therefore avoids diaries, and instead records key moments and encounters in small notebooks he carries with him wherever he goes. (See Stefan Zweig, *Tagebücher,* Frankfurt am Main: S. Fischer, 1984, p. 54.)

4. Rilke's diaries were not included in his *Sämtliche Werke* (1955–66), edited by Ernst Zinn, nor in the annotated edition in four volumes of 1996. The original manuscripts are kept at the Biblioteka Jagiellonska in Cracow (Poland) and are not available even for scholarly work.

CHRONOLOGY

1897

APRIL: Rilke (age twenty-two), in Munich since September 1896 as a "student of philosophy," returns from a trip to Arco (near Lake Garda in the southern Tyrol), Venice, Meran, and Konstanz; later in the month Lou Andreas-Salomé (age thirty-six) arrives in Munich from her home in Schmargendorf.

12 MAY: RMR is introduced to LAS and her close friend Frieda von Bülow (1873–1934), a novelist and companion of Carl Peters, the highly controversial propagandist for German colonization in East Africa, where Frieda managed a plantation. Their meeting takes place at the home of the novelist Jakob Wassermann (1873–1934). RMR is immediately infatuated, and the next day he writes his first letter to LAS, in which he tells her of the profound effect her essay "Jesus der Jude" (Jesus the Jew) in the April 1896 issue of *Neue Deutsche Rundschau* had made on him.

17 MAY: RMR and LAS arrange to meet again, at which time he reads to her three poems from his "like-minded" work in progress, *Visions of Christ.* He inscribes a poem ("Das log das Mittelalter") into a copy of his collection *Traumgekrönt* (1896) and presents it to

her with the dedication "To Frau Lou Andreas-Salomé with gratitude that I was allowed to meet her!"

26 MAY: RMR writes the first of some one hundred love poems to LAS. He would collect them in a manuscript *Dir zur Feier* (In celebration of you) but then refrain from publishing them at her request.

31 MAY: RMR and LAS make a two-day excursion to the village of Wolfratshausen south of Munich near Lake Starnberg in search of a retreat near the mountains for a longer sojourn. During this trip they almost certainly become lovers.

14 JUNE: LAS and F. von Bülow move to Wolfratshausen; RMR first lives in nearby Dorfen before he joins them at the "Lutzhäuser" and, toward the end of July, moves with them to a different house they call "Loufried." The Munich architect August Endell is a frequent visitor. During this "bohemian" period of rustic simplicity RMR, at LAS's urging, changes his first name from "René" to "Rainer." When Friedrich Carl Andreas, LAS's husband since 1887 and a lecturer at the Institute for Oriental Languages in Berlin, joins them (23 July–29 August), RMR leaves for Munich but returns after a week's absence on 1 August. He begins to study Italian Renaissance art.

1 OCTOBER: LAS returns to Berlin, accompanied by RMR who takes up residence there (Berlin-Wilmersdorf, Im Rheingau 8). He enrolls in art history courses at the university, studies Italian, and makes the acquaintance of various poets and writers, among them Stefan George, Carl Hauptmann, and Richard Dehmel. He continues to write poems, novellas, and short plays.

1898

FEBRUARY–MARCH: RMR and LAS decide he should visit Florence to study Renaissance art firsthand. LAS is to join him there later after she sees to family affairs. (Some biographers speculate that LAS arranged this separation in order to secretly terminate a pregnancy.) They plan the trip elaborately together, and LAS instructs RMR to keep a diary, which she will read on their reunion.

APRIL–MAY: Traveling via Arco, RMR arrives in Florence during the first week of April. There the Swiss art collector Gustav Scheeli introduces him to Heinrich Vogeler. He also meets the poets Stefan George and Rudolf Borchardt. In the middle of May RMR departs abruptly for Viareggio, a seaside resort town directly west of Florence, where he stays until the end of May.

15 APRIL: *First dated entry in the Florence Diary.*

JUNE: RMR travels via Vienna and Prague (where he visits his parents) to Wilmersdorf (8 June) and almost immediately on to Zoppot (Baltic Sea), where LAS joins him after visiting Johanna Niemann in Danzig. Their stay together in Zoppot, fraught with tension and frequently interrupted by LAS's trips to friends as far away as St. Petersburg, lasts until the end of July.

6 JULY: *Final dated entry in the Florence Diary.*

11 JULY: *First dated entry in the Schmargendorf Diary.*

31 JULY: RMR and LAS travel from Zoppot to Schmargendorf, where he lives until mid-October 1900 in a rented room (villa "Waldfrieden" in Hundekehlstrasse 11) close to her residence. RMR adopts a regimen that includes daily chores in the Andreas household, barefoot walks in the woods, and a vegetarian diet. He begins to study Russian at the university.

19 DECEMBER: Heinrich Vogeler invites RMR to visit him in Worpswede. After stops in Hamburg and at the house of Vogeler's parents in Bremen (to celebrate Christmas), RMR and Vogeler proceed to Worpswede on 25 December. RMR makes a brief stay there before returning to Berlin.

1899

8 MARCH: RMR announces to Helene Voronina a forthcoming trip to Russia in the company of the Andreases.

18 MARCH: RMR returns from a visit with his mother at Arco and Bozen. In Vienna, accompanied by Arthur Schnitzler, he attends the

premiere of two verse plays by Hugo von Hofmannsthal that leave a strong impression on him. He arrives back in Schmargendorf on 17 April.

EASTER, 1899–AUGUST 1900: RMR is officially enrolled as a student of art history at the University of Berlin.

25 APRIL: RMR, LAS, and F. C. Andreas leave for their trip to Russia, principally to Moscow and St. Petersburg; they return to Schmargendorf on 28 June.

29 JULY: RMR joins LAS and Frieda von Bülow in a small country house on the Bibersberg (Thuringia) that Princess Marie von Meiningen has made available to them. They immerse themselves in Russian studies, which RMR continues at the university after his return to Berlin on 12 September.

20 SEPTEMBER–14 OCTOBER: RMR, now in Schmargendorf, writes the first version of the "Book of a Monk's Life," his poetic impression of the Russian journey. These poems would become the first section of *The Book of Hours,* published by Rilke in 1905.

3 NOVEMBER: RMR resumes his Schmargendorf diary and intensifies his studies of Russian literature and art.

1900

3 MARCH: RMR writes to Leonid Pasternak about his plan for a series of monographs on Russian artists (Ivanov, Kramskoy).

MARCH: RMR reads Nietzsche's *The Birth of Tragedy* and translates Chekov's *The Seagull;* this manuscript is now considered lost.

7 MAY–24 AUGUST: RMR's second Russian journey, this time alone with LAS. They travel from Berlin via Warsaw to Moscow; from Moscow south to Tula to visit Tolstoy at Yasnaya Polyana (1 June); then to Kiev and Kremenchug on the lower Dnieper, through the Poltava region by train to Kharkov, Voronezh, and Saratov; by steamship up the Volga to Kazan, Nizhni Novgorod (now Gorki), and Yaroslavl. From Moscow to the village of Nisovka to meet the

peasant poet Spiridon Droshin, and to nearby Novinki to meet the poet Nikolai Tolstoy. Via Novgorod Velikiye to St. Petersburg, where RMR resumes his studies of Russian art, while LAS travels to Rongas (Finland) to visit relatives.

26 AUGUST: They arrive back in Berlin; the next day RMR travels to Worpswede (LAS has made prior arrangements for him to stay there), where he lives in Vogeler's house, "Barkenhoff."

26 SEPTEMBER: *Final dated entry in the Schmargendorf Diary.*

27 SEPTEMBER: *First dated entry in the Worpswede Diary.*

5 OCTOBER: RMR abruptly leaves Worpswede, and moves into a new apartment in Schmargendorf (Misdroyerstrasse 1). He lives there until mid-February 1901 and renews his friendship with LAS under strained circumstances.

12 NOVEMBER: Paula Becker informs Rilke of her engagement to Otto Modersohn.

22 DECEMBER: *Final entry in the Worpswede Diary.*

1901

JANUARY–EARLY FEBRUARY: first Paula, then Clara Westhoff as well visit RMR frequently in Schmargendorf. 16 February: Clara and RMR inform Paula of their engagement.

26 FEBRUARY: LAS issues to Rilke her "Last Appeal," a long, angry, hurtful (but obviously anguished and concerned) letter expressing grave dismay at RMR's decision to marry, describing his psychological affliction to him in great detail, and releasing both of them to their own separate futures.

29 APRIL: RMR and Clara marry in Bremen and move to Westerwede.

25 MAY: Paula and Modersohn marry in Worpswede despite her new-formed misgivings.

12 DECEMBER: Rilke's and Clara's daughter, Ruth, is born.

THE
FLORENCE
DIARY

All mankind love a lover.

—Emerson

I'm only he who sets the course in motion.

All who go in beauty
will resurrect in beauty . . .

Our will is only a gusting wind
that turns us and urges us,
for in our most fervent longings
we are a field in bloom.

. . . and then I can only keep silent
and breathe—slow, deep breaths.

I simply experiment, an endless seeker
with no past at my back.

—Emerson

"Something simple, beautiful, with a
broad blue sky over it."

—Lou

Florence, 15 April 1898

FROM our winter-shaped terrain
I've been cast far out, into spring;
as I hesitate at its edge
the new land lays itself lustrously
into my wavering hands.

And I take the beautiful gift,
want to mold it quietly,
unfold all its colors
and hold it, full of shyness,
up toward YOU.

I CAN only keep silent and gaze . . .
Could I once also sound?
And the hours are women
who spoil me with all kinds of
blue, shimmering delight.

Shall I tell you of my crowded days
or of my place of sleep?
My desires run riot
and out of all paintings
the angels follow me.

Florence, 16 April 1898

HERE is life's quiet place of sacrifice.
Here day is still deep. Here night builds up
around dreams like a baptistery.
Here life nurtured all its heart and brilliance
and here all was presentiment of its might:
the women's festiveness, the princes' grandeur,
the Madonnas that thankfulness conceived,
and a monk's trembling in his cell . . .

RENAISSANCE I

A deeper hush enwrapped the man of thorns,
fainter and fainter grew his pain.
And the folk were freed to live in joy:
solitary iron-willed figures raised strength's
red banner on the battlements of time.

In white robes they all embark
farther into life and find that land
shimmering with a sense of things to come.
The only one of them already weary—
the Madonna—rests for a moment at its edge.

Florence, 18 April 1898

AND shall I tell you how my day rolls by?
Early on I make my way through shining streets
to palaces where hourly my soul broadens,
and then I mingle in the open squares
with swarthy folk amid their wildest clamor.

Middays I worship in the hall of paintings
before Madonnas of bright noble grace.
And later on, when I leave this holy room,
dusk will have covered Arno valley,
and I become silent, become slowly tired,
and paint myself a God in gold . . .

Florence, 18 April 1898

THAT was a late suffusion in the sun
after a day passed in pale unease;
I don't know where the radiance began,
yet suddenly everything was rich,—
as if in all churches at the same moment
the Madonnas had deigned to smile.

San Domenico near Fiesole, 19 April 1898

RENAISSANCE II

Faith then was not that dreamlike timidity
where all would fold their fingers out of fear,—
it was a hearkening, and love made them
pray pictures and build prayers.

When one felt deep inside: something's growing,—
he delved down into his quiet germination
and joyfully found the god prepared;
he raised the hidden one up out of his doubt
and lifted him, trembling, into glory.

WHETHER I HAVE COME FAR ENOUGH YET AND POSSESS
the calm to begin this diary I want to bring home to You—I cannot
say. But I know that my joy will seem far-off and unfestive as long as
You—at least through some candid, deep-felt inscription of it into a
book all Your own—do not share in it. And so I begin; and I take it
as a good omen that I commence this confirmation of my longing in
these days that by a year's length follow those when, with kindred
longing, I walked toward something vague and uncertain and didn't
know yet that You are the fulfillment for which I was preparing myself in songs of intense listening.

These past fourteen days I have been living in Florence.

At the Lungarno Serristori, not far from the Ponte alle Grazie, stands
the house whose flat roof—both its closed-in part and its part wide-
open to the sky—is mine. The room itself is actually no more than
the vestibule (it also includes the stairwell leading up from the third
floor), and the living quarter proper consists of the high, wide stone
terrace that indeed seems to me so splendid now that I could easily
take up residence here and even receive a cherished guest in proper
style. My room's outer wall is blooming everywhere with yellow roses,
their fragrance at full strength, and with little yellow flowers that are
not unlike wild hedge roses, except that they climb the high trellises
more quietly and obediently, two by two, rather like the angels of Fra
Fiesole bringing recompense and songs of praise for the Last Judg-

ment. In stone bins before these walls many pansies have awakened, and they follow the rousing and resting of my days like warm, watchful eyes. I wish I could always be such that my ways would need never startle them, and that I would seem to them, at least in my deepest hours, a being long their kin, whose final faith is a festive and lucid springtime and far behind it a heavy, beautiful fruit.—But how much does the splendor of this one wall pale before the bright magnificence of the three other sides, in front of which the landscape itself hangs, wide, warm, a bit stylized due to the weakness of my eye, which is unable to recognize more than harmonies of colors and sums of lines. Rich at morning in the glory of a hundred hopes, almost flickering from impatient expectation, rich at noon, sated, heavy with so many gifts, and rich with simple clarity and holy highness in the waning sounds of dusk. It's then that the sky becomes like blue steel and the many things hone themselves on it. The towers seem to rise out of the waves of the cupolas more slenderly, and the battlements of the Palace of the Signoria are as if hardened in their age-old defiance. Until the stillness blankets itself in stars and the mild light assuages everything again with its soft, hesitant tenderness. The great turning-quiet rolls over streets and squares like a high tide in which everything, after a brief struggle, goes under—and at last only a dialogue remains, a to-and-fro of twilight questions and dark answers, a broad murmuring of complementary sounds: the Arno and the Night. Longing is most intense around this time; and if then, deep below, some dreamer happens to improvise a melancholy song on his mandolin, no one would think to ascribe it to a human being; one would feel how it rises directly from this wide landscape that can no longer keep silent in its strange, yearning bliss. It sings like a solitary woman who deep in night sounds the name of her far-off beloved and tries to urge into this poor narrow word all her tenderness and her fervor and all the treasures of her deep being.

Most decorative, though, are the red evenings. Above the Cascine the last, dying blaze still glows, and the Ponte Vecchio, its old houses stuck to it like nests, threads like a black ribbon through silk yellow as the sun. In reconciled shades of brown and gray the city spreads out, and the mountains of Fiesole are already wearing the colors of the night. San Miniato al Monte alone still has sun in its dear simple visage, and I am always prompt to be there to fetch its last smile as a gentle, perfectly concluding grace.

It may surprise You that in Florence nothing as yet has come forth in me but the few insignificant poems that precede these lines. That's because in the beginning I was not alone. During the first two days Dr. L., the correspondent from Paris, was kind enough to look after me and help me find various things, even though his strict demeanor checked every mood that welled up in me. Then, as soon as I had taken up lodgings in the boarding house, it turned out that Endell's cousin, Professor B. from Berlin, was my neighbor, and owing to this surprise henceforth the afternoons at least belonged to him and his wife and the three of us together. Not that I would count these hours among my losses, rich as they were due to the generous kindness of these two good people—but they were without that resonance that extends beyond the present moment. However, it was not just the many people who caused my silence. It was much more the many things. Even though Florence lay spread out before me so widely and invitingly (perhaps just for that reason), I felt at first so confused that I could scarcely separate my impressions, and thought I was drowning in the breaking waves of some foreign splendor. It is only now that I begin to catch my breath. Memories are becoming clearer and distinct from one another. I feel what has been left in my nets and realize that it is more than I expected. I know what has remained my possession and piece by piece I want to spread it out before Your dear lucid eyes. In all ease and comfort, without rushing You from place to place and without trying to be exhaustive, I will show You this and this, tell You what it means to me, and then put it all back among my other things. Whether I will give You a picture of Florence this way—I cannot say; for what I bring You is only, I know, something quintessentially mine; and indeed it now belongs to me and no longer to the bright City of Lilies; this piece of myself, at any rate, I have found in Florence, and that itself cannot be accidental. And besides, You wouldn't expect from me some travelers' handbook, some complete collection, omitting nothing and arranged in strict chronological sequence—would You?

My first evening here and its impact on me remain closest to my memory. Despite my weariness after a trip of many hours, all of them to be endured miserably atop suitcases, I left my hotel and walked down the narrow streets as dusk gathered, found the Piazza Vittorio Emanuele, and quite by chance stepped out onto the Square of the Signoria. Stunning and sudden in its cliff-steep, fortified massiveness, the Palace of the Signoria rises up before me, and I can feel its gray heavy shadow over me. High above the pinnacle-sharp shoulders of the structure the watchtower stretches its sinewy neck up into the coming night. And it is so high that I begin to reel as I gaze all the way up to its helmeted head, and as I glance around, disoriented, looking for shelter, a magnificent wide hall extends its broad arches toward me: the Loggia dei Lanzi. Past two lions I cross over into its twilight, out of which white marble images come toward me. The *Rape of the Sabine Women* I can recognize, and on the rear wall the shadow of the bronze *Perseus* by Benvenuto Cellini takes shape, and I am amazed before its silhouette by the lovely, victorious movement and proud élan of this statue I had never been able to appreciate at a remove, and with every minute I grow calmer and more observant among these high, bright images that seem to me ever more familiar, caringly arched over as both they and I are by this somber, securely extended hall that rests on its strong Gothic columns in perfect confidence. At this moment a figure takes on for me his defining contours: Andrea Orcagna, the creator of this edifice, ceases to be an empty name; I feel over me the clarity of a man and the deep, faithful seriousness of someone who dwells in solitude. A master of life has arched these halls, someone quiet and festive, who created columns in his own image and suspended the roof above them according to life's pattern, darkly weighing down and yet no burden for the assured striving of the sturdy posts. And this is how the first Renaissance man initiates me into the mystery of his time. I have entered into the very midst of it. I sense as it were the rhythm of a deeper breathing, compared to which mine is a tapping of children's feet, and I become strangely free and fearful in this edifice, like a child who carries the armor of an ancestor on his shoulders and who already begins to feel next to the thrill of its brilliance the woeful weight that will soon force him out of his child's pride down onto his trembling knees.—Then, as I step toward the right corner of the hall and glance to the side, a dark empty square opens to me unexpectedly, a narrower St. Mark's

Square without the bright festiveness of the latter's basilica. Two high, silent buildings, rising atop cavernous arcades, run side by side as in continuous striving for embrace, until at the end an impatient arch leaps from one to the other. Above the arch stands some sort of white ruler-figure. And as my eye coasts back along the arcades, there is a movement; out of the dark a line of bright figures emerges, as if they wanted to approach someone. I look around, but there is no one behind me—can their welcome be meant for me? Suddenly I feel it clearly. And with a shy awkwardness I, the small, the nameless, the unworthy one, hasten toward them, and pass devoutly and gratefully from one to the next, blessed by each, recognizing each: Andrea Orcagna first, as I had imagined him, his gaze full of will transcended, raised on high, his forehead a broad expanse for light. And Giotto, deep in thought, and Michelangelo and Leonardo. Then also the poets Boccaccio, Petrarch, and, wreathed in inspiration, Dante . . . And in this way I looked into all their faces and drew strength from their quietude. Then I stepped through the arch at the corner of the square and beheld the night in bloom over the Arno, and the little houses and the tall palaces seemed to me more familiar and understandable than they had an hour ago; for I had seen the people who grew out of the little houses into the tall palaces and beyond them into the one eternal homeland of all highness and magnificence.

On the first evening I was glad to know that my stay here will be measured by weeks; for I felt: Florence, unlike Venice, does not disclose herself to the casual passer-by. In Venice the bright, cheerful palaces are so trusting and talkative, and they linger like beautiful women forever by the mirror of the canal, wondering whether people see the aging in them. They are happy in their brilliance and have probably never desired anything other than to be beautiful and to display and enjoy all the advantages of this possession. Therefore even the most fleeting person goes away from them enriched, richer at least by the festive fronts and their incomparable golden smile, which at every hour of the day remains awake in one nuance or another, and at night gives way to that almost oversweet, surrendering melancholy that has found a place in the Venetian memories of even the hastiest traveler through Italy. Not so in Florence: the palaces raise their mute foreheads toward the stranger in almost hostile fashion, and a wary defiance lingers around the niches and gates, and even the brightest sun does not succeed in dispelling its last traces.—It is a strange sensation, especially amid the open life of the modern streets where the people celebrate their festivals and shout their business, this dense, fortified suspiciousness of the old bourgeois palaces, of the broad gigantic bourgeois arches with their eternal somberness embedded fossil-like in the folds of the mighty ashlars. An occasional parsimonious window, with decoration whose sheen, even when brightest, is like the smile of an intimidated child, interrupts this heavy state of silence and worries lest it betray something of the purpose that animates these walls. With a sharp impatient thrusting-forth, however, the torch-holders and pennant-rings protrude from the clefts in the stone; as if the whole thing were filled with huge quantities of iron, and these molded shapes coiled out of the giant structure as a brazen surplus, warning and watching. And high over the rim a stern and simple cornice, usually with dentils, juts forward watchfully, like a row of poised archers who from their vantage defend the entrance down below. These are the monuments of a potent and pugnacious world, the witnesses to those days of Florentine dignity ascending, when from defiance and sheer know-how the pedestal was built for that serenely cheerful art of its brightest days. And even in the edifices of the later High Renaissance, this old, wise caution still finds place and privilege; it is the element in that succinct, powerful beauty of Florentine palaces that causes one to imagine them inhabited by Michelangelesque figures of unbridled power and prerogative.

But once you have won the confidence of these palaces, they will gladly deign to tell you the saga of their existence in the wonderful rhythmic language of their courtyards. There as well the architecture seems at all times to have preserved its somber dignity until the good monuments of the High Renaissance were completed. But the cold, taciturn reserve has given way to an attitude of conscious, self-possessed confiding, where people of virtue entrust themselves without pose and without anxiety, secure in the feeling that only the best will receive their best; for only he in whom it resonates can make it his possession. In the entire understructure the silent ashlars have been replaced by broad arcades, which watch over a shaded secrecy

and often continue up into a part of the first story, in double sequence with columns, and then they provide a wealth of glimpses
into the interior, all of them like soft, intimate confessions that make
the exquisite relationship to the viewer all the more enticing. The or-
namentation that nestles up against the columns is in the best instances unobtrusive and straightforward, a beautiful thought or a
tender feeling elicited by the column—and thus happily attuned to
the measured festiveness of the capitals, which, often direct from antiquity or freely reproducing it, peel back under the burden of the ar-
chitrave to just that degree natural and necessary to enlist the slender
strength of its shaft in the mute, triumphant battle with the coun-
terforce. Their victory is celebrated, furthermore, through statues
that brighten here and there in the shadowy niches, and through
lunettes and roses that appear in rich and inexhaustible variations between the arcaded arches or at the farther walls of the vault, amid the
pillars or the consoles that catch the ceiling. Sometimes in that wall
that without ornament and arch would appear barren, the earlier
owners' coats of arms, rising in free rows, have been set out in brick
masonry, and then this side can be almost overwhelming in the simple way it tells its story: like a senescent grandson who, as the last of
a noble line, has assembled the deeds of his iron forebears in faultless
memory and talks of their greatness in proud and unapproachable
words, softly as from his own reminiscing and unconcerned if someone hears him.

The most beautiful of these courtyards also show those entering a
portion of the staircase, which then (as in the Palazzo del Podestà in
Florence), contoured to fit the coat-of-arms wall, bordered on its
other side by a broad balustrade, leads upward in knightly steps under
high archways and flows into one of the magnificent bright halls.
Above the moss-covered floor of the courtyard, the bright day is separated from the stone-gray shadow by a single sharp stroke, and that
line appears broken only by the rim of the well that rests atop a few
steps and signifies—the way a small house-altar signifies the heart of
the house—coolness and clarity for those at home here and for the
welcome guest.

Such stone wells are also the focal points of those courtyard spaces
filled out with small gardens—such as one finds, for instance, in the

Certosa of Val d'Ema and in other cloisters. Over the mouth of the well a length of ornamented iron has been arched from one edge to the other as support for the rope on which the bucket descends; or else a yoke, held up by two simple columns, serves this same purpose. In the courtyards of the monasteries greater simplicity and sameness reign than with the interior architecture of those rich patrician houses. One feels immediately that it is not a single individual's will that works here toward festiveness and full pleasure, but that many men are meant to tolerate and grow accustomed to one another's presence, men who gradually forget that somewhere there are still desires outside the solitude and the stillness that tightly encircle the arcades. And since the whole world within this narrow frame wants to gain room and right, little gardens have been placed here with many, many small, white-pebbled paths; between rows of wild roses they intersect one another again and again and finally end at the single cypress tree that rises next to the wall. Longing has led them on along these many branchings; a small, reconciled symbol of the great erring, a remembrance of the many things no longer encompassed by these walks. And among the paths the unspent love of these poor Capuchin hands opens up in cheerful colors and glows and blossoms in all its blessed innocence. And it is then that the early Renaissance appears to me with doubled loveliness: as surrounded by a wilderness of spring. And the masters must have felt this no less strongly than I when they created their mild Madonnas, to whom they gave a piece of blue sky to take with them into the churches' darkness, and whose angels were enjoined with but one task: to bear in patience and beauty the wreath of heavy fruit that is to frame the solitary spring-time Virgin like a sacred promise.

Each day I have had the good resolve to continue with my notes, but it is only now, on May 17th, that I really take up my book again, read through what has happened, lean back, and think quietly out over the Ligurian Sea. This distant surface will dispell the confusion of that network of strange streets from which I finally tore myself as if in sudden flight. I could no longer bear such intensity of looking. After so much art once again nature. After the manifold the one, after the seeking this one great, inexhaustible find, deep within which arts

still untouched stand waiting for their quiet release. I can imagine
that I might endure Rome longer, and that the art of a different era
would have allowed me to trace its general contours little by little, in
daily notes of steadily increasing length. In such a case an image
would have taken form that might capture honestly enough the quality of that first visual encounter, and could thus preserve the highest
and clearest feeling of my impressions, something valuable for all remembrance. But only with antiquity is this first impression also the
clearest and most significant one, and then again with that summit
of the Renaissance as Raphael and a few other artists define it. Not
that a longer contemplation of their works would be superfluous; de-
vout absorption can make many a beautiful aspect more intense and
deeply grasped; but there is no sensation so strong that it will project
beyond the ripeness of that first enjoyment, and the quick word will
be the most fitting one—always provided that its purpose is to convey a pleasure only and not to pass judgment. But confronted with
the works of that age just before Raphael there is no first word—this
is as true for the naive as for the informed viewer—there is only a first
silence. And thus something strange transpires: the relation of image
and guest does not remain one-sided, as for example with one of the
Urbino painter's Madonnas, who accepts the stranger's more or less
sincere admiration with impassible calm; there arises in the first moment a trafficking between the two, quiet dialogues tear down the
bridges between them and a conciliatory silence reerects them. A
becoming-each-other's-opponent alternates quickly with the feeling
of joyful and festive love, and the minutes of lucid understanding are
followed by a fearful alienation. Suddenly we stand face-to-face with
the person who, with rapid or with tenderly hesitant hands, gave
form to a piece of his faith and his longing in the enduring work.
Suddenly we feel that these Madonnas are not monuments of a quiet
gratefulness, that they are only markstones of a dark and somber
path to the sun, and we know that the degree of their beauty will be
the sign of how near or far they are from this goal. For beauty is the
involuntary gesture in which a personality distills itself. It becomes
more perfect, the more hate and fear fall away from it, the more confident the artist grows on the path that leads to his most sacred fulfillment.

No human being can raise so much beauty out of himself that it will cover him over completely. A part of himself will always gaze out from behind it. But in the peak times of art a few have erected before themselves, in addition to their own beauty, so much noble heritage, that the work no longer needs them. The curiosity and custom of the public will seek and of course find their personality; but that misses the point. In such times there is an art, but there are no artists.

There is an ever-recurring cycle of three generations. One finds the god, the second arches the narrow temple over him and in doing so fetters him, while the third slides into poverty and takes stone after stone from the sanctuary in order to build meagre and makeshift huts. And then comes one which must seek the god again; and to such a generation these belonged: Dante and Botticelli and Fra Bartolommeo.

The element of reconciliation and loveliness that one treasures in the works of Raphael is a triumph that only seldom occurs; it signifies a high point of art, but not a high point of the artist.

Pre-Raphaelites: simply a caprice. Tired of smooth beauty, one seeks the effortful—not so? How facile a proposition! Tired of art, one seeks the artist, and in each work looks for the deed that elevated the man, the triumph over something within him, and the longing for himself.

In notes jotted down day after day vis-à-vis the paintings of the quattrocento, I could have offered nothing more than the tourists' handbooks do. For they have formulated with unsurpassable cogency the measure of abstract beauty that inheres in the things. So much so that in fleeting consideration one employs quite unconsciously those infamous half-scientific terms that, once sharp and pregnant, have through so many mindless uses become dull and vacuous.

A handbook on Italy, if it wanted to teach pleasure, would have in it but one single word and one single piece of advice: Look! Whoever has a certain culture in him must make do with this guidance. He will not acquire pearls of knowledge and it will scarcely occur to him to ask whether this work is from the late period of an artist or whether in that work "the broad manner of the master" holds sway. But he will recognize an abundance of will and power that came from longing and from apprehension, and this revelation will make him better, greater, more thankful.

This is the terrible thing: in other countries most people travel sensibly. They often let themselves be guided by chance, discover lovely and surprising things, and an abundance of pleasure falls richly and ripely into their laps. But in Italy they blindly race past a thousand unobtrusive beauties on their way to those official sights that usually only disappoint them anyway—since, instead of acquiring any real relation to the things, they feel only the distance between their peevish haste and the ceremonial-pedantic judgment of the art-history professor, whose verdict the Baedeker has reverently set down in print.

I would almost prefer those who bring back from Venice as their first and most surpassing memory: the fine porkchop they ate at Grünwald and Bauer; for they at least bring back a genuine pleasure, something alive, intimate, and their own.—And within the confines of their culture they exercise taste and demonstrate the ability to enjoy a treat.

This fallacious notion of being "educated" in art has turned all concepts on their head: suddenly the artist is thought of as a sort of uncle who is called upon to perform before his nephews and nieces (the gracious public) a Sunday entertainment: that is the work of art. He paints a picture or chisels a statue, and for what purpose: good God, to delight Tom, Dick, and Harry, about whom he couldn't care less, to improve their bad digestion with a good thought and decorate their parlor with a willing work. . . .

That is how the public likes its artists; thus the philistine fear of the unpleasant in art, of the sad or tragic, the longing and limitless, the frightful and menacing—of which there is more than enough in life. Thus the inclination toward the harmlessly cheerful, the playful, toward what is without danger and devoid of significance, toward the piquant—toward that art of philistines for philistines, which one can enjoy like an afternoon nap or a pinch of snuff.—

The good public itself, though, also likes to pronounce from the judge's bench, and thus when it tolerates the artist as a kind of farceur who is responsible for an uplifting joy or a relaxing pleasure, it is by no means going to be satisfied with just any kind of pleasure. Its judgments foster the illusion that there really is a mutual relation between those who are creative and the crowd; and then there is much gushing about both the educative influence of art and the inspirations the artist receives from the people.

Whole generations grow up, prosper, and age in this attitude toward art. For most of us it was the climate of our own childhood. Thus we have something in us like a spiteful memory that makes us unfair toward many. But we must be hard in order to remain strong.

Know then that art is: the means by which singular, solitary individuals fulfill themselves. What Napoleon was outwardly, every artist is inwardly. One climbs higher with each victory, as if with each new tread of a stair. But did Napoleon ever win a battle to please the public?

Know then that art is: a path toward freedom. We have all been born in chains. A few forget their chains: they have them silver-plated or gilded. But we want to rend them; not through ugly and brute force; our desire is to grow out of them.

Know then that the artist creates for himself—only for himself. What for you becomes laughter or weeping, he must shape with the hands of a wrestler and raise it up out of himself. In him there is no room for his past; and so he gives it a separate, independent existence in works of art. But only because he knows no other material than that of your world does he place them into your days. They are not for you. Do not touch them, and regard them with awe.

There is an unspeakable brutality in the present-day relationship of the crowd to the artist.
  His confessions, which helplessly take refuge in the forms of com-

mon things, are regarded by the many as no different from those things. All have their hands on them; all may pronounce what is to their liking and what does not suit their whim. All take the holy vessel into their hands as if it were an object of daily use, as if it were a possession that at any moment they might break without punishment: defilers of the temple!

Therefore the artist's way must be this: to bridge obstacle after obstacle and to build step after step, until at last he can gaze into himself. Not straining, not forced, not on his tiptoes: calmly and clearly as into a landscape. After this return home into himself, deed after deed will be a leisurely joy; his life will be a creation and he will have no further need for the things that are outside. He will be spacious, and all maturity's extent will be inside him.

The artist's work is a putting-in-order: he places outside himself all things that are small and transitory: his lone sufferings, his vague longings, his fearful dreams, and those joys that will fade. Then the realm inside him becomes spacious and festive, and he will have created that worthy home for—himself.

Often I have such a great longing for myself. I know that the path ahead still stretches far; but in my best dreams I see the day when I shall stand and greet myself.

Once during this last dear winter we talked about it: whether the creative person is qualitatively different from the others. Do You remember? Only now do I know the answer. The creative individual is the more spacious person, the person out beyond whom the future lies. The artist will not for all time endure alongside the man. When the artist, the more mobile, the deeper of the two, becomes ripe and strong enough to engender his own kind, when he lives what now he dreams, the man will wither away and little by little die out. The artist is the eternity that juts into our days.

This development proceeds slowly, but that millennia of artistry have not yet outlined the higher species need not dishearten us. Much noble erring delays the way. And besides, "all time" is a ridiculously small measure for such a goal. If there is a promise for the artist he can trust in, it is this: the will to solitude.

Is the slowness of this development so strange? Is it not that someone with different organs and senses must accomodate himself to this world? And in addition to those conflicts there is that deep chasm that originates in his own inner development and maturing.

Each person creates the world anew with his own birth; for each person is the world. But in addition there is another *historical* world— no, there are a thousand such worlds, and over the agreements that elevate one of these as the world held in common, life's greater part trickles down and its best vigor is exhausted.

Since talk of art's educative influence won't cease: let us grant that it does have a formative effect, but only on the person who creates it; for it heightens his culture.

Every act of art means a liberation, and to possess culture means precisely to be liberated. Thus art is the way to culture for the artist. But only *his* art and only for *him.*

All works are for the artist things of the past and they have for him only the value of fond experiences—a simple remembrance value; therefore it is even conceivable that the creative person may dislike in a work of his something he has since overcome. But it may nevertheless have been an honest and heartfelt work, indeed it may be the work of his that remains—most honest. But that's not what matters. His profit is solely the increasing clarity of his life, for which I have only this name: the way to himself.

You remember how I emphasized so strongly in my lecture on poetry the degree to which each motif can present itself to me as an occasion for certain deeply intimate confessions. Back then it was a matter of the vaguely felt. Now I am more conscious in all these feelings, and thus in my creative work can be more instinctive; for consciousness heightens my culture, and this, in turn, assures me that I am choosing the right bowls in which to place my quiet liberations like flowers and pieces of ripe fruit.

Behold: I had expected to bring home a revelation about Botticelli or Michelangelo. And all I bring back is tidings—about myself, and the news is good.

For a long time I visited the works of art in Florence. I sat for hours before some single painting and formed my opinion about it and later sifted it through Burckhardt's beautiful critique. And behold: my opinion was like many opinions. Then one day before Botticelli's *Magnificat* I forgot for once about my judgment and the judgments of the others. That's when it happened. I looked into a struggle and had the sensation of a victory. And my joy was like no other joy.

That's when the spell was broken: it was as if from that very moment I had become worthy of entering a circle of men whom I had previously heard talk of at tenth remove. How different they were from rumor!

How completely like the best among us they were. *Their* longings live on in *us*. And *our* longings will, when we are used up, remain active in others, until they fulfill themselves in whomever are the last ones. Only these last ones will be a beginning. We are presentiments and dreams.

And if ten thousand times they made Madonnas and saints, and if some of them painted in a monk's habit and on their knees, and if their Madonnas perform miracles into these days: they all had but one faith, and but one religion was the fire of their inspiration: *the longing for oneself.* Their highest ecstasies were the discoveries they made in their own depths. With trembling hands they lifted them into the light. And since the light then was full of God, HE accepted their gifts.

Don't forget that these people were only just beginning to look into themselves. They found there a profusion of riches. A great bliss came over them, and good fortune makes one generous. They wished to be lavish with their treasures, to bestow them on those worthy of receiving them. And there was no one far and wide—but God . . .

Religion is the art of the noncreative. They become productive in prayer: they shape their love and their thankfulness and their longing and liberate themselves that way. They also acquire a kind of short-lived culture; for they cast off many goals for the sake of one. But this one goal is not their only-begotten one, and it is shared by all. But there is no culture that is shared by all. Culture is personality; what one calls "culture" with reference to a crowd is societal agreement without inner justification.

The non-artist must possess a religion—in the deepest sense of the word—even if it is only one that rests on communal and historical agreements. To be an atheist in this context is to be a barbarian.

And suddenly the Church saw that she was only a pretext and arose in anger and hatred: Botticelli and Savonarola. And yet it made so little difference whether Botticelli painted Venus or the Madonna; always this turned into his wounded and tear-stained longing. And he came to ruin because he sought a goal outside himself. He strayed into a dark solitary death.

Savonarola emerges again and again. Be on the alert for his return. Whenever you wish to do without, you disavow yourselves. He wants you poor. But the will of your art is: to make you happy, spacious, lavishly rich.

And if it were only that. Whoever lacks faith, lacks strength. But an apostate draws many along with him, and the many are part of their era. And the authentic ones also must live in this era. And when it is growing narrower and more timorous again, their gestures no longer have room.

Artists shall avoid each other. The crowd no longer touches them once they have accomplished certain liberations. But two who are solitary are a great danger to each other.

Neither shall place his hand on the other's art. For if he takes from one who is greater, he will lose himself; and if he inclines toward the manner of one who is narrower, he will profane himself and rob his heart of its purity; but of the other's culture the artist may gladly and gratefully partake. In this way each may urge the other toward higher humanity and therefore toward purer art.

But did not many of the best take the ancients as their example? Did not the spirit of antiquity awaken just that powerful movement whose eternal testimony I loved and admired in Florence? Exactly because their art was so full of the highest and ripest humanity, it was able to work at the deepest levels in truly formative ways and present art with a new generation. What the creators of the quattrocento imitated in the ancients was more their courage than their manner. In witness thereof: they made their way not really toward the Greeks but toward themselves.

And the same is true of Shakespeare. Whoever is noble and serious does not emulate a personality's small gestures—rather its broad style, which, however, in every great man is: the solitary path to himself.

Fra Bartolommeo I hold in higher esteem than Raphael; for the young Raphael received not only culture from his era but also art. The blame, to be sure, lay with his era—which, flush with its feeling of ripeness, had broken down prematurely the barrier between art and culture, so that the way and the goal appeared the same. The era had just enough strength left to raise one artist out of itself, but it soon died off in a series of pitiful dilettantes.

Artists like Raphael are always high points, but because the path has not reached its end, there must always be a downhill slide afterward and a great erring and a profound discouragement.

The princes and the commonest people have basically the most reasonable feeling toward art: indifference. The rich half-aristocratic and bourgeois middle class simulates that forced partaking of which so much is simply pitiful.

What the prince does for art, he does for the sake of the State. For it is in the State's interest to give art the appearance of something it favors and is pleased to have around, with rights equal to those of the official Church and the other institutions that support its authority. And yet in its patronage it has always seemed to me like republican

France, allowing Napoleon's plans to ripen when by doing so it was lending aid to what would last beyond it. But that's how it is: every state carries a future-state within itself and must, often against its will, provide the embryo with—nourishment.

Unless the prince himself is an artist—as, for example, Lorenzo de' Medici, il Magnifico. And in his case it was actually artistic genius that endowed the prince.

He pronounces the following creed: "All human beings are born with their very own thirst for blissfulness, and toward this end, as toward the only true goal, every human activity strives: but there lies the difficulty: to recognize what blissfulness is and in what it consists; and even when the goal is known, it is no less difficult to attain it; human beings strive toward it on widely divergent paths. And then—after human beings, all of them together, have set this goal for themselves, they begin, each in his own manner, to seek it. And because the general populace branches out in pursuit of these individual interests, and because each individual exerts himself in accordance with his own talents and character: there arises that multifariousness of human activity, and the beauty and the greater richness of life in things desired, similar to the way many different sounds ringing perfectly together become a reconciled harmony." "And perhaps," adds the poet Lorenzo to this humane saying of the prince, "perhaps He who cannot err has for this reason (in order to make the world richer and more beautiful) seen to it that the way to perfection is difficult and dark."

I have been reading almost exclusively in the slender volume of Lorenzo's poems; I have visited the Villa Poggio a Caiano where often that platonic symposium of the Magnifico came together, and to which Marsilio Ficino, Polizziano, and Botticelli belonged. I have tried also—unfortunately without success—to gain entrance to the villa in Caréggi where two ages were juxtaposed. Those about to die often have visions. What is preparing to happen is in an instant completed before their spiritual gaze. As Lorenzo was awaiting death, the future had already been fulfilled; there was no need for a vision. In the figure of Savonarola all the darkness of the beginning age had been amassed along with all the hatred of the days to come. And who would claim that what burned him to death was faith in the light? It was the jealous Church. That is why his spirit spread out over centuries and the smoke from his pyre still hangs over the sun, even in these present days!

Those who have the most longing in them aren't able to say what it is they long for. But then the tempter comes and says: "God it is and his goodness, that is your desire, deny yourselves and you will find him." And so they go off and deny themselves. And before long they have lost their longing.

In the end that is the value of all history: to see that it is never the masses who decide. The struggle that contains within itself the victory and the last decision and the next future is always played out between two solitary individuals. Somewhere suddenly an entire era rebels in *one* figure against another one. But the bearers of the farthest future pass by all struggles with a quiet smile, like monks who have the cloister's treasure in their safekeeping. They have only to protect.

Give art your protection, so that it does not learn of the day's quarrel; for its homeland is the other side of all time. Its struggles are like the storms that bring the seed, and its victories are like springtime. Its works are: unbloody sacrifices of a new covenant.

Here I often think of Goethe, who in his art did not devote a single work to the great heroic uprising of the German people. How could anything that glorified discord have been a building block for a mind by then so rich, mature, and devoid of confusion?

National art! And every honest art is national. The roots of its innermost substance draw warmth from their native ground and receive their courage from it. But already the trunk rises up in solitude, and the region where the crown spreads out is no one's kingdom. And it may be that the dull root does not know when the branches are in blossom.

Each person grows from the many toward himself. If once upon a time someone found himself and greeted himself, perhaps he could return to the many and be their savior; they would crucify him or burn him to death. And out of what remained of him afterward, well, they would make themselves a religion.

But such a person could not have been an artist. For when someone creative has found himself, he will remain in his solitude; he wants to die where he is at home.

If there were gods, we could never experience their existence; for to have knowledge of them is sufficient to destroy them.

That all the great were nothing but parvenus, after all: as proof, note how they always came back to the crowd. Kings risen through the ranks who want to make their relatives into princes and dukes. Kind-hearted ones who from their splendiferous wardrobe give to the poor, and forget that the latter must cut the giant cloaks into pieces before they can use them.

Art at its high points cannot be national. Why? Every artist is born in an alien country; he has a homeland nowhere but within his own borders. And those of his works that proclaim the language of this homeland are his most deeply genuine.

Indeed, I would consider this one of the most profound characteristics of any artist: everyday-man walks away from his homeland into an alien world; he ages, as it were, into the uncertain. The artist, who comes from a dark alien world, from the many enigmas, becomes ever brighter and more cheerful and assured in his stride. All things become more intimate for him, and there is nothing else for him but a great recognizing, seeing-again, and being-welcomed.

And if now the two meet each other on their way—is it still strange that they do not understand each other?

But there *is* a certain point where the two pass each other by; there the one who walks into the alien, the philistine, will try his best to make the other his boon companion and to enlist him as a fellow-traveler. He is always for conviviality and concord.

As I said, the commonest people have, as in so many areas, the most appropriate attitude toward the work of art. In their quiet times they feel its superfluousness, and in their moments of passion they hate all marble images and hurl stones at them. And why not: works of art are the charters of the only sterling aristocracy, the one that has its ancestors still before it.

Whoever comes to Italy for the first time is delighted, especially if he knows Germany, by this intimate communality in which the great works of art and the common people live side by side; some poor devil sleeps off his hunger right under Cellini's *Perseus* in the Loggia of Orcagna, and no chains cordon off the fountains and statues that decorate the great squares. And already one is prepared to believe in a certain sympathy, until one realizes: the common people are no different from the man who lived next to Schubert or Beethoven: first the incessant music bothers him, then it makes him angry, and finally: he doesn't hear it anymore.

The first day I was in Florence I remarked to someone: "Growing up among these things, coming of age amidst all this magnificence, must have deep formative effects even in the most benighted populace. A certain beauty, a certain inkling of greatness must reach down even into their tiredness and poverty and grow up inside them along with their other qualities." I can now answer my own question: The populace grows up amidst this beauty like an attendant's child in the lion's cage. It keeps on thinking in the face of the solemn animal: "I won't hurt you if you don't hurt me." But sometimes art does hurt the rabble . . . and then: Oh, I packed my bags and left Florence when rioting youths hurled stones into the Loggia dei Lanzi.

It has always been thus. Art passes over the people in a high vaulting arch from one solitary individual to another.

It will always be thus. "The people" is nothing more than a stage of development; it is the time of fear and inarticulate dependency when everyone begs his brother to stay with him.

As the expressions of every language rest upon communal agreement, so also with the word "God." It was meant to include everything one sees at work but can't otherwise name or grasp. Therefore: when man was very poor and knew very little, God was very great. With every experience some little piece fell out of his circle of power, and when at last he scarcely had anything left, Church and State collected for him charitable qualities, which now no one is allowed to touch.

That is often the way incapable human beings are, they want their parents to maintain them and take responsibility for them as long as possible. As long as this god is alive, we are all children and dependents. We must sooner or later let him die. For we want to become fathers ourselves.

But he *is* dead; the old story of Kara Mustafa. The viziers of the empire must keep silent about his dying so that the janissaries will not rebel and will continue fighting.

If only the nations had been creative in the first fearfulness of their childhood: then they would have made a *real* god!

God is the oldest work of art. He is very badly maintained, and many parts are later, approximate additions. But of course it is a sign of education to be able to talk about Him and to have visited His remains.

When all peoples were still like one person, they shaped God out of their longing. God will perform a miracle: each person will become like a people.

Everyone comes away from the deathbed of his childhood god dressed in mourning; but as he walks with increasing confidence and festiveness, God's resurrection takes place *inside him.*

The "public," when it encounters the creative individual, will in the end feel only what it feels in the presence of a strange, exotic tribe: their dances have no rhythm for them, and their exaltation is as little like music to their ears as is their longing. Their language sounds strange and unimaginable. In addition one looks just like the other to them and they only distinguish: "old" and "young" and "youngest" and "pretty" and "ugly." . . . Sometimes they can't even tell a man from a woman, what with their barbaric clothes. . . .

Country fair customs and country fair culture is what the people have: ballyhoo and red flag-cloth and Pagliacci. There should be someone "traveling" with Marholm and another with Strindberg and another with Sudermann so that they could all bark out: "Perversions!" Country fair culture this!

Every author who, called by applause, steps out in front of the curtain, should have to do this continually from the moment of his demise until the Day of Judgment. That would be for him a properly mortifying experience and for the people a welcome climax to the act.

But this is not the place to get started on that; "the Stage, considered as an *im*-moral Institution," would fill a whole volume,—and I want to keep these pages clean for happier and more intimate words!

That is why drama is so degrading: because it *needs* the public. And drama's atmosphere, I believe, has infiltrated the other arts as well, so that it is as if a work of art were only there from the moment the crowd ogles and critiques it. On the contrary, there are few works of art that survive this probing without internal damage.

How ostentatious these phrases are! Some artist dies; all of a sudden his works are the intellectual property of the entire educated world. With what has it bought this possession?

Well, the devil, then don't let your books be printed and your works exhibited, if they are none of our business, someone can lecture.— But we must exteriorize our past in works of art, must bring it to a close. They are completed only when they are no longer part of ourselves, when they have been translated into your vernacular—that is, when the book is a book, the painting a painting in your sense. Then there are no longer bridges from us to them, they are behind us, and we can found ourselves upon them.

To the others: For centuries you have been making the world narrow. Now wherever we place some deed, you bump into it: your fault!

Whoever speaks of "art" must necessarily mean "the arts"; for they are all expressive forms of *one* language.

Music alone I hesitate to include here. I have still not been able to approach it, no matter what path I take. But even so I believe its region is essentially different from those of the other arts. The poet of sound does not have to situate his confessions so precisely in the midst of the common world. In his liberations he presents dormant possibilities, and only he who knows the magic word can awaken them into joy and full festiveness.

But especially in this art there is an abundance of complementary revelations. Often it seems to me that music is internal to all the other arts and comes toward us more quietly out of their products. Truly: the mood evoked by a painting or a poem is in so many ways just like a song.

The time will come when I can speak of this also. For I shall go in search of music. I can feel it: simply to let oneself evolve, not to urge, not to ponder. Like a morning every clarity follows every night.

But it is altogether dilettantish in *any case* to seek to align individual arts and bind them to a single goal. Even though all arts have the same end, they cannot attain it at the same time on a single path. In such forced unions one will always constrict the other and exert power over it.

In every work of one of the arts, all effects "of art" must be fulfilled. A painting should need no text, a statue no color (in painting's sense), and a poem no music; rather, everything must be contained in each.

Only a frame so coarse and eager to please as the stage could have advocated a uniting of text and music such as one finds in opera and operetta. That music as the naiver element remains triumphant only testifies to the injustice of such a marriage to begin with.

Such a linkage could of course only arise as a concession to the public, which in its indolence would be delighted to have one art provide a commentary on the other. Speed painters to musical accompaniment, the way honky-tonks stage them, are a perfect complement to the operatic marriage.

The crowd would like best to mix all the arts up together, until art is lost in the process. Listening to good music in a beautiful room is of course another matter; for there exists a decorative employment of the arts completely different from their jumbling-together. Carefully juxtaposed they can work quite nicely as tasteful filling for a space. All arts are then as it were out of action, at leisure, listening, and only involved in the thing at hand with a small part of their being.

The union of decoratively utilized arts takes place, it should be emphasized, not in and of itself but in the sensibility of the person who derives enjoyment from their interaction.

And song? Should it not be sufficiently justified as a popular version of the poem? That in our day it has entered into polite society does not testify against its ancestry and origin. It took the same path as dance.

Lessing (who was as far above his era as he was aloof from any tenderhearted view of art) already sensed clearly the danger inherent in the mixing of the arts, and pronounced many a good dictum in his well-known treatise; his remarks on "the transitional," especially, will never lose their relevance.

There is, furthermore, a peculiar thing about the making of laws—where the arts are concerned. First and always great works must come about, and then, once they have appeared, logical minds can derive rules from them. The era, however, that possesses a priori rules for art is always already a period of decline and—what is even worse—an epoch of imitation.

It is quite obvious: in the work of genius, the law is the necessary accidental. Detached from that one special first case, generalized, it becomes the primary consideration and spawns formalists and fearful pedants.

The public at large would never think to hunt down the laws inherent in certain works of art, but the critics consider this their solemn office; for in this way alone can they discover common points of view among the most heterogeneous artists, and thereby out of many individuals form groups, schools, and circles, an activity that serves to put them at ease and soothe their need for order.

As long as criticism is not an art alongside the other arts, it will remain petty, biased, unjust, and trivial.

How many injustices does the forefather of all art criticism, Vasari, have on his conscience. And yet how high he stands in his naive appreciation above the affected carryings-on of his crippled successors.

The critics are like those schoolboys who whisper the answer to you; they laugh to themselves when the public next to them repeats their inanely false promptings with dumb trust.

Imagine Michelangelo reviewed in some newspaper, never mind whether praised or panned. In those words of Jewish sophistry that have become shiny from so much use. I believe he would have hammered the critic into shape like a block of marble to which the wrong chisel had been applied.

Murat, who was without question a noble hero, said in the face of his judge: "Who will judge me? As marshal of France I can be judged only by marshals, as king only by kings!"

Even posterity would not have the right to judge if it did not have that one advantage: to be able to observe a past era without hatred and without envy. But even this judgment is partisan enough; for each posterity is the fruit of the preceding eras and carries within itself much that they contained. It should be content to love and to cherish those elements of its patrimony that are still *alive in it;* since only they are fertile and vigorous enough to count.

One is inevitably unjust to a work of art the moment one attempts to evaluate it in association with others. In the end that leads to questions like: Raphael or Michelangelo, Goethe or Schiller, Sudermann or————, and the good Germans have always loved such parlor games.

Perhaps people will recognize one day that such questions are a sign of great immaturity. Is it really necessary to judge? Take a piece of music, and almost anyone can relate to it with naive enjoyment: the music drifts pleasurably through his nerves and sets the tip of his toe tapping and he has a quite ordinary good feeling about it all. In front of a painting, though, he gets panicky: I need some quick, quick ideas and something technical like "broad brush stroke" or "diligent labor"—and the second fear: that the judgment he makes will somehow diminish him in the eyes of his companion. Such judgments have virtually attached themselves to the most stellar paintings in the gallery, hanging there like those silver hearts pinned to the Madonnas of Mercy: "For miraculous deliverance from the throes of having to make a judgment."

And there's no doubt: the paintings themselves over time acquire bad habits: the most noble Titians and Tintorettos act as gallery-pert as the most cheeky portraits by Rubens.

The way toward the true value of all works of art goes through solitude. To surround oneself with a book, with a painting, with a song, for two or three days, to become familiar with its habits and to trace its oddities, to gain confidence in it, to earn its trust, and to experience something together with it, no matter what: a grief, a dream, a longing.

In this way I have grown fond of my Grasset, who in the street of flowers observed with watchful eyes the royal houses; in this way I came to love Your *Ruth* before You.

There can never be more than a few such works. They are like pictures of dear people who somewhere in far distant lands yearn obscurely for something which *we* are. We will never meet them; there will always be an aura of much melancholy longing about them.

Only the person who owns a book or a painting can be truly clear about it. Occasionally viewed gallery pictures confuse. Our eyes take in along with them—even when they hang isolated in one room—the impression of this strange space, an arbitrary gesture of the gallery attendant, perhaps even the recollection of a scent, which will all now unfairly insinuate themselves into our memory. This conglomerate, which under certain circumstances might be able to enhance the mood, is in its randomness and cruel lack of style perverse. It is like the visit one pays a great and important man in a hotel. I remember several such visits; with one there is irremediably etched in my mind, alongside the appearance of the personality in question, a bedside chest whose door opened constantly with a little crowing sound, and also some errant slipper; and another I can only think of in the company of a badly ravaged breakfast tray over which a shirt collar had been stretched lengthwise like a bridge.

It is the same with books. A copy I am used to tells me its affair in complete confidence. The more often I use it, the closer I come to telling *it* the story while it plays the listener. A book that is your friend will gladly enter this animated exchange, and many a lovely situation can grow out of it. In time, what is actually printed in the book will have multiplied tenfold; again and again I read my own memories and thoughts along with its text. It is no longer written in the German of this or that author, it is my very own idiom. But the same book in a different edition is like a person whom I encounter in some foreign country and of whom I can scarcely say whether I made his acquaintance in some sort of business or simply passing by.

Toward borrowed books one always maintains a certain formal courtesy. I would never read the book a young woman has lent me in bed or in a morning robe, and a work from the great library of a colleague I would never place in my own slender collection, but assign it a privileged place on my table. If, of all things, I had a superior—that must be like having too low a ceiling—I couldn't possibly use books lent by him except with hat in hand; in short, one develops no intimacy with such books, one always remains on politely formal terms with them.

How much I have grown to like this "Lorenzo de' Medici," whom I have read in Poggio a Caiano, in Florentine churches, at the ocean's edge and deep in the evening of the pine woods.—Always opened at random with indiscriminate grip. The way one leaves meadows and steps into a forest, anywhere. At every place he was an intimate.

That is how one should read all books of poetry. Along the border, a short way into the woods and then back into the summer sun. Then each will retain its own significance: the coolness, the scent, the splendor.

In Florence, where there *are* no woods (scarcely a pair of straggly city trees anywhere), the churches are like woods. In Santissima Annunziata, for instance, or in Santo Spirito, I could sit quite contentedly for an hour or more and read. In Santa Maria Novella, best of all, stay even longer in the old cozy pews of the canons under the Ghirlandaios, and not read. These frescoes seem to me Ghirlandaio's most amiable work: novella-pictures in the fullest sense. Succinct illustrations of Mary's story. Below right: the well-known fresco representing the birth of Mary. The birthing room of a noble Florentine lady, similar to the depiction by Andrea del Sarto in the porch of Santissima Annunziata, told broadly and with patience, in the manner of old people who would like best of all to start from the beginning over and over again. A bit garrulous with its many idle women who look out quite unconcerned into the space of the choir niche, and with its obvious attempt to flatter through this immortalization as many Florentine beauties as possible. Back then—I believe—they already felt it a great hindrance to have to narrate yet again these long-familiar old stories, and they may have also felt how unpainterly it really is to be called upon to present again and again plot instead of situation, event instead of the possibility of event. They tried to find a measure of compensation in portraits, which they had recognized as a worthy and distinguished task, and emphasized them along with architectural elements and the young achievements of linear perspective far over and beyond the event depicted, as if to justify themselves before a different era. This style has something of the so-what shrug of the subordinate who mutters to himself behind the master's back: "Okay then if that's the way he wants it!"

With what cheeky roguishness and with what joyful, self-assured defiance did the incomparable Benozzo Gozzoli make "commissions" of this kind interesting for himself and fruitful for the true idea of art. The frescoes in the chapel of the Medici-Riccardi Palace (corner Via Cavour), which are so luminous in color and conception, appear true hymns of life. The journey of the three Magi from the East has become a hunting portrait of the princely court and its guests, and would retain, even if the crowd of fine portrait heads that give this work its unique stamp were removed from it, its pure and delightful flavor as a work of art. Around that time Oriental princes and their retinue had come to Ferrara to attend the church council there and had preferred—since somber work did not yield tangible results—to join in lavish festivals as guests of the Medici. As in general it was the festive life at which these days excelled. One can see it in these people—how they feel so perfectly at ease in the midst of ostentation and joy, how they wear robes and rings without effeminate vanity as something so self-evidently their own, like a symbol of that bright lordliness they discovered more and more frequently and bravely in themselves. The old Cosimo is all patriarchal dignity and bourgeois goodness, the restless acquirer, founder, and *pater patriae* in every trait and every crease. The man who needs no title because he fulfills all honors in the work he does and would only feel cramped and cornered were he placed in one particular position. He builds no throne for himself, though he could do so daily. He knows: thrones can topple. But by ascending on firm steps he elevates his glory and sits there on the highest; that satisfies his purpose: since from there he can also, as from a ducal chair, survey everything and guide it toward the goal of his own will and of the common good. One can see that this man will forbid a princely burial and will want to sleep, like any other citizen, simply and plainly in San Lorenzo; for only he who earns his glory through daily deeds has a right to it; the idler should keep quiet and ask nothing of life.—How different his grandson looks, the youthful, frail Lorenzo, even in this early painting. The air he breathes is rarified even as he is growing up. Beauty is not for him something one must earn laboriously; for if one did, one would always be afraid of losing it. And a fear—no matter which—would dishonor him. Beauty seems to him the prince's first possession and his proudest right. He does not wear it in his face; for then he might have to be concerned for it: a hatred, a sickness, a harm could have destroyed it. He has submerged it deep into his being from childhood on, and it has woven its roots around what is noblest there, and it drinks strength from that and blooms in his gestures and actions and sayings. But should he want to view its countenance: it smiles back at him in his own blood so intimately and dreamily with the lips of the beautiful Giuliano, his younger brother, and often blesses him out of this pure youthful figure and accompanies him thus—alas for so short a time. In Santa Maria del Fiore the assassin's dagger that Lorenzo himself quick-wittedly avoids stabs the bright Giuliano to death. Amidst his May, in all his child-rich, care-free beauty, ahead of every disappointment and every pain, he is found by the base, cowardly weapon of the undeserved foe, and even then its blind cruelty works as a kindness, as a sheltering providence vis-à-vis this unsuspecting youth who, deeper into life, might perhaps have lost himself and his longing and would have had some day to die exhausted, without a smile. He will remain to me the loveliest figure of life from this era that was itself so life-resplendent; for he is the most consistent and finest of them all, the one most like a dream. There is no shadow over him or in him. No history recorded his deeds and his victories founded no empires. And yet every smile from him must have been a prince's gold-pure gift for those who were worthy of receiving it. His whole childhood resounds in pure festiveness; and each day must have been to his young courage like a new country from which all joy came toward him in bright homage, and each night must have overarched him like a fairy-tale castle with its soft, silk-blue tenderness. And at the border of his manhood he feels suddenly how all this quiet, solitary living-through-life is beginning to stir in his heart, and how his springtime experience is becoming song in his awakened mind. And he bears—he knows no worthier goal— these songs that come to him like first redemptions into one of Florence's darkest streets to a poor girl he loves and founds thereby a church in her heart. . . . And no one ever heard these songs resound except his secret love. They vanished as he himself did, and the son this girl bore him in solitude, weeks after his assassination, never heard them from the lips of his mother; for she gave up her own life for him. Thus Giuliano was the springtime love who had to die when summer wanted to begin. Then his sunny mission was fulfilled.

And in the entire early Renaissance there is something of this blond youth's essence. There is a chaste coolness in their Madonnas and the austere strength of young trees in their Saints. The lines are all like tendrils that close in ceremonial silence around something wholly sacred, and the gestures of the figures are hesitant, alert, full of a trembling expectation. They are all consecrated by longing, but are youthful in all their actions; they find within this longing small, quietly delighting goals and rest in their presence as before the symbols of a different deep fulfillment. They feel a plentitude of eternities, and because they nowhere venture all the way to the borders, they nowhere find barriers. They have a silent and severe will within themselves but it is the same will that is at work in the soft winds and thus they never have to risk movements that are fierce and hasty. They are so entirely one with their time; that is what makes them beautiful. And they are neither hard nor apprehensive; for they have never forced this time into their designs, nor are they its accidental outcome. In a continuous exchange, in willing submission and loving divination, the two have formed one inside the other and ripen and twine about each other toward the same blissfulness. All the exhausting and disheartening inner battles are absent, and the strengths unite, reconciled, in one single broad, patient stream of striving. That was spring. Since then no summer has as yet arrived; and though those may be right who think this Renaissance beyond retrieve, perhaps it is left precisely for our era to begin the summer of this far-off and festive spring, and slowly unfold toward heavy fruit what back then already found perfection in its white blossom.

We have lived through centuries since then. The great spring gradually became a wilderness, without its final beauty ever becoming fruit. Since we now grasp that innermost beauty again, can our love enable it to ripen further?

We have grown older, not only in years, but also in goals. We have gone all the way out to time's borders, and thousands have rattled at its barriers. It is time we reined ourselves in. Spring's pale endlessness we have invented as a lie, and our bleeding hands show the insurmountability of the last walls. But neither may we send our poor dreams out beyond them like doves with olive branches; they will not return. We must be human. We need eternity, for it alone provides our gestures room; and yet we know ourselves in cramped finality. We must, then, create an infinity within these barriers, since we no longer believe in boundlessness. Rather than dreaming of the spacious, flowering countryside, we must remind ourselves of the enclosed garden, which has its infinity as well: summer. Help us to gain it. To found a summer, that must be our goal.

We are no longer capable of an art of flowering. Our art must not just embellish us but also warm us; we have reached the age when one sometimes shivers on early spring days.

We are no longer naive; but we must will ourselves to be primitive, so that we can begin in the company of those who were that way from the heart. We must become men of spring, in order to find our way into that summer whose sovereign majesty we have been placed here to announce.

It is not chance and whim and fashion that lead us to those who precede Raphael. We are the distant heirs whom destiny appointed in the interest of the many legacies.

I often find myself wanting to say to someone (I know not whom): "Don't be sad." And it seems to me as though this were an intimate confession, one that I would have to express softly and tenderly and in deep twilight.

We all have something like a fear in us. We shall be like mothers. For the time being we remain like girls who have burning hands and woeful dreams; but let it be known: we shall be like mothers!

After the new fear comes a new bliss. It has always been that way.

You must learn only to believe; you must become pious in a new sense. You must have your longing over you, in whatever place you are. You must hold it with both hands and carry it into the sun, where it is happiest; for your longing must grow strong again.

If you still have a trembling in you or a doubt, cast it behind you. And even if it grows up behind you on your path: then mountains will stand between you and the past.

How I have admired that in You, my love: this care-free trust in all things, this kindness impervious to fear. Now it is approaching me also, on a different path. I am like a child who was hanging from a precipice. It is reassured when its mother grasps it in dear, quiet strength, even if the abyss is still below it and thorns splay between its cheek and her breast. It feels itself held, lifted—and is reassured.

Since above I spoke of Giuliano de' Medici: a time will come when fate conquers no one before he has borne fruit. Days of harvest will arrive. And each will hear the songs he gave his love waken on the lips of the mother who cradles his son toward manhood. Days of harvest will arrive.

As pure as each loved one was in the Renaissance-spring: so holy shall each mother be in the summer we inaugurate.

Back then you fashioned your Madonnas as maternal virgins; our loved ones shall be virginal mothers.

Oh if I could only tell all of you the kind of time this is! It hurts me that so many are unfestive and without hope. I would like to have a voice like the ocean and yet be a mountain and stand in the sunrise: so that I could shine all of you awake, tower over you and call out to you.

This day a mother writes me, a mother who was deep in many a fear until the miracle befell her. She writes: "Now spring has come to us also, albeit rather stormily and tear-drenched; but I feel now as though I had never seen a spring before. . . . Today I sat all afternoon in the garden with Rolf, and out in the air I felt him opening like a rose; he has become so much more beautiful since you last saw him, his hair is thicker and he still has those big eyes."

I read this like a hymn, Lou. And I long for the moment when I shall read it before YOU; then it will receive melody.

All I need is strength. Everything else that would make me a proclaimer I feel within me. I don't want to journey through all countries and try to spread my teaching. Above all I don't want to let it harden and petrify into a doctrine. I want to live it. And only into Your soul, darling, do I want to pilgrimage, deep, deep inside, where it becomes a temple. And there I want to raise my longing like a monstrance into YOUR splendor. *That* is my desire.

You have seen me suffer and have consoled me. Upon Your consolation I want to build my church—in which joy has bright altars.

Perhaps in spite of everything I am not destined to see that summer I know will come. Perhaps I myself have only springtime strength in me. But I have the heart for summer and the faith of blissfulness.

Those in the Renaissance also received a budding strength that strove so rapidly toward summer: Michelangelo grew, Raphael stood in bloom. But the fruit never came; it was June, hot, bright tempest-June.

They had become so bold after the first fearfulness of beginning. They would have soon lived everything in a single breath out to the end. But the loving order slowed their tempestuous advance. The flowers grew sick and perished, those at least that wanted to become fruit. The cool, exquisite ones waited, as if under a spell, for their release, and are waiting still. Back then it was May, and the world was not meant to have everything simultaneously, time of bloom and harvest—and . . . now it will be summer.

You shall not know them and categorize them and judge them as is your wont. You must *love* them. Can you still do that? That is the test.

What they left behind with a heavy heart, you shall complete with self-assured ease. You are their memorials, and if you wish, you can become memorials unto yourselves!

And you must forget your weariness; you inherited it from those who at the edge of the quattrocento perceived: summer is trying to break through, and we can only blossom—and they became fearful of departing;—and from those who felt: we are being kept from ripening into summer—and they became wild and defiant, and exhausted in the process.—You, however, have no reason to be tired, and no time; for up till now you have only an inheritance and no gain, dreams and no deed.

But you have the mission to *perform* deeds the way deeds *befell* them. They rejoiced so that they could suffer; you suffered toward a new joy!

But you must be worthy, and pure and priestly. You may have no dalliances, only a single love. No longings, only a single longing, and your days may not be full of sensations and confusions; a clear, crystalline festiveness must grow over that, and your figures move about in it with beauty and with ease. But you can have all that, if that is what you long for: dalliances, sensations, intoxications; for you must use what is within you, and to be true is the one commandment.

Be for a single day unfashionable, and you will see how much eternity you have within you.

Those who feel eternity are above all fear. They see in every night the place where daybreak will occur, and are assured.

Summer requires fearlessness. Spring can be fearful; for its blossoms apprehension is like a home. But fruit requires a calm and heavy sun. Everything must be like a reception: broad gates and secure, sinewy bridges.

A generation born in fear comes into this world in exile and never finds its way home.

You shall not hold anything holier than the maternal. Every pain you inflict on a hope-sick woman trembles in advance through ten generations, and every sadness of which you become guilty in her eye spreads its terrible shadows over a hundred timid futures.

Had your parents had more summer in them, you would have attained spring without struggle and would not be weak and dusty from the path back out of the multitude of hateful, alien feelings.

No one will find fruit who lacks reverence. For irreverence is like a storm that rips what is unripe from the branches.

Thus you will live no present, but will be unto yourselves as those who are yet to come. You will walk ahead of yourselves, and therefore you cannot miss the path.

This is something of which the artists of spring were incapable. Their erring, to be sure, was toward themselves. But they knew only dimly where they truly lived, and believed their era with childlike innocence when it told them that the white marble gravestones marked their home. And then they hastened no longer and ceased their urging and walked slowly through sheer light toward the place where they had arched themselves a church over their quiet goal.

We have no need to build churches. Nothing of us must be left behind. We will drink ourselves empty, we will give ourselves over, we will spread ourselves out—until some day our gestures are in waving treetops and our smiles are resurrected in the children who play beneath them. . . .

It was a strange Sunday, this May 22. A deep day. I was even able to record in these pages what I have long felt burning in me, a confession and a clarity and a courage. On a long walk in the festive pinetum the three "Girls' Songs," which delight me with their intense emotion, came to me, along with YOUR high hymn that concluded the new notebook. Everything seemed so ripe for celebration: yet I can have no festival without YOU. And so I moved my high armchair close, dreamed YOU into it, sat down across from You and, as evening deepened outside, read one song after the other and sang the first and wept the second and was pure blissfulness and woe: a toy in the hands of these delicate pale songs that now did to me as I had done to them. All the longing and tenderness I had locked inside them came over me and surrounded me like a wild springtime and lifted me up as if with white, gentle, unseen hands—toward where, I don't know. But so high that the days were like little villages with red roofs and tiny church steeples and memories were like people standing small and silently in their doorways, waiting for something. . . . After I had read through the book and drunk all these feelings of joy and sadness as if from *one* source, I was full of a solemn thankfulness. And I knelt in the midst of the evening radiance that opened up on the high walls of my room like a gold mine. And my shuddering silence was a deep trembling prayer to the holy life to which I was so near in the blissful hours of creativity. That I may become worthy of entering its fulfillments in loyalty and trust, that my joy may become part of its glory and my suffering become great and fruitful like the blissful woe of its spring days. And that the reconciliation be over me that is over all its works like the eternally unchanging, eternally bestowing sun, and that in this gentle light I may walk toward ME, I the pilgrim toward the I who is king and has a rose kingdom and a summer-crown in the midst of life from all eternity.

And that I may become strong and mighty over the passing fears and over all the torments from a single night. And that I may fulfill what I feel to be a mission. And that I may feel, when I do fulfill it, that it makes me richer and more spacious and full of a high, self-effacing pride.

On these days of creativity I can feel it already: how the husks slide off the things and how everything becomes trusting and forgets all manner of disguise. Moments of creativity are like twilights after heavy summer days. All things are like young girls, white and gentle and of a smiling sadness. Until they suddenly nestle up against you with a strange, impetuous tenderness and tremble like does in flight and cry like children dreaming: deeply and drunkenly and breathlessly. As if they wanted to say: "Oh, we really aren't the way we are. We lied. Forgive us." And then you have cool, compassionate, understanding hands that stroke their foreheads gently. . . .

These are moments only, but in these moments I look deep into the earth. And see the causes of all things like the roots of broad rustling trees. And see how they all reach to one another and hold one another like brothers. And they all drink from one source.

And these are moments only, but at these moments I see high into the sky. And see the stars like quiet, smiling blossoms of these rustling trees. And they sway and wave to one another and know that *one* depth gives them fragrance and sweetness.

And these are moments only, but at these moments I look far across the earth. And I see that people are strong and solitary tree trunks that lead like broad bridges from the roots to the blossoms and calmly and serenely lift the juices into the sun.

Yesterday morning something else happened that seems worth recording. I was sitting, as I do every morning, on my wide marble balcony, writing into this book. The garden before me was full of a shy, apprehensive sun, and beyond that, across dunes and sea, there were expectant shadows from a wide bank of clouds. Alerted by a crunching sound on the gravel, I looked down and noticed in the central avenue of the garden a brother of the Black Brotherhood of Ultimate Mercy in his black, smooth robe of folds and black hood that permits only two small eyeholes. As he stood there waiting in the midst of the garden, in the bright red garden with its bear's-ears and poppy and small red roses standing in full spring, he was like the shadow of some second person who must have towered up next to him gigantic and invisible. Or he was like Death himself, but not the one that seizes someone unsuspecting in the midst of life: more like the humble servant voluntarily called, who, appointed to be there at a certain hour, keeps his word, enters calmly, and waits: At your service. And for a moment I waited, with bated breath, to see whether someone would not indeed step from the terrace, some blond girl or a quiet hard man, and deep in thought follow the Black One out of the garden. Simply out of the garden—out of the garden. . . .

There was in all this no fear and none of the feelings that in the days of old superstition would have conquered me. Life in its quiet festiveness seemed at this hour like a wide frame in which everything has room, and the end lost its fear because close beside it stood the beginning and the balancing of the two occurred as if in soft, smiling agreement and like the rocking and lapping of waves. I sensed a mighty reconciliation through this feeling, I was as if kissed on the forehead by a rich and holy consolation whose blessing I would henceforth have for life.

However, precisely because I found myself so far above fear at this moment, I grasped the working of certain strange destinies. The *frate*, who had come to collect for his humble cause, remained unnoticed and rattled his coin box, which sounded eerie and like a chain. After waiting in vain he turned around and strode hesitantly toward the garden gate; then someone below seemed to step out of the vestibule so that with something like haste he turned back this way toward the house. He received a donation from a boy and took an amazingly deep bow before the child, who observed him with curious glances. Then he left, still hesitant, and paused quietly in the middle of the avenue. My image from before reawakened. I imagined that there was standing down below on the steps a white young girl, who hesitated before this summer radiance and could not take leave of all the bright loveliness. And at last through the boy she sent bashfully to the somber, hooded servant, whom she herself had summoned, her little heart; which was meant to say: "I was mistaken, take this, and go on ahead. I can't come yet. I am truly tired, truly. I can't love anymore, take it. But let me gaze a while longer." And I felt, as it were, how two large sad eyes cast the shadow of questions into the bright day: "Only gaze a while longer. . . ." And then he goes, goes reluctantly and in disbelief. Will she not come after all? And he stops one more time at the railing, where the fresh plane tree is full of sun. But the girl remains down below, leaning against a column, and looks past the messenger out onto the green, distant, motionless sea: "Only gaze a while longer." The boy who carried the heart crouches at her side, and cries. . . .

Then I lost the vision; but I thought: he truly did hesitate a long time. If during that time, up above on my broadly visible balcony, deep in thought, I had made some involuntary movement, he would have no doubt taken it for a call and come back; and I know: I would not have in surprised shyness gently said no.—I would have quickly given him something to be rid of him. And he would have then hesitated once again at the door, and somewhere (in a large house by the sea, each moment someone steps to a window) another person would have made a similar gesture, and he would have approached that person, too: at our next encounter we both would have avoided each other and only exchanged glances from afar. And if the two of us were people with many bridges between them, this persistent returning of the Black One would have lain upon us like a danger and a dark premonition. And I imagined a situation that, conjured up by such coincidence, could become heavy and kindred to a fate.

When I stepped into the garden later that afternoon, I was no longer thinking of this apparition. But up ahead by the hall one of our two dachshunds sat and would not be moved at all by those flatteries of mine he usually loves. He seemed immersed in some deep contemplation, even though all he did was stare into the house's wall, which was smooth and barren and without any kind of hold. His eyes, I am sure, were not focusing there; those were the blind looks of someone brooding in earnest, and across the animal's face lay such a stony seriousness, a grim devotion that revealed itself also in the whole strange posture of the body. I stood still, was struck by the oddness of it all, and as I walked on said aloud to myself: "A dachshund with the demeanor of a sphinx. Deep, enigmatic, silent." Said this aloud and forgot it.—Then I finished my songs, and full of sound I left the woods at the first hint of dusk. Somewhere the chambermaid comes up to me and says: "Oh, our Padrone is broken-hearted; imagine, Signorino, the male of our dachshunds, the one he had owned for fourteen years, surely you remember him, today—now—was struck by a horse, staggered, and fell dead on the spot. *Poverino.*" And she greeted me with a smile and passed by.

That's what it finally comes down to: to see everything, all elements equal, *in* life; even the mystical, even death. No one thing may extend beyond a second, each must rein its neighbor in. Then each has its own meaning and, what is most important: their sum will be a harmonious whole full of peace and security and equilibrium.

Only then does the mystical have its rightful place: if one does not grant it power different from the other forces. But the gullible seize on it as the secret cause of all that happens, and those who think they are above it are shattered by the violence of its incursions.

But art also is justice. And you must, if you wish to be artists, grant all forces the right to lift you and press you down, to shackle you and set you free. It's only a game, don't be afraid.

You know that the flower bends when the wind so desires, and you must become like the flower: that is, full of a deep confidence.

After the day of prayer, a day of penance—as it so often happens. I found Your letter after dinner and was dismayed and then afraid. Now I am still full of sadness. I have been anticipating the summer with such joy and felt it like a dear bright promise over everything. And now doubts arrive and worries, and all paths grow entangled . . . leading where?—

Suddenly it is so dark around me. I don't know where I am. I only feel that I must sit among strangers and travel one day and then another and yet a third in order to be with You at last—in order perhaps: to bid farewell to You.

And yet I feel something else in me saying: Wait. There is so much newness crowded before me, I cannot name it nor sort it out. But gaze for a while into forest and ocean, into the great beneficience of this splendor, and wait: clarity will come.

And clarity arrived.

Today there is no more fear in me, only bright joy: to have You again in six to seven days, my darling. I sit amidst this summer morning on my balcony and know only that this deepest of all fulfillments is my next destination. And everything in me trembles toward it.

Joy makes one creative. The two of us shall find through the paradise of having regained each other the surest way into this summer, which no chance occurrence can take from us. To me at least it is like a possession granted by a high power, since I have held it for so long already in day and dream as my heart's innermost hope.

I would travel then with scarcely a longer delay from here by way of Bologna, Verona, Ala, Innsbruck, and Munich to our festival, and place my love, so much richer from memories tinged with longing and loneliness, at Your feet.

Why should I fear a mundane beach in East Prussia! For two whole months I have been scooping beauty with blissful hands; I have enough of it to tower up treasures before You and me so that we will be invisible to whomever else will be there too.

And now I shall use these two or three days—days that I shall urge on toward You by means of dreams, in the fragrance of this blue infinity—to tell You more about the splendors of my days abroad. And as I do so, it becomes increasingly clear to me that I am not speaking about the things at all, but about the person those things have made me. And this change, which goes on quite without my being aware of it, heartens me; for I feel that I am on the way to becoming an intimate of everything that beauty preaches; that I am no longer a mere listener who receives its revelations like mute favors, that I am becoming more and more the things' disciple, someone who heightens their answers and confessions with discerning questions, who elicits from them hints and wisdoms and learns to return their generous love with the disciple's quiet devotion.

And through this humble devotion goes the path toward that longed-for brotherhood and equality with the things, which is like a reciprocal safeguarding and before which the last fear turns into a legendary tale.

Then it's as if we were all of the same nature and grasped each other's hands. And we feel so deeply for each other because we have raised ourselves, each with the other's help, into the happy equipoise of that confidence that makes us brothers.

Even now—and I am still only on the first threshold of all understanding—evenings follow me into the forest and remove from the things around me their reserve—that whole strange reluctance of their hard chastity. They do this as if with gentle chiding: "Why do you cloak yourselves? Don't you see that a friend stands in your midst, someone who won't find his shy beauty unless you doff these everyday masks!" And then all the things smile at me, the way people smile when they remember a warm accord from distant days.

Since I have understood this—to be reticent: everything has come so much closer to me. I was a child even in my deepest feelings and a child in the darkness of my longing when I spent that summer at the Baltic Sea. How chatty I was in the presence of sea and woods, how I sought, full of a stormy vehemence, to reach across all barriers with the heady enthusiasm of my words, and how I nonetheless felt on that September morning when I took my leave of the clouded beach, that we had never given each other our ultimate and most blissful, and that all my raptures were table d'hôte-conversations that touched neither upon my glimmering feeling nor on the sea's eternal revealing.

But now: there are still, to be sure, gentle and rare conversations that build up between the things and my love; but when they want to rise like walls before our eyes, longing is triumphant over all reserve. We extend our hands to each other, and even if this gesture is always greeting and farewell in a single reach, we feel that the silentness between the two will expand with each day and with each deed, and that it will pry open the boundaries that are still superimposed, until there will be as much space between finding and farewell as between morning and the Ave Maria and that in between an entire day filled with eternity will go on and on.

Yesterday toward evening I took a long walk to the beach with my table companion, a young Russian lady, during which we conversed about art and life in those lovely trifles that merely daydream about the things. But there was many a worthwhile remark also. The path led along the woods, and everywhere at its border there were flashes of little fireflies. My potent memories of those shimmering nights in Wolfratshausen may have caused me, lost in thoughts of You, to utter something fervent about nature. Thereupon my companion: "You have always been in such close contact with nature, haven't you—even as a child?" "No," I said—and was surprised at the feeling in my words—"it is only very recently that I have gazed at it and savored it this way. For a long time we walked along next to each other in embarrassment, nature and I. It was as if I were at the side of a being whom I cherished but to whom I dared not say: 'I love you.' Since then I must have finally said it; I don't know when it was, but I feel that we have found each other."

Later the young lady said: "I am ashamed to say it, but I feel almost like a corpse; my occasional pleasures have grown so faint, and I've lost all desire." I acted as though I hadn't heard anything and then pointed suddenly in quick delight: "A firefly, do you see it there?" She nodded: "There, too." — "And there—and there," I added, carrying her away. "Four, five, six—," she kept on counting in excitement; then I laughed: "How ungrateful you are; that's what life is: six fireflies and more and more. And you want to deny it?!"

When I think that I myself was once one of those who look on life with suspicion and mistrust its power. Now I would love it regardless—rich or poor, vast or narrow. However much belonged to me I would love tenderly and allow all that was latent in my possession to ripen in my inmost being.

With Herr K., who is here now as companion to Professor Brentano, I had a long conversation about this odd, many-sided man, about events of current interest, and finally about Leopardi, whose pessimism struck us both as inartistic and embarrassing. It was mentioned that he had always been sick. "Yes," I said, "and one of the things I find most moving is the way people with infirmities manage to embrace life, and from the small cool flowers by the wayside reach conclusions about the vast splendor of its great gardens. They can, if their souls' strings are finely tuned, arrive with much less effort at the feeling of eternity; for everything we do, they may dream. And precisely where our deeds end, theirs begin to bear fruit."

It requires a great fineness of mind and disposition to take that piece of life that cramped corporeality grants sick people and regard it, in all the naive gladness of the heart, as if it were a whole. To find in this, as it were, all the tools required. It is like a meagre paint box for traveling; the resourceful artist will find ways to mix all the colors he needs from the available tubes. And it will not concern him that there are other boxes with richer selections.

It is also one of life's basic laws: to regard every possession as a whole; then every supplement will appear a surplus, and of riches there will be no end.—

Herr K. also described to me the current season's exhibit of modern paintings and sculptures in Florence and lamented having visited this inventory of modern decline in good taste. "A genuine foreboding has kept warning me away from it," I said, "and I have gladly complied. Dante's cenotaph in Santa Croce, the monument to him by Pazzi on the square facing it, and many another current disaster (which will remain forever current and therefore never become eternal) have been enough to make me wary of all that. It's too bad that the Florentines, when they were running out of artistry and good taste, didn't also run out of marble. But nature is too rich and simplehearted to contrive so devious a providence, and so bunglers defile the same material that their ancestors ennobled. As alas it always happens. Even all that profuse creating of the Renaissance artists seems

to have been motivated by a dark foreboding—as if they were trying
to leave the quarries in the mountains of Massa and Carrara empty
for their grandsons!"

On the way to Pietra Santa there is a bleeding mountain. It pulls the
olive trees away from its stone-gray body like a dusty pilgrim's frock
and displays to the sleepy valley, which did not want to believe in it,
the wound in its breast: red marble, ingrained in age-old flesh.

The trip to Pietra Santa, which I undertook while still in the company of the dear old Austrian couple, offers a wonderful variety of
views. The landscape is on the whole flat and amiable. Only a few
areas in the valley appear hemmed in by the blue mountains, which
distinguish themselves from the sky in modest, beautiful transitions.
Olive groves, with sheep pasturing among them, are the constant
companion of the straight road, which finally breaks through the
city walls of Pietra Santa and flows into the main square of this little
town; on it of course a monument, a Palazzo Pubblico with modest
Renaissance-recollections, a "cathedral" that a native artist has decked
out with various marble works—choir balustrade behind the main
altar in the manner of Rovezzano, as well as a baptistery that is said
to house certain works by Donatello. From there, the long uniform
streets branch out, clinging jealously to the cool shade. They take a
break now and then from their long journey in a small town square
(inevitably with a monument to Garibaldi or Victor Emmanuel) or
else seem to linger before one of the many commemorative tablets or
corner Madonnas (in the manner of Robbia but without his depth of
feeling). That is the basic character of all these little towns, from the
poorest all the way up to those that at one time were even the center
around which a dukedom was destined to spread: such as Lucca.
This latter town is especially distinguished by its walls—which, as testimony to a peaceable time, support avenues of bright plane trees—
as well by as its churches, most notably the cathedral that houses (in
the second chapel left of the choir) Fra Bartolommeo's flawless masterpiece, the purest of all those Madonnas that precede Raphael and
the one in which all that is best in Raphael has already found solu-

tion. The two great paintings of this master (in the Palazzo Pubblico) complement wonderfully the strength of this personality, in which peace and reconciliation were so deeply ingrained that the paintings, in spite of these qualities, remain individual confessions, and produce a deep, unforgettable effect through the assurance with which the worldview of the triumphant, enthroned majesty is again and again pronounced. This God-the-Father in his great gesture is just as much confession as the two holy women who kneel in tender piety beneath his glory and with their hearkening, devoted beauty frame a piece of light Leonardesque landscape: blue-tinged mountains, tender-stemmed, trembling trees, and a river that winds its way shimmering past sun-drenched cities. Angels lift those praying gently aloft, angels who are just this moment beginning to form from clouds, while other fully shaped angel-youths warm themselves in the radiance of the solemn father. The nobility of the composition, the peaceful absorption of the personalities in their settings, and not least the festiveness and grave magnificence of all its colors raise this painting to a significance that yields nothing to the first miraculous works. The appeal of the other painting (in the same room)—*Madonna Pleading for the People of Lucca*—lies not, by contrast, in the total configuration but in the charming, copious treatment of individual groups. The movement of the Madonna is a little too vehement for the tired woman, who would stand out more effectively from the many anxiously awaiting worshipers were she to intercede out of a quiet, deep confidence instead of with such imploring. In addition, the bat-wing-like drop of her dark blue mantle has the bothersome effect of mere drapery, and the Christ who, hovering horizontally toward the foreground, so that he overshadows her supplication, is not sufficiently modeled to make this difficult perspective seem natural. The painting looks like an experiment into which such a king of technique, for all his earnestness, could have easily been lured by his time. But in those other works where he is not bent on creating challenges to his ingenuity, he solves the most difficult problems with unselfconscious ease and has—to repeat—attained in ultimate perfection everything that, combined with Perugino's depth of feeling and Raphael's youthfulness, yields that immortal triad which rang with highest purity in the Sistine Madonna.—

Next to these paintings my strongest and most fruitful impressions are of: Giorgione's *Concert,* with its supreme glorification of a silent dialogue among three people, in style and mood and manner and motif so consummate that it will probably never be surpassed, no matter what degree of insight we may some day attain into this holy quietness. A state of being and yet an eventful action (emotionally speaking), a group and yet a differentiation between three distinct personalities, a narrative and yet a pure painterly idea: that is the *Concert.* The belonging-together and the being-in-exchange of the three figures is indicated most subtly by the *one* twilight, so that they all, as three solitary, unequally mature people, follow *one* fading sound along different paths. The player so easefully that he, having already arrived where he wants to be, looks back toward the friend who has fallen behind, while the third makes his way full of meditative strain. Yet one feels (and this is the discreetly promised intensification) that they are each the other's equal and will all come together again somewhere in a final bliss that will redeem them all.

It must have been very superficial observers who felt even some slight resemblance between Lorenzo Lotto's portrait-heads of the players (tellingly designated *The Three Ages of Man* by a later era) and this masterpiece. It strains belief that even Giorgione's other works (aside from some beautiful male portraits) were truly his or issued from an early time. I would much rather have a delightful *Santa Conversazione* (given by the Uffizi to Bellini) attributed to him. Regardless of whose it is, it is so exquisitely confessional a work that it achieves a personality in and of itself and does not require some other work to complement it. Background: mountainous landscape (terra ferma), peacefully inhabited by hermits and characterized by farming and herd-keeping. A peculiar little temple closes off the background against a dark green lake, before which the setting of the painting proper—a broad, festive marble terrace—spreads out. A balustrade of simple design fences off this terrace from the lake and the edges, and it rises on the left toward a throne on which the Madonna, soft, sorrowful, in a black-and-white gown, holds her melancholy dominion. A female saint stands at her side, perfectly still and waiting, and in this subtle figure one feels most richly the festiveness that weaves its way so variously throughout the others. Behind the balustrade, deeper within the painting, a male saint stands with an alertly resting sword, and next to him St. Peter leans with both arms, as befits his pensiveness, against the stone railing—in front of which, at the extreme right, a hermit and a magnificently reconciled St. Sebastian, who allows the arrows to rest in his wounds, stride toward the solitary princess with hesitant steps. In these two figures, absolute calm rises to a soft rhythm and then breaks in the center of the painting into cheerful movement, with the play of a few naked children who in richest spontaneity wind their intense joy around a clipped laurel tree.

Off to the side hangs a Vittore Carpaccio one could almost mistake for a better work of Dante G. Rossetti, so fairy-tale-like and mysterious is it in form and color.

But what is this fairy-tale quality of the Venetians, even if only darkly expressed (but expressed nonetheless), compared to the hidden mysteries that in the paintings of Botticelli compose the very essence of the work.

The mysterious does not conceal itself here in deep and heavy darkness. It has revealed itself brightly and majestically to some being. But that being, in which the happiness of this unveiling still trembles, is much too helpless and primitive to echo back somehow the depth of the confession. She feels immeasurable wealth inside herself, but when she tries to give freely from it, she cannot lift a trace of its fullness out of her soul. She remains poor because she is not able to consecrate anyone as an accessory to her treasures, and solitary because she does not succeed in building a bridge out from herself. And so these beings go through the world without ever touching it, carrying inside themselves the mute stars of which they are able to tell no one. That is their sadness. And they are also haunted by a fear: that they themselves will come to mistrust these stars when they will be exhorted to believe so completely in nothing other than their glory and their goodness. And for all that they are illumined through and through by their inmost possession of this solitary brightness, which would make them blissful if they were more courageous and without pity.

That is the apprehension of his Venus, the fear of his Primavera, the weary mildness of his Madonnas.

All these Madonnas feel their unwoundedness like a guilt. They cannot forget that they gave birth without suffering, just as they conceived without passion. There is a shame about them that they did not with their own mighty effort lift the smiling salvation out of themselves, that they became mothers without the daring of a mother. That the fruit simply fell into their arms, into these yearning girls' arms that hold it as something undeserved and heavy. What they bear, finally, is only the weight of the presentiment that the child will suffer because they did not suffer, will bleed because they did not bleed, will die because they did not die. This reproach overshadows all the light from their heaven, and the candles burn dimly and anxiously in it. —There are moments when the splendor of their long throne-days places a smile about their lips. Then the tearful eyes strangely harmonize with it. But after a short absence of sorrow, which they experience as happiness, they are startled by the strange ripeness of their spring and long in all the hopelessness of their heaven for a hot summer joy full of earthly passion.

And just as the weary Madonna regrets that she missed the miracle for the sake of the miraculous and laments her powerlessness to lift out of herself the summer whose seeds she feels in her ripe body, so his Venus fears that she will never be able to dispense all the beauty she brings among those who are thirsting for it; and in the same way his Primavera trembles, since she must keep her ultimate splendor and her deepest holiness an unspoken secret.

And so charged are all these works with this single schism, that one recognizes it even in the way that they are constructed, worked out in detail, and presented: one sees the artist's trembling hands, fighting and straining to lift the gold-pure weight of deepest fulfillments all the way out of his soul, and yet again and again growing exhausted from the stubborn impossibility, and at last tearing desperately at the secret riches. With that the hands clench violently and twist the contours into acerbity, into misshapenness, into spite. And then Savonarola releases the convulsion and conflict from them. He lifts them out of the depths of what is secret into the ecclesiastical twilight of renunciation. And there they grope uncertainly and aimlessly like sedated madmen at the edge of old memories and simulate dead longings with numbed humility. And that is the end. That is the manner of someone's dying who had the longing to bear fruit, but whose strength reached only to the marches of spring, to that region where he is heavy with sweetness, deep with ripeness, and poor in the presentiment of someone who is to come. . . .

And if I am not mistaken, if we (or those behind us) should be the ones who have (or are acquiring) the strength for summer to match the longing for summer, then it is imperative that we not only better understand Botticelli, erect monuments to him, and deck his immortality with wreaths, but also love him like a dearly departed, who fell because he fought so far ahead of us for *that* victory—which for us is still dream and goal and longing in our creative days.

Oh this touching sorrow of those arrived too soon: they are like children who find their way into the Christmas-tree room before the candles have been lit and the objects cast their aura. They want to turn back and flee the threshold and yet they remain standing in the disenchanted darkness—until their poor eyes grow used to it.

Fra Angelico is the sharpest opposite of Sandro Botticelli. He is shy like the very first moment of spring and just as full of faith. Whether he paints Madonnas or the legends of whatever saints he takes as pretext (*Cosmas and Damian* in the Galleria dell'Accademia), he avows in them again and again in trembling words the creed of his own humility. And yet he is a latecomer with the gestures of the very earliest, with the coolness of their feeling and the boundlessness of their devotion. Only girded by San Marco's intimately sheltering cloister walls could this art break open and flower and wilt away in such forgotten purity, leaving nothing more behind than perhaps a May-morning memory in the hearts of a few special masters who, in their thirst for life, grew out beyond this strange blissfulness. And it is odd that of all people Benozzo Gozzoli should become the freest and happiest proclaimer of earthly joy, he who even in the very midst of those contented saints was Giovanni Angelico's youth and disciple. On the Campo Santo of Pisa he has left behind shining evidence of his outlook, his aptitude, and his inner riches; the one side wall is decorated almost its entire length with his frescoes, and one marvels at the resourcefulness with which he drew splendor and humanity from the sparse biblical material and at the unswerving lightheartedness with which he covered over the wall of a graveyard with endless triumphs of life, as if he wanted to spoil and make irksome the dominion of he who is absolute ruler here. Even the old master of the *Triumph of Death* and of the *Last Judgment* (Vasari refers to him as Buffalmacco), whose close presence he must have felt like a constant admonition as he went about his work, could not in the least trouble his naive intentions. He came and painted life and its enjoyment, and the spring, framed by the high Gothic arcades, built its cheerful roses in the middle of the Campo Santo's courtyard as one who shared his outlook.—And thus, thanks to this alliance, life seems to rule victorious here even to this present day. There is nothing of the dark severity of a monastery courtyard, either in the hall's boldly arched-out vaultings or in the self-admiring column-architecture of the windows (whose inexhaustible vistas continually surprise); and even the painting of the triumph of death seems put there only to emphasize the happiness of a hermit's active existence and the reconciled harmony of paradise. This latter portrayal, most likely by Orcagna, exists like a medieval love song turned painting amidst the oppression of the most ghastly, nightmarelike scenes.—Over all these figures there lies something of that festive leisure and ease that is like a resting after long travels. All are quiet and thankful for this common solitude and heavy as if with a sweet languor, which in the noble folds of their glowing garments mysteriously reveals itself. There is nothing yet, as in later representations, of that banqueting or dancing or telling stories or singing at any cost; one celebrates easefully and delights in the consciousness of one's sleeping strength or dream-struck longing. And something of this instinctive attitude remains alive in the common people, as I was able to observe recently on a Sunday. How the mothers and old folk and children take their whole life, with all its small joys and stunted hopes, out of the week's darkness and place it in the sun—as if they were carrying it into a temple. On chairs, small stools, and benches they all sit in front of the doors, depending on age and inclination silently or gossipy, pensively or watchfully, and with their cheerfulness embellish for the whole length of all these narrow streets the inexpressive brows of their poor houses. And then it is quite something to drive by them in a carriage; the coachman snaps his whip above the clattering stones and puts all his pride into trotting by at a furious clip. And they all look up, curious and indifferent and annoyed and waving. It is as if the cramped dwellings had been turned inside out by some magic word, and you now drove past all sorts of naked destinies that offered themselves up willingly to your gaze. But later, in the afternoon, you can come across blond and dark girls in the forest, and watch the way they hold hands and in almost total silence stride hesitantly in long lines between the steep pine trunks; occasionally one of them will slowly begin to sing, softly, as if out of a sweet remembering, and then two or three of the others will join in with louder voices—as if in confirmation. And after a few paces the song will subside again into their movements, from which it had seemed to free itself, and they will wander deeper into the woods. That is their Sunday.

The sea also plays a part in this molding of an unassuming festiveness. All these people, men and young girls, have no idea how deeply they are its pupils and its children and how closely connected they are in mind and mood with its beauty and with its anger and with its vastness. There was a day of abundant fishing: in the evening they gather on the pier, which goes out along the canal toward the landing, and they wait there and guess the names of the boats that with steep, narrow sails like cypress trees appear on the horizon and two by two grow larger until they are like an avenue leading out into infinity. There is a bright joy on their watchful faces, and the deep sun traces the line of its smile far away onto the housefronts of Viareggio, so that they too seem full of happy participation. But at the end of the pier, where the reception begins, ladies and fishergirls, soldiers and monks, children watched over by the Black Sisters stand as in the old operetta, while from the farthest piling some brown urchin lets his sandhard little legs dangle as a pennon of welcome. And in soundless dignity the boats steer with broad, sated evening-sails into the black lapping of the canal. All the crew stands around the mast. Laughing boys, stout men, quietly leaning against the trunk, and very old men with wrinkled faces crouch in bright patchwork at the tiller: all their old strength seems concentrated in the sinewy, hairy hand that grips the steering shaft as if it were the hilt of a sword. In this way they glide in as after a long journey, as if they had aged out there and now for the first time found that beach again from which they had set out when they were full of young darkness. All have something of the seriousness of eternity about them, and one can see by their chests that they have grown broad and brave in the strong fear of danger.

As in the southern Tyrol here also: only the mothers appear tired and prematurely aged. As long as they are still in spring, they are light, bright, smiling girls—and then their summer-strength fails from the many children and the endless work. Finally they are nothing but tough tenacity, rough resistance to a death that wants to tear them prematurely from their house and its indigence—only a daily revolt against the tempting weariness with which it seeks to seduce them— nothing beyond that. What lies over the decline of this people is what brought about its bloom: the incapacity for summer. It created the cool beauty of its springtime art and now is guilty of the careworn autumn of its living-to-the-end.—

In the small villages along the Arno—in Rovezzano and Maiano, and then by the bright rose-slopes of Fiesole—you can meet childlike young girls who replicate exactly the Madonnas of the early flower-ing. They are like late godchildren of these white marble Marys of Settignano and Da Maiano and Roselino. In these masters the sculp-tural quality of spring seems to me to have found its most beautiful fulfillment—remembering also and only the Robbias, who in their best works (the tabernacle in S. S. Apostoli) preserved for eternity all the magic and confidence of their time. There is already a growing-riper and a growing-warmer in the bright colors of these works in clay, a quiet humanizing of the miraculous, which descends from the smooth, royal marble into this rough clay, from the unapproachable palace into the festively decorated hut that stands in the people's midst.

And scarcely have they ventured this step forward when already a premonition of summer coils around them in fruit-wreaths strong with color, frames them and at the same time circumscribes—strange symbol—their cheerful splendor.

These Robbias held fast for over a century to the full loveliness of their sentiment, unconcerned with taste and fashion. They recognized the value of a form once discovered, and sensed that they could not venture out beyond it without forfeiting the reconciled unity of their circular reliefs. They had a small repertoire of motifs and a humble material: but because they went so deeply into both, they extracted from the figures the most heartfelt tenderness and from the clay its most delicate effects. Especially where, as with Andrea, Luca, and sometimes Giovanni, the colors still exhibit a modest restraint, where the most ravishing blue appears to transfigure the blinding white of these angels' heads and otherwise partakes only along the edge, for example in the wreaths, adding to this purest harmony a gentle animation, like a pious hymn from more colorful days—there one will feel a magic that outlasts all ages. Or these tabernacles with their deepening central perspective toward which all figures tend in gentlest piety, and these naive-intimate babes in swaddling clothes on the facade of the Ospedale degli Innocenti, and so many other of these delightful surprises that populate Florence and its environs in such profusion. One imagines that these Robbias created a Madonna in the likeness of every woman in Florence. And even if their Madonnas never performed any great miracles (if one wanted that kind, one had only to bestir oneself to the white ceremonious ones in the churches), they yet listened to each girl's prayer each morning and answered: "You are lovely and luminous and life is your home, for it is bright and glorious like you. Go forth and be happy in it." And they went forth and were full of beauty and happiness. And that is miracle enough.

Lorenzo il Magnifico's "Canti" comes to mind, with these lines of jubilation that contain the kernel of all inner workings and essences:

Quant' è bella giovinezza,
che si fugge tuttavia.
Chi vuol' esser lieto, sia!
Di doman non c'è certezza.

[How beautiful is the time of youth,
even as it flees life's course.
He who wants to be gay, let him be so!
For who knows about tomorrow.]

But the impending end, far from being a source of fear, was the ground of all quick gaiety and bore no seeds of sentimentality.

The latter was something invented for the first time in the era of fatigue; when one no longer possessed the courage for great pain and the trust in joy had slipped away from people, then somewhere in between they found sentimentality.

In Botticelli there is no trace of it; instead there is the deepest pain overshadowing the ever-again desired consummation. In his paintings there is no lingering in tender, soft-hearted melodies; there is the leave-taking of a dying bliss.

In the gallery of Prince Corsini, where a Botticelli (also a beautiful Raffaelino da Garbo, by the way) hangs beside a spate of late Italians, one can grasp his sorrow in its full extent. It is like a martyr's death juxtaposed with the "beautiful dying" of a play-actor.

How could these primitives come upon sentimentality, when it arises only where small, intimidated feelings are no longer capable of filling the emptiness of a human being; then one supplements one's interior architecture with statues in the swollen style of Bandinelli. They fill out.

Sentimentality is premised on weakness, and on fondness for suffering. But in no one so much as in Botticelli does one perceive the struggle *against* pain. And this pain is not a dull, aimless dejection (as I have tried to indicate), but the feeling of this unfruitful spring that exhausts itself in its own treasures.

One could in fact more nearly call Michelangelo sentimental, if one wanted to talk merely of his form. As in his work the concept is always huge and endowed with the fixity of finished sculpture, so the line of even his most peaceful figures is always restlessly active. It is as though someone were speaking to deaf people or recalcitrants. He can never emphasize strongly enough, and the anxiety of not being understood colors all his confessions. Thus finally even his intimate revelations have the look of manifestos that had demanded to be erected at the far corners of the world, visible to all.

What saddened Botticelli, the more subtle, more exquisitely observant of the two, caused him to lose his hold on himself, and when Sandro's hands were shaking with a sense of dread, his fists hammered an image of his anger into the trembling stone.

Had Michelangelo been left alone for only a moment, he would have set his chisel to the world and sculpted out of this pinched sphere a slave. And that figure would have then had to crown the sculptor's tomb.

Now *that* was someone with the strength for summer. But there was no space then and no example. When he gave his boy David the limbs of a giant, he only made us see more clearly the unripe youthfulness of this figure.

And if the trees were to arch their blossoms out over every mountain, the season would still be only an immeasurable spring without the power to fetch the summer from the sun.

His Madonnas deny their springtime. They feign, to be sure, the happiness of a completely earthly fulfillment. One could almost believe them—that they had given birth to the Redeemer in grief and labor-pain. But this lie makes them hard and unfeminine, and they get beyond virginity *and* maternalness with one violent shove, to arrive at a kind of defiant heroism.

Michelangelo did indeed, because he failed to find his way into summer, often go beyond it altogether. And both his imitators and his fellow strivers confirm with all their mediocrity the decline that this genius announced in such desperate shouts.

Yesterday's evening produced two excellent conversations that touch so closely on my mood and meditations that I want to record them briefly. At half past five, in the midst of my Michelangelo-thoughts, Herr K. came to see me. I could not pry myself loose instantly from what had been the joy and effort of my afternoon, so I kept on talking and musing until finally I was unfolding to him in broad outlines the notion of that contemporary summer art that is to fulfill the quattrocento springtime. He was quite taken by this, for all his intellectual reserve, and I needed all my strength to control my enthusiasm for this doctrine and not preach at him out of all bounds. I must have talked nonstop for two hours or more, all the time watching with intense pleasure as his eyes brightened and his whole demeanor warmed. I wanted so—quickly, quickly—to come to You, for I am aware of something inside me that You don't know about yet, a new great brightness that endows my speech with power and a full complement of images. I sometimes catch myself now listening to my own words and learning in startled awe from my own conversation. Something is sounding from deep within me that through these pages, through my tender songs, and through all my plans of future deeds wants to reach people. It is as if I must talk, now in the moment of strength and clarity when more speaks out of me than I myself: my bliss. It is as if I must convert all who are holding back and having doubts; for I have more strength in me than I can contain in words, and I want to turn them to freeing people from the strange fear out of which I came. And that must be apparent in me; for today my Russian neighbor, when we were walking to the seashore at nine this evening, offered me her confidence in all manner of lovely indirectnesses, so that I felt like a father in my will to protect and in my power to do so. And I resumed talking exactly where I had left off with Herr K. And it was as if I were merely translating into words the great soundings of the solitary moonsea at our side, and we were both listeners. I said: "You must find the confidence for everything, and the place where there is space for all your riches. Otherwise you will pass life and yourself by. That would be a great pity. There are such golden treasures in both. You should leave home. Not just for six to seven weeks. Leave. There is a great difference. For a short trip you will only take along a few things. You will select what is most necessary, and finally, when you are in that foreign place, you will find yourself lacking certain things. Nothing weighty, but something dear: a picture, a book, a remembrance; some small trifle that you would hardly think of at home. Now you miss it. It's the same with one's spiritual luggage and the soul's provisions: you take along for six to seven weeks only what is most suitable. You arrive at a foreign place and remain a foreigner there because you don't have enough home with you to spread out around yourself. And then that being-limited: when in that distant country something really comes toward you, something that demands much, that demands *You* of yourself, then you don't have yourself with you and begin thinking: 'Why risk it, I'll be traveling back tomorrow toward the old things anyway. . . .' " And I went on in this vein, saying things that by now I have quite forgotten, and then: "I wish I could show you something from out there like a gift one brings back from a fairy-tale people and says with shuddering wonderment: 'Yes, such things do exist there.' That's the way I'd like to show you something."—As we stood by the gate at half past ten, the lady said: "And you don't consider that unfeminine?" "Oh," I said, "a man can be rich in possessing, but a woman forgets her wealth if she is not allowed to give freely of it. You must have space to place something out of yourself. You must experience some form of motherhood. A day must come that wants something of you, and a second and a third: each with a different wish. When you finally see how you can accomplish everything, there will be no end of self-confidence and joy. Try it. Go away and don't think of coming home. Go as one would like to walk by the sea at night, forever on and on under the many silent stars. Try it." "I will." And she gave me her hand full of a deep gratefulness.

A good conclusion to a day—was it not? I leaned back in my tall armchair for a long time, and with a flickering candle at my side I thought: "Lou—how splendid You are, what space You have opened up in me." For if the Italian days showered me with treasures, it was You who created room for them in my soul—where the dreams crowded, and the many timidities. It was You who made me festive.

To return to You so clear, my darling: it's the best of what I'll bring You.

I know: not everything will remain a hymn in me, as in these days; darknesses and confusions will come. But deep within me I have a small garden surrounded by solemn festiveness, and no fear will ever reach down that far again. And if you wish, each year we shall extend this garden's markstones.

Is it not thus: deep inside, everyone is like a church, and the walls are decorated with splendid frescoes. In first childhood, when all the festiveness still lies open, it is too dark inside to see the paintings. And then, as it grows lighter and lighter in the hall, the adolescent stupidities and the false longings and the craving shame take control, and they plaster over one work after the other. And many will go far into life and through it without even suspecting the old magnificence beneath the somber dearth. Fortunate, however, the person who feels, finds, and secretly uncovers it. He bestows gifts upon himself. And he will return home into himself.

Ah, if our parents were only born with us, how much bitterness and retracing of paths we might be spared. But parents and children can only walk along next to each other, never with each other; a deep trench runs between them, across which they can now and then extend each other a small tenderness.

Parents should never try to teach us life; for they teach us *their* life.

Mothers, however, are like artists. The artist's task is to find himself. Woman finds fulfillment in the child. And what the artist wrests out of himself in bits and pieces, Woman lifts out of her womb like an entire world, full of powers and possibilities.

Woman has not then reached the goal, and may not give the child her own life. Because now her path toward the child begins.

A woman who is an artist is no longer compelled to create once she has become a mother. She has given her goal a place outside herself and from that moment on may in the deepest sense *live* art.

That is why Woman is richer by so much: she truly reaches that fulfillment toward which the artist may only ripen. That is why to the creative man she can be like a prophetess who through her love recounts to him the goal's splendor.

Woman's way goes always toward the child, before her motherhood and after. The moment she grasps herself, she removes her goal from herself and places it into the midst of Life. For her path is meant to lead into Life.

Those women who bear the many children accompany each one only to the threshold of Life; there they must turn back around and go meet a new child coming toward them. And so the children become orphans and the mother hastens impatiently back and forth along the borders of Life and lacks festiveness and joy and grows old and tired.

If one wanted to indicate somehow the ardor of our time, one would have to speak of the painful bliss of its artists. And the book would be titled: *The Maternal in Our Art,* but it would be a betrayal, this book.

How typical it is that others deemed the human the universal—the place, so to speak, where all find and recognize one another. One must learn to see, on the contrary, that it is precisely the human that makes us solitary.

The more human we become, the more diverse we become. It is as if beings suddenly were faceting a thousandfold; for a collective name that earlier arched over thousands is rapidly becoming too cramped for ten people, and one is forced to consider each in isolation. Imagine: when instead of peoples, nations, families, and societies we shall some day have human beings, when one can no longer combine even three under a single name! Will not the world then have to grow larger?

We are a long way from that, of course: for the present the need to close ranks, to set common goals is still—and above all in Germany—very great. Whereby of course the responsibility of the individual is greatly reduced, while his strength is artificially heightened through the noble feeling of competition.

But that in art of all places the forming of "societies" still flourishes is a depressing sign of immaturity. These pamphlets constantly keep appearing that are tastefully and modestly made up of endless variations on "We want . . ." Just the other day the same thing again: "German Theatre Society." Ten privy councillors and retired officers and university professors, who occasionally feel obliged by their social status to do something for this poor, needy art that is demure and well behaved like a candidate for a teacher's position, band together and in addition to other weighty pronouncements turn out— once and for all—yet another version of this: "We want an art for all the people." What a rash presumption, since "the people," who to be sure *are* the greater authority, decree daily: *"The people want no art at all."*

This at a time when we are just beginning to enjoy the fact that our art can be redemption only for the artist himself, and that only very few initiates who gaze into these mysteries can participate in them with full happiness!

The artist can leave a lasting imprint on wider circles only through his personality, through the art now in his past—which I, as earlier, would like to term his culture. His works are experiences, told to a few deepest intimates in hours of sacred twilight. And situating them among the many will not make them more effectual; for those who are without love will not come near them.

But in our museums crassness reigns. As if someone blindly tore pages out of different books in different languages and pasted them together into one huge luxury volume.

Torn away from the place to which all their inclinations and aptitudes bind them, all these works of art are now homeless and stand next to each other like orphaned children. And one reacts the same way one does when confronted by a troop of such uniformed children. One does not see the blond child, the sad child, the pensive child, and the quietly clever child; instead one says: Twenty orphan children.

If, at all events, the works of *one* artist are forced to put up with each other in a single room; then something does arise from their involuntary cooperation that is greater, more eloquent, and more revealing than any one taken by itself. I am thinking of the Donatello room in the Bargello.

But what would all those statues be without the polychrome portrait bust of Niccolò da Uzzano. It is one of art's most extraordinary revelations. Donatello the realist came to feel quite naively that he would be unable to capture the personality of this man without giving him, in addition to all the life of the lines, the color needed to complete him. And thus this wondrous work. A head in which energy competes with a certain *laisser-aller;* one that is not quite witty, but that nonetheless turns toward you with such full engagement that you suppose some question must have passed you by and, embarrassed, seek quickly for an answer. You feel as though you have known this man a long time and delight in seeing him again. And he confirms in you this feeling; for his friendly interest seems vividly to return it.

Polychrome sculpture. Of late we have often attached a question mark to this notion. I am convinced that sculpture, in order to achieve its ultimate goals, must often reach for color (which is not to say that it should get its color from the art of painting). When it is a matter of portrait busts, it will be up to the artist to determine whether an individuality, for its full realization, requires color—and as with all things of art the deciding factors will be the particular case, the motif at hand, and finally the material, not some universally valid law. It might be possible, for instance, to repeat the bloom of a pale young girl in softly yellowish marble; even the small gray veins of the material might be cleverly exploited, assuming a deeply insightful artist is at work. Perhaps a very old man or someone afflicted with an illness could be more richly portrayed thus in white marble, in which case the vacant eyes would nicely further the impression of a standing-above-life. I can imagine, for example, a bust of Jacobsen made from this material. For a beautiful and mature woman, a bluish-white marble of sheen and gentle smoothness will be appropriate, and contrasts will lend clarity to the conception—for example, a subtly golden, stylized employment of jewelry, or a hint of color in the hair. As in general the intermittent use of color can be one of the most subtle means of characterization. Combining mineral, bronze, and metal with stone in a single figure, however, will always seem dilettantish and contrived. It should only be employed in small, elegant works—as in one of those exquisite pieces that require the interplay of gold and ivory or silver and ebony to achieve their ends. But how ridiculous the effect of these bronze chairs and metal wreaths of all our white monuments! The material that almost calls out for color is clay, and it is strange that our time remains so incurious about its potential. Even though we know that the Greeks regularly polychromized their statues, we anxiously avoid this possibility, fearing that a colored statue would have the look of a wax figure. With the same logic one could contest a painting's color, fearing that it might approximate an oleograph.

Clearly, there is much still to be learned here, and color is not the only factor; one will have to attend to the characteristics of the material and submit oneself to its will—even, up to a point, to its whim. As far as portraiture is concerned, one will know whether marble or bronze or clay is more suitable for describing a certain individual's personality. One will further weigh that person's closeness to life or his distance from it and will represent someone who was solitary differently from one who found his greatest pleasures in sociability. One will have to consider whether the purpose is to provide a confirmation of immortality or an image for the family, along with a thousand other things. If, moreover, a large monument is to be erected, the decorative intent comes much more into play than otherwise. One will conceive of the town square as an integral space—something difficult, admittedly, with our town squares—and heighten this impression through the monument one entrusts to its center. The stranger who visits the town should constantly find himself imagining that this significant immortal had always been there, and that the houses had congregated around him one by one to form a reverential circle.

Here one might speculate more generally about portraiture and its place within art. It seems at first glance that with portrait-painting the subjectively confessional, which for me determines the rank of every work of art, has withdrawn before a purely material-objective task. Absorption in someone else's individuality appears here to take precedence over one's own self-clarification, thus putting the whole notion of art advanced here into question. Even more damaging is portraiture's character as a means of income, which plays havoc with all the crucial tenets: it would be difficult to maintain in this context that the public is superfluous, just as it would be hard to believe that any sincere artist had felt the compelling need to "confess" himself a councillor-of-commerce or an archbishop.

But if one reconsiders a bit less prejudiciously, it turns out that a head can become a pretext for certain deeply personal confessions just as readily as, say, a landscape, and that a distinctive face, with its depths and hidden intimacies and its alternating disclosures and concealments, is certainly no more confining a space than an ocean mood or a forest motif. And whoever regards the necessity of resemblance to be an arbitrarily imposed restriction might want to consider that its achievement requires the development of a whole array of the most subjective qualities, and that the task of making "lifelike," not the momentary demeanor of a person, not his occasional face and one of his everyday gestures, but a distillation of all the phases of his personality, admits of *only* a personal solution.—Every artist, almost as a matter of course, searches out all traces and presentiments in a face that auspiciously approaches him as motif, in order to study them patiently or (depending on his mode of creating) identify and subdue them at a stroke. And when he uses them as the basis for certain expressions of his own, far from jeopardizing their particularity, he will actually illuminate and exalt it—lift it, as it were, out beyond every doubt. For there is room left for personal confession only where the subject has been grasped in all its depth and subdued in all its resistances. And here it seems to me that even the ocean in its boundlessness is no broader a frame for the abundance of confessing than the human face and figure, where the means are more concentrated and more intricately related. And if to the true artist the face will appear spacious enough for all the possibilities of his own feeling, there may still be those who conceive of their job as "filling in" the portrait, just as one might, given a predetermined rhyme scheme, "fill in" a poem, and so go about satisfying the requirements of this quaint amusement with either more or less technical skill. Which doesn't mean that it isn't good enough to be paid for according to how big it is and how many different colors it contains.

Judgments about resemblance or the lack thereof are relevant then *only* with reference to photography. Artistically conceived resemblance is to the actual look of a person as ecstasy is to lassitude.

Does Botticelli in his portraits become a groveler or a self-renouncer? The subject presents for him the same challenge as his Madonna and his Venus. He masters it in order to get through and beyond it to himself.

Perhaps the best thing about Lenbach is that he takes the names away from all his portrait heads—no matter how heavy the crowns that may rest on them—and simply turns them all into Lenbachs. Which in this instance, however, may not mean for all of them a heightening. Just think of Titian or of Giorgione or indeed any of our best contemporaries.

That many an artist experiences the portrait, apart from the prejudices attached to it, as a confinement, may lie in the fact that his contemporaries appear to him so narrow. In all other motifs he experiences the eternities. From their faces, however, his present era looks back at him soberly through fearful boundaries. So it is, I think, with Böcklin.

Those in the quattrocento were able to live free of this apprehension. If their era also gazed back at them out of all these facial traits, there was more eternity in their era. One finds oneself marveling: how much space for sun there was on all these foreheads!

Of course one enjoyed perusing oneself; but one preferred letting oneself be painted, together with and next to others. The statue effected an isolation. And in a painting one always got one's whole era in the bargain, a golden background that was a realm of riches in its own right. One loved this era and wanted everyone to know that one was a child of its strengths.

And so one placed in one's background some piece of architecture, a bright hall, a proud tower, a defiant wall. And one never forgot the garden. As in a grave one wanted to be together with one's favorite things.

And even at a time when one was already quite sophisticated about perspective, one blithely painted people and towers and houses side by side at equal height. "Oh," says the good public in front of them today, "these little towers!" Instead of saying in amazement: "Oh, these huge people!"

Sculpture in those days kept its distance from portraiture, no doubt because of its preference for the nude per se, perhaps also because of its primarily decorative intent. And then: in the midst of time and life one wanted to display to all the many viewers the descendant who *in this frame* was noble and dignified. In the durable stone, in this white, timeless solitude one wished to represent only those ripe for eternity. And since standing is part of life and well suited to its narrow days, but altogether too profane a posture for the boundless, one chose for these figures a ceremonious sleep. The easy relaxedness in these limbs dispels any thought in the viewer's mind that they might ever grow tired. But also no note of impotent decrepitude inflects the state of bodily death; there is in this deep immobility a soothing, standing strength that better than anything transmits the impression of eternity.

Such is the spirit of the magnificent Renaissance monuments of the bishops and princes and statesmen: those by Settignano and Roselino in Santa Croce, and Roselino's masterpiece in San Miniato al Monte, which remained exemplary for a vast array of Italian funerary monuments.

That is no accident; for the seriousness and solemnity achieved through its noble simplicity of material, profiling, and ornament are unsurpassable, and they could not but satisfy the highest need so long as what one wanted from a funerary monument was reconciliation and hopeful, high serenity—not mysticism, sentimentality, and painful distortion.

Our time could not slap itself in the face more insultingly than by installing next to these homes of death—which are like the keystones of noble, ripe attitudes toward life—its own pitiful marble phrases, and then having the nerve to use these latter to try to celebrate Dante!

All fear of death falls away from one in the face of these tombs. The archfiend appears vanquished exactly where life comes to celebrate him so simply and naively with all its love and lightness. Death is as if put to shame by magnanimity and, in a gesture of renouncing, places his hard hands into those of his conqueror. And says: My strength henceforth be yours. It is the only one you still lack. You must wield *this* power also; for since you build and create, you alone can know as I do what is worn and weary and in need of passing on.

This reconciliation culminates in the quiet rounded shape that arches over the sleeping marble figure to protect it and conclude it and make its white peace even more ceremonious and solitary. These people were not vanquished by death, and no trace of resistance, no remembrance of a struggle, clouds their foreheads or makes the folds of their garments hard.

Only rarely do Gothic elements make an appearance on these sepulchres: various cheeky little turrets or wind-bag arches that try to make promises out beyond this reconciled ending. But the Gothic also exists in this same relationship in the greater architecture. *It* is the guest that must adjust itself to the customs and legends of this sunny country, and where it recklessly tries to outstretch and display its entire being, there arises high up in the vaultings, at the capitals and along the cornices, a battle in which the healthy and proud strength of the Renaissance ideas, effortlessly smiling, prevails.

Yes, it is quite comical to see these many tamed arches with their pointed tops and the frightened little turrets that are like actors who forgot their lines in the middle of their scene. A great impotence came over them. Suddenly they lack proof of the heavens they were meant to proclaim, and they stand in adolescent embarrassment before the mature, compassionate forgiving of these marble-clear earthly thoughts.

What could promises mean for an era whose every wish fulfilled itself each day? It had raised the heavens out of itself, and had caused longing and bliss to be merely like things among the other things, merely like colors among the many colors, merely sounds, neighbors to one another, in the hymns of their festiveness; and by conquering all might and by shepherding each joy or fulfillment into its own bounds, it became so spacious that it seemed limitless, and the splendors in it became deeper and holier for its holding all of them in its arms with warm love.

What remains for an era that believes that the purest bliss is in the timeless heavens and that the bloodiest suffering is somewhere in burning hell? Splendor and darkness, love and hate, longing and despair, fulfillment and eternity, anger and timidity—none of that belongs to it. It lies poor and colorless somewhere in the middle of it all and a single twilight blurs its night and day.

Zoppot, 6 July 1898

Here at the edge of a cooler sea I bring to an end this book, which I have denied more than three times; for much fear and poverty lie between back then and right now: days like flat country roads with poor leafless chestnut trees on either side, thoughts like endless villages passing by with dull lifeless doorways and windows ruined by rain. And yet all this *had* to come, and I am like this not because it came but because it happened *now,* at a moment when I wished nothing more than to bring You so much festiveness, unspoiled and holy, and surround You with it as with a dark niche that receives its statue. But I was like the child who for love of his desperately ill little sister runs to the city from the dark farmstead through night and need to fetch her medicine, and in the light of morning, enticed by childish games, forgets the very purpose of the trip and cheerfully returns without the longed-for cure. . . . This cheerfulness will become a weeping, and a despair stands behind it: I know too well.

And furthermore: the circumstances under which we first saw each other again were such that I perceived in You only various things from the world of yesterday; something past, something overcome, something narrow that had been hurtful for us both crowded in on me and blocked the memory of our solitary happiness that is timeless and not tied to any "once." I knew only that You patiently listened to my innumerable small complaints, and suddenly I noticed that I was complaining again and You were listening again, just as before. That made me so ashamed, it almost embittered me. It was much like the people of Prague, who for their entire lives live their own past. They are like corpses who cannot find peace and therefore in the dark of night live their dying again and again and pass one another by across the hard graves. They have nothing left; the smile has wilted on their lips, and their eyes have drifted off with their last crying as if they were floating on twilight rivers. All progress in them amounts only to this: their coffin turns to rot and their clothes fall to pieces and they themselves grow crumblier and wearier and lose their fingers like old recollections. And they tell each other the story of this in their long-dead voices: that's how the people of Prague are.

Now I came to You full of future. And from habit we began to live our past. How could I observe that You became free and festive through the confidence in this book, since I did not see YOU, but only Your forbearance and gentleness and the endeavor to give me courage and raise my spirits. Nothing at this moment could more incense me than this. I hated You like something *too great. I* wanted this time to be the rich one, the giver, the host, the master, and You were supposed to come and be guided by my care and love and stroll about in my hospitality. And now in Your presence I was again only the smallest beggar at the outermost threshold of Your being—which rests on such broad and certain columns. What help was it that I put on my accustomed holiday words? I felt myself becoming more and more ridiculous in my masquerade, and the dark wish awakened in me a desire to creep away into a deep Nowhere. Shame, shame was all there was inside me. Every reunion with You made me ashamed. Can You understand that? Invariably I said to myself: "I can give You nothing, nothing at all; my gold turns to coal when I hand it to

You, and I become poor in the process." Once I came to You in such poverty. Almost as a child I came to the rich woman. And You took my soul in Your arms and rocked it. That was good. Back then You kissed my forehead and had to bend far down to do so. Do You understand that at Your side I grew up until it was only a short distance from Your eyes to my eyes? But that I wanted in the end, stem-strong, to bend down toward Your lips exactly as Your soul once bent down toward my forehead? I didn't want to be embraced by You, I wanted You to be able to lean against me when You are tired. I didn't want to feel Your consolation, I wanted to feel the power inside me to console You, should You ever need consoling. I didn't want to find the memory of our Berlin winter days still inside You, I wanted You to be more than ever my future, since I had the faith for happiness and the confidence for fulfillment. And meanwhile this book told You what happened to me down below, and You lived through it like a deep dream and became the future. But then I no longer believed in it. I was blind and bitter, full of helpless and hateful thoughts and day in, day out tormented by the fear: that now You, with the riches I had brought You and that You so quickly raised and made Your own possession, could begin presenting *me* with gifts, and already I felt in the best hours how I was beginning to accept as alms of Your untiring goodness what I had fetched in blessed victories. I had brought golden bowls to You, bright vessels of festiveness, and then I had compelled You with my neediness to mint from this noble treasure small coins for everyday use, and thus slowly pay me back the gift. I felt myself becoming so pitiful and wretched as this happened that I threw away or lost the last of my own wealth and in my desperation felt only the vague imperative to flee the environs of this goodness that was humiliating me.

But during that time, in the midst of this very convulsion, I realized that were I to shake off my paralysis and gather myself in a resolve: each of my deeds, all movement in me, would strive toward You; then, when for the first time after this dull sadness I was forced to think again about tomorrow, when behind Your figure Fate stood and through Your estranged voice put to me the iron question: "What will you *do*?"—then everything inside me was as if freed from ice; the wave sprang from the floe and cast itself with all its might toward the shore—without delaying and without doubt. When You asked me about the future and I lay helplessly and remained awake that whole night wracked by this worry, then I knew, when in the morning I found You again, that You are the ever New, the ever Young, the eternal Goal, and that for me there is one fulfillment that includes everything: to move toward YOU.

If my beloved were a poor, slight girl, I would have had to take leave of her forever; this girl would have loved the past and always tied my young roses with the faded ribbons I brought her once in May. That is why young men so often must appear ungrateful and inconstant, especially vis-à-vis these tender and gladly sacrificing beings who have given them everything; these girls are violins with one single song, and they don't know when it has ended.

Your strings are rich; and however far I may go—*You are always there before me*. My struggles have in Your case long become victories, and therefore I am sometimes so very small in Your presence; but my new victories are Yours also, and I may present them to You. I traveled across Italy on the long path toward the summit, which this book represents. You flew to it in swift hours and stood, before I was all the way up, on its clearest peak. I was far up, but still surrounded by clouds; You waited above them in the eternal light. Receive me, darling.

Be always thus before me, You dear, peerless, sacred one. Let us go upward together, You and I—as if up to the great star, each leaning on the other, each reposing in the other. And if sometimes I have to let my arm fall from Your shoulders for an interim, I fear nothing: on the next height You will smilingly receive the tired one. You are not a goal for me; You are a thousand goals. You are everything, and I know You in everything; and I am everything and direct everything Your way in my moving-toward-You.

I need not say: Forgive! For I ask that from You in every silence. I need not ask: Forget! For we want to remember these hours also, in which I tried to flee from You in shame; and on my blind flight I was always running toward You. Nor do I want to say: Trust! For I know that this is the language with which we recognized and greeted each other in these new sanctified mornings after a long being-distant and an estranged being-close that was our last separation and my last peril.—And now in the end, this book's ultimate worth lies in the knowledge of an artistry that is only a path and at last fulfills itself in a single ripe existence. With each work that one raises out of oneself, one creates space for some new strength. And the last space, which comes after a long process, will bear everything within itself that is active and essential around us; for it will be the greatest space, filled with all strength. Only one person will attain it; but all who are creative are the ancestors of this solitary person. There will be nothing else but him; for trees and tall mountains, clouds and cascading waves have only been symbols of those realities that *he* finds in himself. Everything has converged in him, and all powers that before had fought one another in scattered battles tremble under his will. Even the ground beneath his feet is superfluous. He rolls it up like a prayer rug. He no longer prays. He exists. And when he makes a gesture, he will create, will fling out into infinity many millions of worlds, on which the same game begins: more mature beings will first multiply and then withdraw into solitude and after a long struggle at last bring up one again who has everything within himself, a creator of this type of eternity, a very great one in space, one with the gestures of sculpture. Thus every generation sends its tendrils like a chain from god to god. And every god is the entire pastness of a world, its ultimate purpose, its uniform expression, and at the same time the possibility of a new life. How other faraway worlds will mature toward gods—I do not know. But for us art is the way; for among us the artists are the thirsty ones who drink everything into themselves, the immodest ones who nowhere build huts, and the eternal ones who reach across the roofs of the centuries. They receive portions of life and give life. But when once they have received life and bear the world within them with all its powers and possibilities, they will bestow something—beyond that. . . .

As for ourselves: we are the ancestors of a god and with our deepest solitudes reach forward through the centuries to his very beginning. I feel this with all my heart!

THE
SCHMARGENDORF
DIARY

11 July 1898, in the evening

Do you know what is happening here? these pages are streets down which Your words were supposed to go. White and festive, they waited eagerly for the procession, which they already saw approaching: black rows in a tight throng and in front, over the incense, holy flags waving. Flags taken from an old church treasure, pale blue damask with silver symbols. And distant voices, asking and hastily conferring the way they do just before their singing. . . . But suddenly late this morning the group dispersed before it turned into this street through which now, timidly and full of shy surprise, my thoughts wander.

Thoughts, what kind of thoughts? As of late they have all been practicing that odd trick of changing clothes, again and again changing clothes on the high wire of distractedness, and they haven't even left me enough introspection to observe them inside some mask. They have left me no memory at all, not of their royal moments nor of their needy phases. It was like after a great and perilous time of rain: what drifts downshore on the wild, alien rivers could, if salvaged, no doubt serve a certain comfort and satisfy many a need; but it is all estranged property, torn loose from here and there and half-destroyed.

And if an unsmashed cradle should wash ashore to someone out of this crazed flight, he would scarcely be tempted to make it a bed for his child. One stands there at the edge with folded arms and lowered forehead and sees the things floating by and doesn't reach one's hand toward those that pile up in the shorebushes. But neither can one return to one's cabin and, once inside, bend over one's work. One waits. And the things swim about in the sunset and appear larger and stranger, and only occasionally one of them comes drifting in out of the night on white ripples like a slowly landing boat.

I remember once when as a child I couldn't tear myself away from a river on whose broad swollenness beams and barrels and pieces of furniture and roofs were drifting; all of course are in themselves uninteresting things, but then there really is something quite remarkable about seeing a roof, which one would otherwise find always and only in its appointed place atop secure walls, traveling with such alacrity and so liberated from its sense of duty and playing catch with the next barrel. And then: even if this is a board and that is a tub and the other thing, which looked so fantastic from far away, is an old broom—it might well be that behind these bizarre workaday objects something tremendous and unheard-of could come along—could it not? And even if nothing does come, if merely the evening sets over the unaccustomed landscape, does not all dead apparatus come alive and light up as if a great colorful parade were passing by on a broad thoroughfare all decked out in purple bunting? And just at this moment all happiness and movement get lost in the heavy twilight, and a solemn funeral procession seems to fade away toward the night. But when the moon breaks free of the clouds, are not hastening hordes and towering horsemen fleeing across white steppes? And if at that moment you have come far enough in your history lesson, you will think: Napoleon is returning from Russia—or something similar.

Among these three or four images, however, lie ten or twenty other transitions—wild spectacles full of grotesque surprises, tragic destinies, and witty genre scenes. All of world history's great dramas of heroic ambition you can observe in a single evening sky, more festive and frightful than they ever came to pass. But if your soul does not feed on these things of the past, if it apprehends motion even where motion is not expressed as the jostling of masses, then it has space and power to discern in each hour a pure, more elemental action in which solemn and calm forces enact selfless gestures without posture and pomp. It will observe that there are far deeper and more unsettling sensations than being reminded by a group of rushing clouds of Lützow's Hussars or by a mighty river of a dark pirate ship, and it will feel clearly that such memories are signs of a certain immaturity and lack of independence. Why listen so intently to the breathing of yesterday and the day before—since both of them are sleeping and the present moment is awake? Is it any different from thinking, in the face of a mighty and proud granite rock, of the rain that washed over it yesterday?

In this way people betray themselves to be false aristocrats. They believe their wealth consists in celebrating and praising the memory of great ancestors. While all the time they could be so much richer if they celebrated and praised their own possibilities.

For those who talk about a great departed know nothing about him except anecdotes. But those in whom a great ancestor resurrects keep silent about him.

That is why every real one must feel himself to be a first one; for the world whose inception he is knows no history; the fathers and forebears from whom he receives culture and strength and style and aptitude are contemporaries of his soul and are at work *in* him, not *before* him. All the others, alas, lived on other stars and died on other stars!

As in general a history of the present would have to comprise whatever things of the past became productive and apparent in later fruitions. What belonged solely to one era gained significance solely for that era, and the so-called historical value is a collector's price not everyone is willing to pay.

What remains to be feared about history and its effects is that things of the past appear in dimensions beside which each contemporary moment, no matter how near and mobile, stands small, constricted, and, as it were, helpless; the encouragement and the ambition that great figures from the past arouse in an emulous posterity appear impotent and insignificant compared to that vacuous space, surrounded only by idle admiration, that remains behind every hero.

People are often so taken aback when someone powerful and great arises from among them that long after he has passed away they forget their daily work and stand around the deserted spot with weighty words and empty gestures.

Indolence also enters in here. People are simply required to expend a certain portion of energy, no matter how they do it. And now if a statesman or a field-general or a king puts forth a potent will, the others will feel unburdened and relieved of their duty. For they are convinced at heart that it was, after all, they who raised the hero out of themselves, and think: that's enough now for a while, and let themselves go. (A pupil who has done the homework for the entire class. Paris, June 1903.)

Among the quotidianites and those who live in life's poorhouse, historicism finds its best welfare; for those who feel themselves barely tolerated by the present swell in the consciousness of being the protectors of an expired greatness.

France, for example, still feels exculpated for its current insignificance by the fact that *it* possessed Napoleon. Such an attitude is not totally groundless. National heroes and statesmen have nothing to offer but their great will; their richness and potency, however, are the strength of the people, whose scattered rays they unite in their energy. So that if a man like the first Napoleon places himself over a people who have squandered their strengths for centuries on frivolous whims, he cannot but take a whole century's strength from the crowd as an advance lien and use up the means of a whole future in one great moment.

And perhaps it is the tragedy of nations that precisely the best princes use up a portion of their people's future in their present. The strength of the crowd, however, is a capital that can absorb a great many losses but not experience increase through anything; for the unity and therefore the power of the many does *not* increase in concert with the strength of the individual; on the contrary, the two are irrevocably opposed. The stronger person always becomes the more solitary person. Weakness and weakness and weakness, tied firmly together, yield finally a unified small strength; strength and strength and strength, summed up, produce: several strengths.

That the state should further the welfare of the crowd by granting the needs of the individual their greatest possible satisfaction must remain therefore nothing but a fond cliché. Union of individuals takes place only at the most elemental and again at the highest stage of development. First, where each single person is merely the duplicate of his fellow creature, and then again, after millennia have passed, between the most mature and sublime individualities, each of whom represents a world in himself with all its powers and possibilities, so rich and self-contained and saturated with being that none any longer poses a threat to the others.

16 July 1898, Zoppot (Talmühle)

THE CHURCH-GENERATION

OUT of that spacious, proud resplendence
they pried God and forced
him into their time . . .
And they surrounded him and hymned him
and now he's all but vanished
into their darkness.

And they light candle after candle
in that darkness and pray
that the flames won't all flicker out
before they see some trace
of God's heart . . .

23 July 1898, Oliva

HUMAN beings who have that deep silence
are like boys who own violins
passed down from their great-grandfathers;
and they never play those violins:

their hands, which labor on in darkness,
became too hard.
But the violin cases are like forests,
and something strong roils through the branches
and the grandsons feel: behind them
lies the sea . . .

In the high beech-tree alcove of the park at Oliva we two put the finishing touches on this poem together:

THESE are the fearful twilight dramas:
characters removed from days
long for the nowhere-realm,
suddenly all names become burdens
and beneath their weight
the tame, tender things suffer so.

Can you feel how all transitions
hesitate between one state and the next?
The suns were like a chorus . . .
And suddenly all leanings stop and hearken
and you're alone with your fear.

1 August 1898

I have been in Berlin since yesterday evening.—I came through the
city early today; the first thing I discovered was: Bismarck has died.
The portrait of the chancellor by Lenbach is in the display windows,
and above the heads of the curious, veiled flags fly at halfmast. Extras
are being cried out, and certain people wear important expressions or
a black frock, well-to-do patriots both. As for the rest, however, the
mood is: Bismarck is dead—long live—Berlin. The newspapers tell
of "muffled mourning". . . , but all that is muffled is what always remains muffled in the workaday world and among the crowd. Just
how tastefully the grief—which one is meant to notice wherever one
goes—proclaims itself is indicated by a new phrase that flew along
Friedrichstrasse shrieking out of twenty hungry muzzles: Bismarck's
deathbed postcard!

From a letter:

10 March 1899, Arco

. . . for in our gazing lies our truest acquiring. Would to God our hands were as our eyes are: so ready in grasping, so bright in holding, so carefree in letting all things go; then we could become truly rich. But we do not become rich by having something dwell in our hands and wither there: everything is meant to stream through their grip as through the festive gate of entrance and homecoming. Our hands are not meant to be coffins; rather beds, in which the things engage in twilight slumber and accomplish many a dream, out of whose darkness their fondest secrecies speak. But the things are meant to wander on beyond our hands, sturdy and strong, and we are meant to retain nothing of them but the courageous morning song that floats and shimmers behind their fading steps.

For possession is poverty and worry; having *had* possessed is the only unconcerned possessing.

From the same letter:
. . . And I say to reassure myself: desires are the memories from our future.—

From conversations and in their background:
(Sensuality. Chance. Forgetting.)

That sensuality is not a secret flame that always breaks out in the same place—let that be our pride and our strength. We want it to become a cheerful torch that we hold laughingly behind all the transparencies of our being.

For the solitary person there are no chance occurrences. He feels encircled by laws, feels conditioned and sustained by them, and even in its dangers still loves the law. With each *meeting* chance begins. It exists where two or three are together in its name, and its power increases with the number of those assembled.

To embrace forgetting as solace and reverie is a form of lassitude and denial of life. What I can forget I have never lived. But what I live I want to keep as my own and have around me as treasure and usage. My happiness is my gold and—who is so rich that he may forget his misfortune?

Why say what *is?* Why afflict the things with their meaning? I can imagine only a longing that with continual wandering traverses the world. All things are so ready to host for a short time our many and often confused thoughts and desires.—I want to rest for one night in each thing when by day I have gone with my doings through the other things.—I want to sleep one time beside each thing, grow drowsy from its warmth, on its breathing dream up and down, sense in all my limbs its dear relaxed naked being-near and become strong through the scent of its sleep and then in the morning, early, before it wakes, ahead of all farewells, pass on, pass on. . . .

3 November 1899

I love the outsets, despite the fear and uncertainty that attach to all beginnings. When I have earned myself a joy or a reward, or when I wish that something had not existed, when I want to deny an experience its right to remain in my past—with that instant I begin. Begin to what? I begin—period. I have already begun a thousand lives this way. I feel as though a whole generation must arrive to complete all these lives, for they cannot linger indefinitely in daybreak; but I fear at the same time: it will be an unhappy and dissatisfied generation, the one that torments itself over these thousand lives, that grinds itself down and falls out with itself on account of their thousand senses.

All the same, I am perhaps already in the process of having begun *my* life: the life one doesn't let go of until one has completed it; unless one should die over this honest work; but then this life that one nevertheless possessed as one's own descends on someone else or on a landscape or on God. Once you have led it up to a certain point it will complete itself at any cost—whether in your present time or sometime later—so why be afraid?

3 November 1899, at night

The greatest portion of fleetingness, frailty, and instability is a consequence of the not-having-been of so many people. It is not enough to have been born in order to be. One must splice oneself into some great circuit; but one must also insulate oneself, in order not to mischannel, not to use up, not to lose the current that one carries. To pass it on is everything; but without seeing the one to whom one passes it, to stretch oneself taut over landscapes and people with a hundred shining wires out to the next pole; is that not it?

I think about so many things, even though my thoughts are like children at a fireworks show. They stand in tight clusters, gazing into the night and waiting for the rocket. And they hear their hearts beating as they watch and can feel them all the way up in their craning necks, and sometimes the blood is pounding in their eyelids as they wait. But at the very moment when the rocket rises, peaks, and explodes, they had to turn and tell one another something and missed it all. And now they stand there again, with eager hearts, and wait, and they see only the night and the quiet, friendly stars.

But these stars are *more* to them than to the others, who are pampered and spoiled from the red and blue and silver lightfest of the fireballs. And sometimes my thoughts go out even beyond the stars, when the nights darken behind them and become deeper. Then I hear a voice that chants:

> After the last sound has long withered,
> a silence remains, deep and broad:
> the stars are only many names
> for one single darkness.

There is still much about me that I dislike; and yet I feel already that these qualities are *foreign,* contingent, not really connected to me. From this comes a certain confidence, a certain strength.

Whether I will succeed someday in going about entirely in my own clothes—I do not know. At any rate, I want to start off by becoming naked, then everything else will take care of itself.

When I consider world history—I find it not unjust but impoverished. It must limit its notion of experience to what can be told as a story.—It is a child whose finger travels on a map: there it is a short way from Italy to Denmark and a quick, commodious trip.

Better that we regard our chance occurrences as our experiences.

That way our life remains pure and unbetrayed, but also something unexpected and strange for us.

In all my best hours I shall take your smiling as a city, a distant city that shines and is alive—I shall recognize a word from you as an island on which birches stand or pines but at any rate quiet and festive trees. I shall regard your glance as a well in which the things have gotten lost and over which even the sky trembles with blissfully fearful thoughts of falling in—I shall know that all this *exists,* that this city can be entered, that I have often beheld this island, and that I know exactly when it is most lonely at the edge of the well; but if you ask me, you will see me hesitate: I don't know for certain whether the forest we walk through is not merely my mood—a dark, shadowy mood. Who knows: perhaps even Venice is only a feeling.

3 November 1899, at night

Why am I suddenly writing so much? Because I once again: begin. Today, suddenly—"today" is a beginning, a one. Beginning of what? A one before what? Before a long number, before millions perhaps. And one doesn't know from which numbers the great sum came. I have never added up—but occasionally I'll find a result at the edge of a page and turn and not transfer it onto the new leaf. What for? It is all *one* book.

3 November, near midnight

I fear in myself only those contradictions with a tendency toward reconciliation. They must occupy a very narrow spot in my life if the idea should occur to them to extend hands to each other, from one edge to the other. My contradictions shall hear of each other only rarely and in rumors. Like two princes from distant lands who suddenly feel an enmity between them because they are both setting out to woo the same young girl. The young girl, however . . . but why reveal everything? Sometimes one can simply say: I am happy. And whoever understands you will need only that to be the confidant of your joy. Or else you say: I am sad, and your state is just that—a simple being-sad that admits of no other name. But between these two

moods there is a whole range of nuances, transitions, hesitant feelings
with long trails of echoing sounds. In order to name them you say: I
am . . . , no, you are more likely to say: there is . . .

There is, for instance, an evening in a room; before the windows
bright twilight, accented by the vague outlines of treetops. Inside, all
the light is a shade deeper, calmer, nobler. A handful of young men
are assembled there, and their conversations have just fallen silent.
They stand together in their high-collared, carelessly unbuttoned
uniform frocks, forgetting one another, as it were. Then suddenly one
of them makes a movement as if he wished to flee, but instead turns
abruptly to his companion, a pale blond youth with large, pensive
eyes. "Play something, Sascha," he says overloudly and as if far past
him. With that the others also come to life, and they urge the youth
with the sad, pensive eyes toward the small, old-fashioned piano and
place his hot hands on the keyboard. And the youth can sense, in this
strange room in which the others—God knows why—are standing
together and becoming aroused, who it was that played these keys *before* him;—he feels two hands next to his own, as if teaching, but with
such tenderness, and he has a vision also of the face that accompanies
these two hands. A young girl's face, sketched by soft, gentle lines. It
stands out against the twilight of a window, almost pure silhouette
and yet something more; one sees also a lowered eye, almost veiled by
its lid, and the forehead above it quiet, shadowy up to the edge of the
tangled hair, in which a wind has settled. And so Sascha now plays
this young girl's song acquiescently, as the keys dictate it. On and on
he plays, on and on the song of this absent, unknown, perhaps already long-deceased young girl. And thus darkness comes over this
room. The others move about almost lost in the dark, for they have
lowered their faces listening. Only occasionally a forehead shimmers
here and there. Whenever any two of them shudder and look up simultaneously and with dark questioning meet each other's gazes.—

And more and more often I find myself, when I want to say: I am . . . ,
having to say instead: there is . . . , but at those times I usually just
say nothing.

Our feelings all seem to me like curtains before actions. All it takes
is for a light to rise somewhere in the background, and immediately

large and mysterious shadows move across the curtain's surface.—
And we would do well to make this the model of our feelings, and
only let them expand across us when they are either so simple and
modest that we live them in our movements and bearings, or so vivid
and deep that we could narrate them like something that happened
to our ancestors—once upon a time . . . in wondrous days.

That is our progress: the material itself is not so weighty, so important anymore; we may *use* it and create whole dramas for no other
reason than to become conscious of one single feeling, i.e., to become
richer by a new feeling.

Noon, 5 November

So, without suspecting it, I have been approaching your mood in
these thoughts. And whatever else I might have written here, now I've
told You in person, which I had much rather do anyway.—

Strange, last night the military novel suddenly became so pressing
that I thought I would have to begin writing it—if not that instant,
then at least today. But of course in the new day everything looks
quite different; what seemed so necessary in the middle of the night
appears now no more important than two, perhaps three other sub-
jects and is not even an intense inner need but a dry literary intention—and thus I am not at all inclined to pursue it. The project
itself, no matter how deeply I immerse myself in it, still seems to me
impossible and ill-formed; I don't yet feel adept enough to show this
society of boys in all its brutality and degeneration, in this hopeless
and melancholy cheerfulness . . . to let this whole mass, *as such,* constantly be working its effects, seems to me as important as it is difficult. For each of them, taken by himself—even the most
depraved—is after all a child, but what takes shape from the con-
glomeration of these children—this would be the dominant impression—is a frightful totality that behaves like some dreadful organism,
stretching out with its desires first this and then another arm. The
scene that occupied me in the beginning is the one with Karl Gruber, the pale sleepwalker with the flat chest and the voice that wades
in its spit.

Gymnasium. The class stands in their bright drill shirts, lined up

in two rows beneath the large gas chandeliers. The gym instructor
with the hard tanned face and cold mocking eyes has ordered exercises and is now dividing up the sections. "First squad—horizontal
bar, second squad—parallel bars, third squad—vaulting-horse, fourth
squad—climbing. Dismissed!" and the boys quickly disperse on their
light, rosin-dusted shoes. A few stay behind in the center of the hall,
hesitant, as though unwilling. It is the fourth squad, the worst gym-
nasts who find nothing fun about working out on the equipment and
are already tired from the twenty kneebends and a bit dizzy and out
of breath. Only one of them, the one who is usually the very last on
such occasions, Karl Gruber, is already standing next to the climbing-
poles that are installed in a dusky corner of the hall, close to the
niches in which the uniforms are hung. He has taken hold of the
nearest pole and jerks it forward with extraordinary force, so that it
hangs quivering in the area reserved for this exercise. Gruber doesn't
remove his hands even for a moment; he leaps straight up and remains quite high, his legs locked instinctively in the correct climbing-
grip (for which he had previously shown no aptitude), clinging to the
bar. From there he waits for his squad and observes—so it appears—
with special pleasure the surprised vexation of the little Polish non-
commissioned officer who shouts at him to jump down. But this
time Gruber is having none of it, and finally Jastersky, the blond
noncom, shouts: "All right now, either you'll come down or you'll
climb up, or I'll report you to the first lieutenant. . . ." And now Gruber begins to climb, first violently, recklessly, hoisting his legs under
him and directing his gaze upward, gauging with a certain anxiety the
immeasurable length of pole still ahead. Then his movement slows,
and as if he were relishing each grip as something new and pleasur-
able, he hoists himself higher than the exercise normally requires; he
ignores the agitation of the already piqued noncom, and climbs and
climbs, his gaze steadily directed upward, as though he had discovered a way out in the ceiling and were striving to reach it. The whole
squad follows him with its gaze. And even from the other squads
boys turn their attention toward the climber who had always before
scarcely managed to climb a third of the way up the bar, panting the
whole way, red-faced and with angry eyes. "Bravo, Gruber!" someone
shouts over from the first squad. With that several of them turn and

look upward, and for a time the whole hall grows silent—but just at that moment, as all gazes are hanging on the figure of Gruber, he makes a motion up there under the ceiling, as if trying to shake them off; and apparently failing, he knots all these gazes onto the naked iron hook up above and slithers down the smooth pole, so that everyone is still looking upward while he, dizzy and hot, is already standing down below, and staring with strangely lusterless eyes into his burning palms.—Then one of the comrades standing next to him asks him what has gotten into him today: "Trying to make the first squad, are you?" Gruber laughs and seems about to reply with something, but he thinks better of it and quickly lowers his eyes. And then, as the noise and commotion pick up again, he withdraws quietly into the niche and sits down and looks around nervously and takes a breath and laughs again and tries to say something . . . , but already no one is paying attention to him any longer, and only Jerome sees that he is looking at his hands again, bent down deep over them, like someone who is trying to decipher a letter in poor light. And he comes up to him after a while and asks: "Did you hurt yourself?" Gruber is startled: "What?" blurts out of him in his usual gargly voice. "Let me see!" and Jerome takes one of Gruber's hands and turns it toward the light. It is scraped a little and bleeding around the palm. "I can give you something for that," says Jerome, "if you'll come with me after class."—but as far as Jerome can tell, Gruber doesn't hear: he looks past him into the hall as if he had seen something, perhaps not in the hall, perhaps outside by the windows, even though it is dark outside, and late, and autumn. And just then the noncom shouts with his usual arrogance: "Gruber!" Gruber doesn't react; only his feet, which are stretched out in front of him, slide forward a little on the parquet floor.—"Gruber!" screams the noncom, and his voice cracks. Then he waits for a moment and says quickly, without looking at the boy he's shouted at: "You'll report after class, I'll have you . . ." And class goes on. "Gruber," says Jerome, and bends down to his comrade who is leaning back deeper and deeper into the niche, "it was your turn to climb again, up the rope, go ahead, try it, or else Jastersky will make an affair of this, you know . . ." Gruber nods. But instead of getting up, he suddenly closes his eyes and slides away under Jerome's words as if a wave were carrying

him—slides slowly and soundlessly deeper, deeper off his seat, and
Jerome doesn't know what is happening until he hears Gruber's head
bang against the wood of his seat and fall over. . . .

"Gruber!" he shouts hoarsely. At first nobody notices. And Jerome
stands with limp hands and shouts: "Gruber, Gruber!" It doesn't
occur to him to prop Gruber up. Then he feels a shove, someone says
to him: "Stupid!" Someone else pushes him away and he watches
them lift the unmoving body. They carry it past, to wherever, probably into the small room next door. The first lieutenant comes running and gives orders in a tough, overbearing voice. His command
cuts off the buzzing of the many chattering boys instantly. Everything
becomes quiet. Only isolated movements continue here and there; a
belated laughing breaks out of someone who doesn't know what's
happening. It jumps headfirst into the silence and drowns instantly.
Then rapid questions: "What? What? Who? Gruber?" And more and
more are inquiring. Then someone says loudly: "Passed out."—And
noncom Jastersky with his red face runs after the first lieutenant and
shouts in his vindictive voice, trembling with anger: "A malingerer,
Lieutenant, sir, a malingerer." The first lieutenant pays no attention
to him. He looks straight ahead, gnawing at his moustache—which
causes his hard chin to jut forward even more forcefully—and from
time to time giving terse orders. Four cadets who are carrying Gruber disappear with the first lieutenant into the small room. Shortly
afterward the cadets return. A servant runs through the hall. The
four are being pressed hard by the others: "How does he look? Is it
bad? Has he come to yet?" None of them can say anything for sure.
And the first lieutenant is already shouting into the gymnasium that
exercises aren't over yet, and he gives the command over to Sergeant
Goldstein.—And so they are back to their exercises, at the parallel
bars, at the horizontal bar, and the small chubby members of the
third squad creep across the vaulting-horse with outspread legs. But
all movements are somehow different from before, a listening has
settled over them, the rotations at the horizontal bar suddenly break
off, and at the parallel bars only half-hearted little exercises are being
carried on. The voices sound less confused, sharper, as if all were
continually saying only one word: "This, This, This . . ." Sly little
Krix meanwhile has been listening at the door to the room. The non-

com from the second squad chases him off, raising his hand as if to smack him on his behind. Krix jumps back like a cat, his eyes flashing deviously. He already knows enough now. And after a while, when no one is watching him, he whispers to Pavlovich: "The regimental doctor has arrived." And of course everyone knows Pavlovich: with his usual effrontery he marches straight across the hall, as if he'd been ordered to do so, and announces loudly from squad to squad: "The regimental doctor is inside." And even the noncoms seem intrigued by this piece of news. Glances are turning ever more frequently toward the door, the exercises are being performed ever more slowly, and one small fellow with dark eyes has remained crouched high atop the vaulting-horse and stares open-mouthed toward the small room. And something immobilizing seems to lie in the air. The strongest of those in the first squad still put forth a few exertions, they work their legs, and Pombert, the powerful Tyrolian, flexes his arm and watches his muscles stretch broad and taut against the fabric of his gym uniform. Yes, even little Baum continues to do a few more rotations on the horizontal bar, and suddenly this vigorous movement is the only one in the hall, a large flickering circle that takes on an uncanniness in the overall quiet. And with a sudden jerk the little fellow flips himself into a standing position, allows his knees to give, and makes a face as if he had contempt for them all. But even his dull little eyes are glued to the door.—Now one can hear the singing of the gas flames and the simple ticking of the wall clock. Suddenly the bell rasps, signaling the end of class. Its sound is new and peculiar today, and it breaks off as if startled halfway through a word. Sergeant Goldstein, though, knows his duty. He calls out: "Fall in!" Not a soul hears him. No one can remember what this phrase meant—before. Before when? "Fall in!" the sergeant croaks, and now the other noncoms are shouting too, and even some of the cadets are admonishing as though in some dream: "Fall in." But at heart they all know that they still have to wait for something. And then at last the door to the small room opens, and for a while nothing, and then First Lieutenant Wahl steps out, his eyes are wide and angry, his stride in perfect control. He marches the way he does when he is passing in review: "Fall in!" he says hoarsely. With indescribable speed they all stand in rank and file. No one moves, just as if a general were there.

And then a command: "Listen up!" and from far away hoarsely and hard: "Your comrade Gruber just died. Heart failure. Dismissed."—Recess.

And after a while the soft, small voice of the cadet on duty: "Left face, at the double, company march!" Slowly and in loose formation the whole class turns toward the door.—Jerome is the last. No one looks back. As the cadets start down the corridor the air that meets them is cold and musty. One of them thinks it smells of carbolic acid. Pombert cracks a loud crude joke about the odor. No one laughs. Jerome suddenly feels his arm seized, as if he had been pounced at. Krix is hanging onto it. His eyes are gleaming and his teeth are bared, as if he wanted to bite something. "I saw him"—he whispers and squeezes Jerome's arm, and there's a laughter inside him that rattles him back and forth. "He's all naked and sunken and very long. And on his feet he's been sealed!"

And he giggles and sinks his teeth into Jerome's sleeve.

I am too tired today to work on the next scene (Gruber's burial and the night preceding it). But after our talks a different scene occurs to me. To wit:

Between the castle rocks of Arco and the Dosso di Romarzola, a mountain ridge that leans toward Lake Garda like an awakening thirsty dragon, there are three villages. All share the same name; they are so poor that none was strong enough to distinguish itself permanently from its neighbor. At the edge of the first village there is a church, white and new, yet already dirty a third of the way up its walls, like a dress that has been dragged along on the ground. It was built for the benefit of all three villages, though the inhabitants of the town farthest away would rather go to the mendicant friars in the old monastery of Santa Maria della Grazia to pray and sing. At the edge of the second village there is an inn, often frequented in the afternoons by the visitors to Arco and thus transformed over time by these visitors, a bright house with inscriptions, terraces, and small oleanders (sometimes even marked by a flag). And beside it looms a massive, many-windowed steam mill that blocks out the little houses and their sky. It was built by the innkeeper and owes its existence to the soiled money of the vacationers in Arco, who pay dearly for his sour *vino santo.* And each person who comes there and drinks, asks the waitress her name, and writes a joke in the smudged guest book, adds without knowing it one more stone to this mill, for each year it puts forth some new little house or at the least a young wall.

I happen to know that the first village is called Chiarano, the one with the shared little church at its border. I thought I was well acquainted with its few houses; for a steep stone conduit runs through the middle of it into the olive forest that veils the background slopes with its gnarled silvery branches. It was this very trail I thought I was taking one morning in March. Through the wispy, undulant fog that had absorbed the whole strength of the sun, so that it seemed much closer than when it becomes outlined somewhere in the sky, I had glimpsed a moment earlier the first olive trees, shining, their trunk and leaves of the same, almost untinted paleness. But suddenly a wall that ran from who knows where across the whole breadth of the street stopped in its tracks before me. And so I turned off to the left. I was so open to the morning's whims. But I did have the feeling that I had been walking so long in this new street that the village must have surely come to an end; instead of which there stood in my way again this rough old stone wall, hovering in the fog, almost breathless, as if it had rushed ahead on a different path to get there before me. And I turned left again. That led me to the dark broad arch of a gate above which the wreath, the sign of a *vendita di vino*, was still hanging. But it had faded, and the wine had run out. In the courtyard lay frames of doors and windows, torn out by storms or young boys, and through the empty doors one gazed into pure desolation. Beyond the courtyard was a second gate, at the end of a rather long, dusky hallway. And just then in front of this gate a young girl passed, or perhaps a woman. Slender and in the black dress that these peasant women wear almost daily. As I stepped out of the house she disappeared toward the left into the fog. I walked in that direction. And now constantly, both left and right, small narrow side alleys were opening as if the houses moved to the side, and out of them came young girls and women just like the first, and without speaking to one another they all followed in her footsteps. For an instant I could see their young awakened faces or their pensive eyes or their small brown foreheads across which their black hair was blowing lightly and freely; then the fog dropped quickly, like a curtain to hide them, and only the many wooden clogs clattered somewhere up ahead. And this clatter was so invigorating that I began to smile. It was just the thing I would expect in these streets. And with a smile I stood and unraveled from the thinning fog as if from soft tangled hair: a well with a stone rim, yes, even with a relief, a small St. Mary's column of weather-beaten stone and with a small round roof above—but this column was only the beginning. It formed the corner of a very small church. On the walls one could make out the remnants of an old fresco painting, perhaps of the Last Supper, and on the side of the entrance door, the head and arms and a piece of the sturdy legs of a St. Christopher—in such large proportions that the figure of the saint appeared bent not just from the burden of the Child Jesus but also from fear of the encroaching roof. The roof itself was very makeshift. It must have had many cracks in it, for over the young girls and women who were now sitting inside in the pews pieces of brightness rained down—many small lights that fell from their hair onto their shoulders and clung there like so many petals of a large rose that was slowly tearing apart. The altar was almost dark; the thin, paltry candles cast a sickly light and flickered restlessly before the blackened pictures. A small old man in a chasuble of pale blue taffeta was reading the gospel. He stood with complete calm, his round, light-blue back turned to the women as if he were asleep, and only his white-haired head trembling from the words of the gospel. Or perhaps it just appeared that way in the shimmer of the candles.

When I turned around, the square was clear, and the fog lay damply on the stones like a fleeting splendor. I walked through two or three streets. In the houses left and right the men were stirring, curses could be heard, and here and there a hoarse song began. But the voices were still heavy with sleep. A lad with a red face was driving a donkey out of the stable. An old man angrily kept calling: "Gita, Gita!" But nobody answered. I could have told him where Gita was. For I had seen where the women are before the men waken.—Immediately after that I was among olive trees. I paused in the woods and looked back. Again the poor cottages with bad roofs, weather-beaten walls, and red aprons drying on the railings. At the edge, the ugly new white church in which each Sunday morning at nine o'clock high mass is held. Perhaps the little church would grow dark and gloomy were it to learn about this rival. But there is an hour before daybreak when it is like the only church in the world, like a cathedral, and like a great forest. And while the women are inside it, none of them will say a word to her neighbor about the new church. They are in fact completely silent, as if none were aware of the others. Even the old priest doesn't know whether or not people are present. He reads the gospel and muses only occasionally in the midst of doing so, when he feels the stones' coldness in his feet: "Wasn't a carpet here yesterday? . . ."—but actually it was sixty years ago that a carpet covered the steps.

I have never gone back to Chiarano, for fear of not finding this little church again.

7 November, in the evening

I will try to jot down here briefly another little episode.

In San Rocco the old gravedigger had died. There were daily announcements that the position was open. But three weeks passed without anyone applying. And since during this whole time no one in San Rocco died, the matter didn't seem pressing and so people simply waited. On a morning in May the daughter of the mayor encountered a man she didn't know standing in the hallway of the house where she lived with her father, the stout Gian-Battista Lecconi. And yet she felt as if she had seen him many times before. He was tall, slender, and had a clear, cheerful forehead. That was the most conspicuous feature in his quiet countenance. But his lips were also familiar to the young girl when he asked: "May I see the mayor?" The young girl nodded. Then the stranger said: "You are his daughter?"—"Yes"—"And how old are you?" She laughed. "Almost seventeen." Then the stranger smiled and walked on. Suddenly, as if alarmed, Gita shouted after him: "Mister, who are you?" She heard the stranger pause at the end of the dark hallway, and after a while he said in a bright, pleasant voice: "A gardener."

This was the new gravedigger of San Rocco. He had an odd conception of his office. He rearranged the whole churchyard, worked day and night to prepare the old existing graves as if they were one large bed in which May slowly and with sleep-drenched movements awakened. Opposite the graves, on the other side of the central path, there had always been wild grass, unkempt like the hair of a young lad fresh out of bed. There the strange man created many small plots, so similar to the graves across the way that the two sides of the churchyard looked like sisters. On both parts May was equally rich and resplendent, and the people who came out from the town always had to search to find their graves; indeed, many a dear old widow knelt over the empty beds on the right side of the path and wept, without, however, this prayer being lost on her son, who far away on the left lay under the bright anemones.—But because of this, the people of San Rocco also ceased to feel the whole weight of death. Whenever someone died (and it was mostly the turn of old people this spring), no matter how sad the path on the way out might still be, once in that place outside there was always a small and quiet celebration. The flowers seemed to press in from all sides and come so quickly to stand before the dark hole that it was as if the black mouth of the earth had opened only to articulate these many blossoms.

The stranger's most frequent visitor was Gita. She stood by his work and listened to what he said. His talk was like his face, strange and yet at the same time deeply akin. He never spoke of people, not of the general populace nor of individuals—not even of the great Condottiere Bartolommeo, with whose fame every beggar was acquainted. And yet personalities formed behind his words, whole eras arose, prospered, and decayed, and behind his thoughts millennia seemed to run their course.

When summer came, Gita was in the churchyard almost every day. At home they warned her, they reproached her for it, they tried to hold her back by force: it was all for naught. She still found her way there and forgot, once she was out there with the stranger, every hardship and the anger of her father, of whom she had previously been so frightened.—

But one day in August when it was so oddly heavy and oppressive in the streets and even outside the town no breeze would ever gather force, the stranger was waiting for her by the churchyard door and said urgently: "Go home, Gita, you mustn't come here any longer until you hear me call you back." Then they both gazed for a long time into each other's eyes. And then Gita went back into the somber, sunless town and paced to and fro quietly and without laughter in Gian-Battista Lecconi's house. But the stranger kept gazing after her, and when she disappeared his work began in earnest. Every day three, sometimes four funeral processions came out. Many citizens went along, and all the burials were beautiful and rich with nothing spared in the way of incense and singing. The stranger knew, however, what no one had told him yet: the plague had gained its foothold in the town. And the ever more stifling days with the hot standing skies fell ever more silent, while in the nights, the fearful nights that trembled before morning, a scream rose here and there, rose high up and seemed to fall back all the way from some star with its forehead shattered. While the horror and the fear in the town paralyzed all hands, the arms of the stranger grew stronger through the greater demands on his office, and there was even a certain cheerfulness about him, the cheerfulness of working, of moving, and the clear chant of his blood filled his veins in the few hours of his sleep.

Then, when he awoke one morning, Gita was standing before him. He was startled and only gradually took in her words: the people of San Rocco are coming. They plan to kill him; for they say that he has brought this plague upon them, by devising on the other, empty side of the churchyard all those little hillocks, those graves. He has summoned the corpses with them, the many hundred corpses that are now being carted out to him each day. "Save yourself," and Gita embraces him with wild strength.

Just then he sees a dark throng swelling toward him on the road from the town. Dust in front. Already individual threats can be distinguished amid the hollow murmuring of the crowd. Gita tries to pull him away. But he orders her abruptly into his house. And with trembling she obeys.—Then a stone flies and a second one. They hit the wall somewhere. Gita hears it; she leaps out with wide, terrified eyes, and the third stone crashes against her temple. The strange man catches her and carries her into his small dark house. Outside, crowding up against the low wall now, the people are howling. But suddenly the little scrivener with the bald head, Theophilo, clutches his neighbor, the strong blacksmith from the side street Vicolo Santa

Trinità. He staggers, and his eyes roll weirdly. And at the same time, a youngster, Alonso, begins to totter in the third row. And toward the rear a woman lets out a piercing scream and falls. In a frenzy they all scatter. The blacksmith quakes with his heavy shoulders and makes furious movements with the arm to which Theophilo has been clinging.

After an hour, when the gravedigger steps out of his door, there is emptiness everywhere and space in the field for the red evening. He digs a grave there at the end of the central path, in the white glittering gravel. And later, when the moon comes, it is as if he were digging in silver. He fills the grave with armloads of flowers and then he lays Gita inside and covers her up with more flowers. And for a while he stands bowed over her, and his hands tremble. But immediately thereafter, as if the quiet made him afraid, he begins to work. Seven coffins still stand unburied. They had been brought out in the course of the previous day. Not with much of a retinue, even though in the one especially broad oak coffin lies Gian-Battista Lecconi, the mayor of San Rocco. Everything has changed. The honors and titles have ceased to work. Instead of a single dead accompanied by many living, now *one* always comes who is alive, black Sicco, and he brings three, maybe four dead along with him. And the stranger gauges how much space he still has on the right side of the churchyard. He counts room for some fifteen graves. And so he begins his work, and his light spade is the single voice of the night. Until that frightful moaning begins again, louder and with more desperation than ever, as if there behind the nearest darkness a gigantic wounded monster were writhing in its death throes. But the stranger keeps digging quietly. He has the feeling: as long as he is master here, within these four hedges, as long as he can create order here and build and at least outwardly, at least through the flowers and beds give meaning to this senseless contingency and reconcile it with the land all about, then the Other is not yet almighty, and there may come a day when he, the Other, will tire, will give in. And in no time two of the graves are ready. Then voices approach. And one hears a cart creaking. The cart is piled high with corpses. Naked and clothed, some in velvet and some in rags, young ones and old ones lie tangled up in one another as if stiffened in a horrible debauch, in this dark night. And black Sicco has found accomplices. Red drunken louts with naked laughter and bare arms. And they reach blindly and greedily into the heap of flesh and yank one out who seems to resist and toss him over the churchyard wall. And then another. The stranger quietly puts them away. Until the body of a young girl lands at his feet, naked and bloody. Her poor mistreated hair still tries to cover her small young breasts. Then with a dark voice the gravedigger shouts a threat into the night. And he tries to go back to his work. But the lads are just not in the mood to take orders. Black Sicco bobs up again and again, raises his flat forehead and throws a body over the wall. And so corpses pile up around the quiet worker. His spade grows heavier and heavier as it moves. The dead themselves seem to be pulling against it with their hands. With that the stranger pauses. There is sweat on his brow. In his chest something tightens. Then he steps closer to the wall, and when Sicco's black round head lifts up again, he swings his spade, feels in his body the shock with which it crashes down, and as he pulls it back still sees that it is black and wet. He throws it away in a wide arc and lets his forehead drop: a man defeated. Then he steps slowly out of his garden and walks into the night. (Toward what destination, no one knows.)

Its title, if one wishes to consider it a story: "The Grave-Gardener."

8 November 1899

THE CARDINAL: A BIOGRAPHY

He is the son of the beautiful princess of Ascoli. His father was some rank adventurer, who back then called himself Marquis Pemba. But the princess loves this son most of all. He reminds her of a garden, of Venice, and of a day when she was more lovely than ever before or since. That is why this son shall have life and a name: Marchese of Villavenetia. The Marchese is a poor student. He loves feeling the falcon on his hand. His teacher asks him once (and the teacher knows little about hunting): "What if some day the falcon doesn't come back?" "Then, then . . ." responds his charge, full of agitation, "then I shall feel wings myself." And he blushes all over, as if he had betrayed himself. Later, around his fifteenth year, he becomes quiet and studious for a while. He falls in love with the beautiful Duchess

Julia d'Este. For a year he loves her with unrequited passion—then he goes off and takes his pleasure with a blond servant girl—and has cured himself of love. Now quick, tempestuous days begin. His sword is scarcely ever sheathed. He comes to Venice and must remember a garden. For a year he searches for this garden: then he finds Valenzia. She is golden, magnificent, and proud. The thought of her excludes all other women. He doesn't really think of her at all—he kisses her. But she has a lover. They also say she has a husband, but the lover is more dangerous. The Marchese has long been aware of him. For a century paintings of him have been hanging everywhere. They hang in the darkest halls, usually over a door, so that the children won't see them. They have the evil eye. And the Marchese feels himself pursued by it. He sees reflected in every wineglass: this dark, mysterious, tight forehead and the straight black eyebrows along its edge. He becomes easily frightened. At the slightest occasion he is startled and then laughs too loudly. One night, when the curtain of the broad bed has stirred, he jumps out of the window of the Signora's palazzo into the canal. He hears shots, but makes his way out to the piazzetta, where fishermen come to his aid.

Ten years later he travels to Venice, for the sole reason of examining that window. It is of the most delicate style, a pointed arch with decorations, not overly ornate. That satisfies him. He is still young, secretary to Cardinal Borromeo, and rediscovers Venice. At a festive occasion he also sees Valenzia. She is just as she was back then, she approaches him: but he is a different person, he bows deeply and withdraws with Senator Gritti for a serious conversation. Just before Easter he is made a cardinal. On Resurrection Day he feels the heavy purple silk ripple from his vigorous shoulders. He delights in the beautiful pages who carry his train, he delights in the brightness, in the splendor, and the singing goes to his head like the scent of vineyards. The year after, the cardinal is absent during the Easter celebrations. He lives on one of his estates and decorates his gardens. On the great Sunday he is sitting over the designs for a new château. Perhaps Sansovino can still be persuaded to build it. Toward evening one of his favorites remembers that it is Easter. The cardinal laughs. A festival is rapidly prepared, and young girls from Carmagnola come, twice fifty girls.

The cardinal is renowned for his hospitality. Everywhere they tell stories about him. The people regard him as a wizard. Twenty painters surround him, ten sculptors work in his parks, and every poet compares him to some god. One day he receives Valenzia. The Signora is more radiant than ever. Each day he devises new entertainments for her. In the midst of the most beautiful of these fetes, a messenger on horseback arrives with a letter for the cardinal. He reads, turns pale, and hands it to Valenzia. That evening the Signora travels back to Rome. She has friends there among the cardinals.—At night the cardinal wakes up. He reads the letter again, as his favorite young page holds the torch. The last words are: The Pope is dead.

Three days later the cardinal receives a letter from the old Duchess of Ascoli, his mother, who writes from Rome. It is the first letter she has ever sent him. She congratulates him on something. He doesn't quite understand. But that evening he is summoned urgently to Rome. Then he understands and resolves to give his mother a Giorgione.

8 November 1899

A few more notes on the following incident.

Every summer Frau Blaha, who was married to Wenzel Blaha, a minor official of the Turnau Railroad, vacationed for a few weeks in her native village. This village lies in the flat and swampy part of Bohemia close to Nimburg and is quite poor and nondescript. When Frau Blaha, who by now had for the most part come to regard herself as a woman of the city, saw all these small miserable houses again, she felt herself in a position to attempt an act of charity. She entered the home of an old acquaintance, a peasant woman who she knew had a daughter, and proposed to her that she take this daughter into her service in the city. She would pay her a small, modest wage, and on top of that the girl would have the advantage of being in the city and learning all sorts of things there. (Exactly what sorts of things, Frau Blaha was not sure.) The peasant woman discussed this proposal with her husband, who all the while kept squinching his eyes and at first only left to take a good spit. But after half an hour he returned to the room and asked: "Well, and you did tell this woman that Anna is . . . ?" And as he said this his brown wrinkled hand swayed back and forth in front of his forehead like a wilted chestnut leaf. "Lummox," muttered the peasant woman, "not on your life!"

And so Anna came to live with the Blahas. Most of the time she was there all day by herself. The master, Wenzel Blaha, was in the chancery, the mistress went sewing in other people's houses, and there were no children. Anna sat in the small gloomy kitchen, which had a window into the shaftlike central court, and waited until the organ-grinder came. That happened every day just before twilight. Then she leaned in the little window, bent forward so far that her pale hair was hanging in the wind, and felt herself dance inside, until she grew dizzy and the high, sooty walls began to sway dangerously toward and away from each other. When that frightened her, she started walking through the whole house over the dark filthy stairs all the way down into the smoke-filled street-tavern where now and then someone sang in the early phase of his drunkenness. On her way she always found herself among the children who milled around the courtyard for days on end without ever being missed at home, and oddly enough these children always wanted her to tell them stories. Sometimes they even followed her into the kitchen. But then Anna sat down by the stove, covered her pale empty face with her hands and said to herself: "Think." And the children were patient for a while. But when Annuschka kept on thinking, so that it became all quiet and scary in the dim kitchen, the children ran away and were not there when the girl began to cry softly and mournfully and was all small and helpless from pure homesickness. It's not clear what she longed for. Perhaps partly for the whackings. Mostly, though, for something vague that once upon some time had existed—or perhaps after all she had merely dreamt it. In the course of the many thinkings that the children demanded of her, it came to her slowly. First red, red, and then many people. And then a bell, a loud bell, and then: a king—and a pawn and a castle. And they speak. "Dear King . . . ," says the pawn. "Yes," responds the king in a very proud voice: "I know." And indeed, how should a king not know everything a pawn has to tell him.—

Not long after that the mistress took the girl along shopping. Since it was evening and close to Christmas, the shop windows were very bright and filled with magnificent displays. Inside a toy store Anna suddenly saw her memory. The king, the pawn, the castle . . . Oh, and her heart was pounding louder than her steps. But she glanced quickly away without stopping and walked on at Frau Blaha's side. She had the feeling that she mustn't give anything away. And thus the puppet theater, as if shunned, remained back behind them; Frau Blaha, who had no children, hadn't even noticed it.—A few days later Anna had her free Sunday. She didn't come back that evening. A man, whom she had seen before down below in the tavern, joined up with her, and she couldn't remember exactly where he had led her. It felt to her as if she had been gone a year. When she came into the kitchen early Monday, tired, everything was even colder and grayer than usual. She smashed a soup tureen that day and was roundly scolded for it. Her mistress, though, hadn't even noticed that she had stayed out all night. Thereafter, up until about New Year's, she stayed out three more nights. Then suddenly she stopped walking about in the house, anxiously locked the doors of the apartment, and sometimes didn't even go to the window when the organ-grinder played.

Thus winter passed, and a pale hesitant spring began. That time is a season all to itself in the back courtyards. The houses are black and damp, and the air is bright the way often-washed linen is. The badly cleaned windows twitch with sheen, and assorted scraps of refuse are caught up in the wind and dance their way past the building's stories. The sounds of the whole house are more audible, and the keys jangle differently—more brightly, at a higher pitch—and the knives and spoons have a different rattle.

At this time Annuschka gave birth to a child. Its arrival took her completely by surprise. After she had felt thick and heavy for weeks, it pushed itself out of her one morning and was in this world, God knows from where. It was Sunday, and everyone in the house was still asleep. She looked at it for a while without her face changing in any way. The child hardly moved, but suddenly a sharp voice started up in the little chest, and at the same moment Frau Blaha called and a bed creaked inside in the room. With that Annuschka grabbed her blue apron, which was still hanging by the bed, tied its waist-strings together over the little neck and put the whole blue bundle into the very bottom of her trunk. Then she went into the rooms, opened the curtains, and began making the coffee. On one of the next mornings Annuschka counted the bit of pay she had managed to save. It came to fifteen guilders. Then she locked the door, opened the trunk and put the blue apron, which was heavy and motionless, on the kitchen table. She slowly untied it, looked at the child, and, using a measuring tape, ascertained its length, from the top of the head to the feet. Then she put everything back in its former place and left the house. But, what a pity, the king, the pawn, and the castle were smaller by a good bit. She brought them back with her anyway, and other puppets as well. Namely: a princess with red round daubs on her cheeks, an old man, another old man who had a cross on his chest and because of his big beard looked like a Santa Claus, and two or three other less beautiful and distinguished ones. Also a theater, whose curtain went up and down, making the garden behind it alternately materialize and disappear.

Now Annuschka had something for her loneliness. Where was her homesickness now? She erected the large, beautiful theater (it had cost twelve guilders) and positioned herself, as one is supposed to, behind it. But sometimes, when the curtain had just been rolled up, she ran quickly around to the front, and now she gazed into gardens, and the whole gray kitchen had disappeared behind the high, sumptuous trees. Then she stepped around to the back again and brought out two or three figures and let them speak their minds. This never turned into an actual play; but there was talking and talking back, there were even moments in which two puppets suddenly, as if startled, bowed to each other. Or else the two of them bowed to the old man, who couldn't bow back since he was carved out of wood. And so he showed his gratitude each time by falling over.

Among the children a rumor spread concerning these games of Annuschka's. And so the children of the neighborhood, at first suspiciously, then more and more unguardedly, flocked to the Blahas' kitchen and stood, as twilight set in, in the room's corners and kept their eyes fixed on the beautiful puppets who always said the same things. One evening Annuschka, her cheeks hot with excitement, said: "I have another puppet, a really big one!" The children quivered with expectation. But Annuschka seemed to have forgotten about it. She placed all the personages in her garden and the ones that didn't like to remain upright she leaned against the side wings. In the midst of this a harlequin with a large round face appeared, and the children had no recollection of him at all. But even more excited by all this pomp, the children begged for the "really big" one. Just once, the "really big" one! Just for a moment: the "really big" one.

Annuschka went around back to her trunk. It was already starting to grow dark. The children and the puppets were standing opposite each other, stock-still and similar. But out of the harlequin's wide-opened eyes, which looked as if they were awaiting something horrible, such a completely unanticipated fear came over the children that they gave a sudden scream and ran away, every one of them. Annuschka returned with the big blue one in her hands. Suddenly her hands were trembling. The kitchen had become silent and empty in the children's wake. But Annuschka wasn't afraid. She laughed quietly and pushed the theater over with her feet and stomped to pieces the various thin little boards that had been her garden. And then, when the kitchen had turned completely dark, she walked around and split open the heads of all the puppets, the big blue one's included. (Frau Blaha's Servant Girl)

9 November 1899

Next comes the story of the Duchess of Villerose, which I was not able to include here, since I wrote part of it on the way to the city, part of it during the lectures. Last night I wrote the ending and this afternoon I connected and revised the three sections.

10 November 1899

CHANSON ORPHELINE

Où veux-tu que je m'en aille?
Partout m'attendent ces mots . . .
Après tous les jours de travail,
après toutes les nuits de repos,
après toutes les larmes et les rires
qui se sont écoulés,
après tout que je hais, que j'admire,

dans ce chaîne de change
revient le refrain étrange,
qui me fait désespérer.

Est-ce toi mon père? Tu te vantes
que toutes les femmes charmantes
le long de ta vie t'aimaient trop . . .
Est-ce ma mère, qui chante
dans son pauvre tombeau?

Tuesday, 21 November 1899

CHANSON ORPHELINE

Wer rät mir: Wohin soll ich fliehn vor dem Schall?
Sind diese Worte denn überall?
Nach den Arbeitstagen, den wachen,
nach Nächten, trübe von Müdigkeit,
nach jedem Weinen und Lachen
(und beides scheint mir so weit),
hinter dem Hassen und Staunen her
auf den Wegen der Wiederkehr
kommt ein fremder Kehrreim, und der
macht mir das Leben leer.

Sprichst du, mein Vater, rühmst du dich so:
"Ich liebte die Frauen, bis ich sie floh,
weil jede mir alles gab",—
oder singt meine Mutter irgendwo
in ihrem armen Grab?

ORPHAN'S SONG

[Whose voice is it? Where shall I flee the din?
Are there words wherever I go?
After the wide-awake days of working,
after nights dark with fatigue,
after all the weeping and laughing,
(and both seem so far away),

> behind all the hatred and marveling
> on the paths of return
> comes a strange refrain, and it
> makes my life void.
>
> Is it your voice, father, are you boasting thus:
> "I loved women until I fled them,
> since each gave me all,"—
> or is it my mother singing somewhere
> in her unquiet grave?]

French poem born on a walk to Halensee and just now (laboriously enough) translated.—In the meantime there also came to me: *The Book of the Good Lord and Other Things* and a novella: *The House.* A few things more are likely still on their way. Perhaps even something for the stage.

Tuesday, evening

> THE song of the refrain also touches me,—
> after all true days I feel
> the muffled impotence in all I do.
> Why in the times of resting
> no rejoicing,—
> why not in my hands a present instant
> (each wants to sleep) held like something wakeful?
> Since all of me *trembles to give form*—
> and since even now Death may be learning my name
> along with those other names
> he has to memorize for his next trip.
>
> O NIGHTS, nights, nights,
> I would like to write
> and always, always remain hunched over pages,
> and fill them with intricate symbols
> that are not from my tired hand.
> That reveal me to be the hand of someone
> doing wondrous things with me.
> Thus in the darkness dimensions rise

and strengths that, as I serve, make use of me,
and words whose last syllable I veil
mysteriously with my life,
and silences that let me dive
so deeply into what's without sound
that I relax under all waves,
and no one notices when I stir,
and even in a smooth pond
my movement would make no rings
since I'm so deep now
in the dark realm of the ground.

WHERE am I, where? Perhaps in a room, / and a lamp's yellow glare grabs my face / to examine my gaze: / . . . Is this what you are always, always? . . . I'm not that at all.

I range through the heath. / And around me all storms break loose; / I'm as if in my childhood suit / and growing smaller, and the wind is growing vast.—And when it's grown so vast / that the stars tremble / and hang mutely in their skies, / I see the goal of my heath-roaming / through its darkness, / and it's still far, far away.

Where am I, where? Perhaps in a name? / And it presses round me like an old frame / which fears secretly that it no longer holds its portrait.

It does hold the portrait, but he whom it pictures / in the garb of immaculate short hours / has changed, his face has grown wild, / and his hands are alive to the night. / And as the night rises as if made of laurel walls / and as it grows on endlessly,—only then / does he feel the clay in his hot hands, / and outsiders don't know his fulfillment.

Where am I, where? Perhaps in a womb. / And my limbs remember the woman / in whom they sprouted, and the shrub asks me, / pointing back to the ground, "do you remember that too?"

But I *don't* remember it. I can only take on faith / that I existed long before I began. / I am Gold, and the hastening minutes rob / me from the chests in which I mused Sun. / And bury their booty until it rolls / out of their dead hands again. / And the minutes collapse exhausted, / let go of me, and I am Gold.

I have written nothing on the drama and have spent the whole day in idleness. This has to have been the last day of this kind; I must learn to exploit even my weariness, even my *justified* weariness. Otherwise the song of the refrain actually will come true in me. Each single day must and shall have its meaning, and it shall have it not from chance but from me—tomorrow more!

Wednesday, 22 November 1899, in the evening

All human beings are occurrences, but they happen to no one.

The song of the statue, written on Saturday, the 18th of November, at night:

> WHO is there who so loves me, that he
> will forfeit his own dear life?
> If someone will drown for me in the ocean,
> I will be brought back from stone
> to life, to life redeemed.
>
> I long so for blood's rushing;
> stone is so still.
> I dream of life. Life is real.
> Has no one the heart
> that I wish for in this beauty?
>
> And if once I do find myself in life,
> given everything most golden,—
> - - - - - -
> then I shall weep
> alone, weep for my stone.
> What good will my blood be, when it ripens like wine?
> It cannot scream back out of the ocean
> that One who loved me most.

Friday, 24 November 1899

Yesterday I tried, all tiredness notwithstanding, to write down the sketch of the monks in the Cloister of Our Lord the Redeemer in Val d'Ema. Well, the result was thoroughly awful, and what I did come up with can at best be considered only the barest setting down of the basic material. It would well deserve a full treatment. Today I am with Lou (noon till evening late) and tomorrow: ?

The "Bridal Couple" material is still keeping me at arm's length—all the same I will attempt two or three scenes of the first act tomorrow and perhaps something more for the "Connections."

> Je vois deux yeux comme deux enfants
> errant dans une forêt.
> Ils disent: Qui nous mange c'est le vent, le vent,—
> et moi je réponds: Je le sais.
> Je connais une fille qui pleure, son amant,
> il y a deux ans, s'en allait,
> mais elle dit tout doucement: C'est le vent, le vent,—
> et moi je réponds: Je le sais.
>
> Souvent dans ma chambre en m'éveillant
> il me semble qu'une langue me parlait.
> Toi, mais la nuit murmure: Le vent,—
> et je pleure dans mon lit: Je le sais.
>
> [I see two eyes like two children
> straying through a forest.
> They say: What gnaws at us is the wind, the wind,
> and I, I reply: Yes, I know.
> I know of a girl who weeps; her lover—
> it's been two years—went away,
> but she says so sweetly: It's the wind, the wind,—
> And I, I reply: Yes, I know.
>
> So often I'll wake up in my room
> thinking a voice spoke to me.
> *Yours,* but the night murmurs: the wind,—
> and I weep in my bed: Yes, I know.]

24 November 1899, at night

Car tu ne peux pas consoler aucun de tes amis inconnus autrement qu'en parlant ce seul mot: Je le sais. S'il est vrai que comprendre c'est pardonner, aussi avec quelque droit on peut affirmer: Savoir c'est consoler.

[For you cannot console a single one of your inscrutable friends except by saying these two words: I know. If it is true that to understand is to forgive, then one can also claim with a certain right: to know is to console.]

24 November 1899, at night

MADNESS

She must always brood: I am . . . I am . . .
    And who are you, Marie?
"A queen, a queen!
On your knees before me, on your knees!"

She must always weep: I was . . . I was . . .
    And who were you, Marie?
"A no one's child, all poor and bare,
and words can't tell you, how."

And such a child has now become
a queen, to whom one kneels?
    "Because the things are all different now
    from how a beggar's child sees them."

So the things bestowed your greatness,
And can you still say, when?
    "One night, one night, in the space of one night,—
    and they greeted me a different way.
    I stepped out into the sleepy street, and look:
    it is stretched taut like strings,—
    then Marie became melody, melody
    and danced from edge to edge.
    The people crept past so cravenly,
    as if they were rooted next to the walls,—
    for only a queen has license
    to dance in the city's streets, dance . . ."

Saturday, 25 November, early morning in the woods

Aucune de mes amies
ne m'a compris,
quand je pleure dans l'église,
elles me disent:
C'est la vie.

Aucune de mes jours
ne prend par la main,
j'attends en vain
ce que je crains:
l'amour.

Aucune de mes nuits
ne m'apporte quelque chose:
une tendresse,
qui me presse,
un rêve, une rose . . .
Je n'ose
de croire que c'est la vie . . .

[None of my girlfriends
understands me;
when I weep in church
they say to me:
that's life.

None of my days
takes me by the hand,
I wait in vain
for the thing I dread:
love.

None of my nights
brings me some benison:
a caress
to hearten me,
a reverie, a rose . . .

I can't possibly believe
that that's life.]

Saturday, 25 November 1899, at night

CHANSON ORPHELINE II

I WOULD like just *once* to be proficient
and accomplish a *real* task!
Not so that afterward I can rest.—
no;
so that I can say to you with blissful senses:
Now let me begin.
What *must* be done is done,
and what comes now is the overplus.
With the rest I worked my way toward freedom,
now I am alone with my strength.
I saw it once before at night (as if I had
wakened to it), my eye managed to endure it:
and it was supple and girl-like
in countenance and shape.
If young people were to ask me,
I'd tell them one thing:

Whenever you long for the boon companions,
go ahead and give them your days.
But keep the nights quietly for yourselves
and lock out foreign footsteps.
Bear in mind: then many a person prays alone,
and many a person lets Death in,
and many a person stays awake creating;—
all's different from at day;
from clockstroke to clockstroke
sheer migrating strength.
So hearken and don't go in droves
in this sanctified time—
if someone shouts coarsely at night
he wakens his dead mother.

And his dead mother comes and beholds
a child who no longer kneels,
and, blinded by this sorrow, can no longer
find her way back into that bliss
that envelops her so gently.
Nights are not made for the masses,
the night cuts you off from your neighbor,—
and you are by no means to seek him out.
And if at night you light your room
so that you can look people in the face,
then you'll have to consider: whom.
People are horribly warped by the light
that drips from their faces,
and if at night they have gathered together,
then you'll see a wavering world
all heaped up at random.
On their foreheads yellow glare has
driven out all thought,
in their eyes the wine flickers,
from their hands hangs
the heavy gesture by which they
understand one another in their talks;
and by which they say: I and I,
and mean anybody.—
How will you usher into *this* night
that one person, the very One
whose single glance transported you
to ecstasy or tears;
so much foul laughter sticks to it
and so much bad smell from the clothes
and the voices of gossips and naggers
and nonsense and nausea—
where will you go with this one person
if you've used up your night?
He is your *first* guest,
the first who truly knocks at you,
who wants to *be* with you

without laughter or lampwick.
But rapaciousness already dwells there
and lounges about in your nights,
and there's no place for your solitude—
about which the uncloaked one
keeps inquiring.
And when he ponders and says:
"Since that last prayer you prayed,
which left you some time ago,
has someone come into your night—
and may I ask his name?"
It's then you feel: into your paradise,
from which no one expelled you,
you yourself have introduced exile,
long before you recognized
misery's blossom and felt its touch.
What good now are the sanctities
with which a stainless life comes toward you?
There's nowhere to safeguard its gifts:
you've betrayed your night.
You have no space left for a quietness
and no womb for a seed,
and even your will
is exiled.
And you must tell that One: "I'm sorry,
my life might as well be over,
nothing can happen to me anymore.
For my night is no longer mine,
I called all these strange people in
and there's so much noise now
that I can't understand what I say . . ."

Night, 25 November 1899

If god has made a law, then it is this: Be solitary from time to time.
For he can come only to a single one—or to a pair between whom he
can no longer distinguish.

2 December 1899, evening

THE stormy night is like a great gesture
in which God sweeps up the many things;
the sky stands, stammering faint stars,
and seeks in this great flight a fixity.

But God cares nothing for this stock.
Forest and wall are faltering and pale.
And through all earth's streets
hundreds of dark stallions stampede:
shadows of God's roaming hand.

YOU must construct an image for each feeling
you wish to give to many strangers;
for one must firmly frame what one imparts;
in children's words or summer lime trees
there must be some likeness that will shape it.
You mustn't *say* what secretly you *have,*
your life mustn't trickle out upon your lips,—
you must bear your blossoms like a bough,
then all breezes will proclaim you . . .

If the poet does not come to the land that raised him, then that land
will come through all things to the poet. I dreamt this recently as material for a story.

These last few days I have immersed myself in Russian, which had
been neglected far too long. I read also to my great profit: Melchior
de Vogüé, *Le roman russe.* I've excerpted everything notable in this
fine book. It takes one from the earliest beginnings up through Tolstoy, whom it treats with great insight.

Immediately after that I read Dostoyevsky's first novel, *Poor Folk,*
that book which Nekrassov and Biélinsky praised so lavishly. And—
I can think of no comparable book. Today is not the time to write
about it; but it will remain with me. And immediately after that the
fragment from Richard Beer-Hofmann, *George's Death,* came into
my hands, and now I can scarcely put it down. I hold it like a letter;

a typeface that is part of the content, the paper, the scent released as the pages turn,—all this gives the feeling of something confided, addressed to us and to many toward whom we shall proceed like messengers and forerunners.

2 December 1899, at night

WHO are we then, with all our wisdoms,
how does song enter our souls?
and our hands move about so slenderly
amid plans and sketches, as if along a colonnade.

Our thoughts, impatient, rushed past
the momentous and trivial alike,
but stopped dazzled before each *thing*,—
for there was none that wouldn't veil its face,
as if it were to blame for its beauty.

The things, though, compliantly must hold
what someone put into their hands;
there a glass tells me what moved my forebear,
a book betrays to me his hidden passion,
and this satin, which, when brushed by shapes
of long-deceased women, rustled with excited flair,
always falls again into the old folds.

What sleeps in us keeps awake inside the things:
out of them dark eyes gaze after us
and accompany our gestures for a long way:
The first endure, and we are second . . .

In the night of my 24th birthday

At first everything seemed intent on concealing the things' beauty from me. Gradually I learned to experience it as an exception. And now, in these present days, I see ever more clearly that it extends everywhere with its own infinite laws, and it seems to me a cruel lovelessness of the eye to make distinctions among the things between what is beautiful and what is not. Each thing is only a space, a possibility, and it is up to me to fill it perfectly or poorly. For since human beings and circumstances are so capricious and forever in turmoil, by what is one to measure oneself if not by the willing things?

Night, December 3–4, 1899

This is the first presentiment of something eternal: to have the time for love.

A person and an unpleasing landscape: it is always the *person's* fault.

Have you not noticed how scorned, lowly things revive when they come into the willing gentle hands of someone solitary? They are like small birds to which the warmth returns; they stir, waken, and a heart begins to beat in them, rising and falling in those hearkening hands like the utmost wave of a mighty ocean.

12 January 1900

Of the educator. An educator must make it his task to transform the crowd of children entrusted to him into many, and many different, human beings; better to commit the error of splitting one person into two who disagree with each other, than to perpetuate that quotidian goal of molding all his pupils into a single species.

12 January, evening

Through Lichtwark's books a host of new interests are entering my days, which are much too narrow as it is for the burgeoning experiences that keep arriving unexpectedly from all things; it looks as though the book on Meister Francke has succeeded in steering me toward a new feeling for German art! What an infinite host of new beauty still awaits me! Before these works I have been a stranger until now and someone born blind, but in ever so gentle healings the growth of my soul continues, and it is as if a mission had been reserved for me that requires that I learn to embrace every beauty and the beauty in everything. As if the feeling of its ubiquity should then reveal to me my mature task, about which I would rather not inquire,

not just now at least, but toward which I am moving ever more trust-
fully, in quiet preparation.

12 January 1900, at night

A Poem at the *Edge of Night:*

> MY room and this vastness,
> awake over the darkening land,
> are one; I am a string
> and stretched taut over wide,
> raging resonances.
> The things are violin-bodies
> full of grumbling darkness:
> in it dreams the grief of women,
> in it the grudge of whole generations
> stirs in its sleep . . . I shall
> vibrate like silver: then everything
> beneath me will live,—
> And what wanders lost in the things
> will strive toward that light
> that from my dancing tone—
> around which the heavens pulse—
> through thin, pining rifts
> into the old abysses endlessly
> falls . . .

12 January 1900, at night

> ONE single poem that comes off well—
> and my boundaries fall as in the wind;
> there's no thing of which I'm not a part;
> it's not my lone voice singing: there is sound.
> The things grow brighter and metallic
> and as they breathe they touch in space
> and become like bells whose long silken strings
> fall into the hands of children playing;
> the children, surprised to find them there,

begin to pull in unison on all cords,
so that before Heaven's doors—which swing open
much too slowly—the sounds already throng.

13 January 1900, at night

From a confession of a young man:

... THERE'S something fatherly, far off:
in glassy nights my soul
—as with the breathing of a star—
became small and clear again.
I'm alone here in life;
and besides me there's one other,
and I'm afraid, because I'm much farther
from him than he is from me ...

24 February, an evening walk in calm, soft, darkening air, Dahlem Street.

WHOEVER you are: In the evening step out
of your room, where you know everything;
yours is the last house before the far-off:
whoever you are.
With your eyes, which in their tiredness
barely free themselves from the worn-out threshold,
you very slowly lift one black tree
and place it against the sky: slender, alone.
And you have made the world; and it is huge
and like a word that goes on ripening in silence.
And as your will seizes on its meaning,
tenderly your eyes let it go ...

Sunday, 25 February, at noon

EACH Sunday the orphan boys come down
the narrow streets, grayly, in cloth rotundas;
the blond ones are like far-off, wind-blown leaves,
but the dark ones are even more forsaken.

The squares become more vacant where they walk,
the streets lead deeper into open spaces,
and—the way a curtain drops from facing sides—
the avenues close shut behind them.

Sometimes a child presses against the panes
in a gray house by the ancient moat,—
and thinks and thinks why the orphan boys,
who do have such a lovely garden,
would not, of all times, stay home on Sunday . . .

21 March 1900

THE darkening was like treasures in the room
in which the boy, so deeply hidden, sat.
And when the mother entered, as in some dream
a glass trembled on the silent shelf.

She felt how the room was giving her away,
and kissed her boy: So you're here.
Then both gazed anxiously toward the piano;—
for on some evenings she'd play a song.

And this song was not just melancholy,
it was completely dark, the way a thing is;
The boy's gaze shuddered
when her hand, bent down by the ring,
as if trudging through deep snowdrifts
traveled across white, white keys.

Thursday, 21 March, in the woods

By the new lake in evening, splendor, and storm. It was there that the
lute-motif came to me:

. . . this lyre was built
from the pure undesecrated wood
of a tree felled by storms.
One which by day, aloof,
withdrew its senses from time.

And only a few knew that each deep night
melted its blooms' heavy jewelry
into flooding scents . . .

But the wood's smooth surface
was not aroused,
only moved as by evening breezes:
noble-veined and clear . . .

YOU have made a lute of me:
now be a hand.
Across the chasm of my night
you've stretched strings
on which other hands would quickly
succumb to vertigo;
and so forever unapproached,
stars arching over it:
that dark shore
on my music's other side.

YOU came toward me for a long time
before as voice and shape
you reached me; what appeared to me
a forest was already you.

And what in my intensest griefs
grew audible in every calm,
was not my blood and was your stride,
and already that stride was you.

I had been garbed in waiting
and my cloak was heavy;
the whole world was a coming-close,—
and through it all came you.

O how my senses watched for you!
Awakened, straining far from body's reach,
as brides, O Night, desiring you,
lean from windows high . . .

Saturday, 24 March 1900

Afternoon before Beethoven's *Missa Solemnis*.

> DON'T be lured by those sounds
> that fall to you out of the full wind;
> wait, see if your strings
> will attract hands that are eternal.
>
> Those evolving are expelled by Time;
> for Time is nothing but decay.
> You can only grow in the Colossal,
> only be solitary in the All.

Sunday, 25 March

Yesterday evening listened to Beethoven's *Missa Solemnis*.—Found especially stirring the jubilation in the Credo and in the Gloria. The soul's growth toward jubilation.

> OUT of the high jubilation-sounds
> thronging to pass through heaven's gate
> rise steep voices, transitions,—
> and all at once the storms are still.
> From the angels' bright brows the sounds
> cast themselves freely into death;
> different jubilation rises in the harps,
> not so passionate and red.
> Silver comes and with quieter light
> threads through words as through darkling vales,
> and they all seem smaller and slimmer
> and like girls with softest eyes.
> But all these girls can feel how love
> unites them with its silver sound,
> and across intervals they extend each other
> their voices—clear, all tears wept.
> And what before was all confusion, woven
> into words of those unused to bliss,
> is now, as by a thousand hands, being raised
> quietly, deftly, sweetly into the sun!

Tuesday, 3 April 1900, at noon

ENCOUNTER

"What a stroke of luck; how good
to see you again."
"To see?"
          "Yes, most fortunate:
people have been asking about you."—"About whom?"
"So tell me, what are you up to?
have you been away traveling, or are you
still working on that novel?
You seem preoccupied. Am I wrong?
And you've changed so
since last we saw each other.
At the theater—remember?"—"No."
"I recall it like yesterday:
You chatted with my wife and me
about Rubinstein.
She'll be glad to see you, too—
have tea with us today."
"And so nothing has changed here with you?"
"What should have changed?
You're a most excellent prophet,
you and all your doom.
Among us, God be praised, things
are just as always . . .
we're all prosperous—but where are you off to? . . .
Mind if I come?"—"Yes."
"And what do you mean by that?
Come, stop your jesting . . ."
"You are?"—"Good Lord man, like you I am
a writer."
          "A wanderer, I."
"And your name?"
                    "That was long ago."
"And so who are you?"
                    "Someone different
from whomever you suppose."

It was after this that we had our conversation about the relationship between apparel, comportment, lifestyle, and raison d'être. The above poem (or better, conversation) is like a preface to it, a preface, regrettably, that says somewhat more than it should. (Tuesday evening)

Friday, 6 April 1900, returning home through the first soft spring rain

AGAIN the woods smell sweet.
The soaring larks lift up with them
the sky, which felt so heavy to our shoulders;
through the branches one did see the day, still empty,
but after long, rain-filled afternoons
come the golden sun-drenched
newer hours,
before which, on distant housefronts,
all the wounded
windows flee fearfully with beating wings.

Then it grows still. Even the rain runs more softly
over the stones' quietly darkening gleam.
All noises slip entirely away
into the brushwood's glimmering buds.

6 April 1900, in the evening

THE evenings are warm and tender,
and in their gentle presence
all the things are good;
each tilts its head and listens,
and through their quietness
their keeping-silent rushes like blood.
In these light hours
time grows powerless and tired:
the things bestir themselves, released,
and each wanders unopposed
to its eternity.

7 April 1900, after the morning

Vitali awoke. He couldn't remember if he had dreamed. But he knew that a whispering had wakened him. Without thinking he glanced toward the clock. It was a little past four. The twilight in his room was giving way to a brightness that spread steadily everywhere. He got up and walked to the window, still in the white woolen sleeping cowl that gave him the look of a young monk. There outside lay the little garden—quiet and empty. It must have rained during the night. The dark soil was visible through black, leafless branches, and it looked heavy and sated—as though the night, seeking refuge, had sunk into it instead of rising into the sky. The heights were desolate, overcast, and jostled by high winds. But as Vitali let his gaze drift aimlessly across the clouds, he heard the whispering again, and only now did he realize that it was the first, faraway larks, rejoicing in the dawn. Their voices were everywhere, far and near, as if dissolved in the soft, saturated air, so that one heard them more with one's feeling than with one's ear. And he grasped suddenly that this hour full of voices can be called by no name and read from no clock. That it is not yet morning and no longer night. He felt closer to the little garden beneath the windows, as if he now better understood his sight; and his eyes came to rest on what he hadn't noticed earlier, the stout shrub on whose branches flower buds the size of small birds were sitting and waiting. And everything on the ground was expectation and patience. The trees and the small round flower beds—which had already been prepared for something new—awaited the day from the skies, and to be sure no sunny, radiant day, but a day from which rain fell, fell without hurting itself, because everything in nature was a hand that received it. That was how moving the patience of this little garden was. But Vitali said aloud out over it: "I gaze as through a Gothic window." Then he stepped back and returned quietly to his bed. Without resisting he let sleep wash over him. But he still heard the roaring outside as a great rainstorm came down.

7 April, toward evening

After the commotion of the city to see these high waiting woods again! How noble this standing is, this calm. Perplexed by the furious gestures of human beings, one comes to feel that there are only two great and related movements. The wingbeat of a high bird and the swaying of treetops. These two gestures are meant to teach one's soul how to move.

I am still too much among you when I am with you, you people. Because these streets are yours, because it is not possible to walk through them—other than behind you, in front of you, next to you, a hastener among hasteners, a single one among different ones. Some day, when I return from the land that is Foreignness for you, it will no longer perplex me to walk through your streets, someone different among different ones.

> YOU must leave behind those musty habits
> you see in all these mindless streets,
> and shut out all their rote compliances,
> on which currently you still rely;
> not till you've doused all those mendacities
> in which you trust, will you at last be
> at your self's beginning and stand
> beside a sea on which you'll calmly walk,
> not knowing that you work miracles
> that sever you from all mankind forever.

Everyone who gazes will sooner or later feel the urge to go out into the desert. With scant nourishment to sit on a rock and think weighty thoughts, so weighty that they press down upon one's eyelids. Yet all who have gone into the desert have sooner or later come back to those they once left. And they all wanted to teach solitude to the communalists; thus they grew tired, despaired of themselves, and died the small tormenting death. But one must go out beyond the desert, farther, always in the same direction. Only he who does that will know what lies on the other side of solitude—and thus why one seeks the desert. And he will not become lost and will not grow tired and his death will not act as though he had never existed.

For the desert is only a gate, and those who come back from there are like beggars who turn around at the church door once they have been given their alms. Receiving such charity has only made them poorer, and the copper piece in their hand is only misery given concrete form. Had they but gone into the church, they might have wandered out beyond the altar with empty hands toward the East, and they would have never been seen again. But as it is they behave like all inveterate teachers, who also are beggars: they come back with alms and have words of blessing on their lips, which hastily and helplessly tag along after the givers, who treat them as an embarrassment and a nuisance.

7 April

I am currently reading *War and Peace.* I am in volume one, and my fullest sympathies are with Prince André. All the best passages I have marked.

11 April, evening

In the city (in Café Bauer) read Georges Rodenbach's drama *Le mirage* full of emotion—as if in a state of breathless listening.
On the way home:

> YOU live reclusive, so that Life often
> turns to the things, to inquire
> if they know you from those sudden days
> in which your childhood left you.
>
> If they still remember how you seized them
> so you could gaze into their faces for a long time
> and then with steps freed of your burden
> leave them far, far behind . . .

Then a quiet evening walk with You in the fields, during which I recounted to You the plot of Rodenbach's drama; the scant content of the four acts, the scent of which sank so deeply into me that I can't give it off. Not yet!

On the evening of 12 April 1900

> WHEN you return from deserts, long off alone,
> enriched by your silence's weight,—
> it may be that you'll know yourself well
> and feel: I am a teacher of mankind.

Yet nothing corrupts so much as *this:*
to approach people as instructor.
You stand at the edge of their looks
and read their hidden hatred.—
And you interpret it to your advantage.
But you're lying: they despise you.
And ever since that lie crept up on you,
you've grown devoid of mastery,
and your house is just like the others.
Whoever would truly master people,
let him go far away from them, quietly,
and let his serenity be unvoiced;
for no one can penetrate the workings
of his own time. To every sage
its fate, its sorrow, is an enigma.
All he experienced is that force
from which the times, departing quietly,
make their way toward mankind.
And forever branded by this knowledge,
he may not ever grasp the others.
That's why to this very day
no word of any triumph has arrived:
no teacher has ever kept silent,
and no wisdom has ever been attained
by this wavering one, by shame.—
Thus we became dreamy violinists
who softly step out of their doors
to make sure, before they pray,
that no neighbor eavesdrops on them.
Who only, when all people have dispersed,
behind the last sounds of evening
play the songs behind which—
like woods in the wind behind fountains—
the dark violin-case murmurs.
For voices are only worth anything
when silences accompany them;
when behind the speech of the strings
rushings remain as if from blood;

and unendurable are those times when
behind all the vanities and strutting masks
there is no ruling force that rests.—

Patience: the gentle clock hand circles,
and what was promised will come about;
we are the whisperers before the silent one,
we are the meadows before the wood;
they still resonate with a dark humming,—
voices everywhere and yet no choir—
and they help prepare us for the mute, deep,
everpresent holy groves . . .

On the same evening

AND if sometime you *have* to teach—
because you have a child, one who sits waiting,
or because in the evening a guest,
one dark with grime,
walks up to the edge of your lamp,
or because your stride
falters once
and you have to stay until daybreak
among strangers,
or because a friend from times past, one who feels
the long-ago friendship tottering,
implores you
to write him sometime soon—
that's when you'd better whisper to yourself
what "teaching" means:
with words that are at your call
to say: I am.
And then furthermore
what teaching *doesn't* mean: to lecture
every man on the tumble of times,
on the how and wherefore of their succession;
teaching means: to ask of each person
what he feels closest to in silence . . .

Riva on Lake Garda, in April

From a girl's letter:

. . . when everyone was asleep I rose quietly and opened my window. It didn't rattle like all the windows at home. It turned softly in its hinges, not so much pulled by my hands as pushed inward by the scent that had been gathering on its other side. This window opened like a bud. . . . Its wings parted from one another like hard, lusterless outer leaves, and now I gazed into the depths of the blossom, into the night's dark calyx that innumerable petals keep secret.

So this is what they call "traveling," Helene. What a mundane title for such a magical book, whose first page rustles in my hands because I hesitate, out of my old childish fear of marvels, to turn it. So all this they simply call traveling. Another name needs to be found for it, don't you think? Help me invent it, dearest. Or better yet: help me keep it a secret if I should unexpectedly come upon it—now or while dreaming. What is dreaming? What were all the dreams we told each other on those long afternoons when we wandered through the rooms, slowly, idly, all caught up in our lassitude? Even Your dreams, dear Helene, for all the splendor and beauty with which they outshone mine, here even Your dreams would be like a Christmas tree in the light of day, dark and paltry. Forgive me: but perhaps it isn't wise, the way You invest so much in your dreams. You often wake with difficulty and live an entire forenoon with Your face turned backward, and Your brow is pale all over, as if illumined by a different light that hasn't yet set for You. Then all Your thoughts reach in that direction, there is no room in Your eyes for the day, and Your hands (so slender!) stand around in their work like orphans whom no one oversees. Your hushed mouth is pale, a little opened, like those beautiful mouths made of white stone from which brooklets stream in bright self-wasting, unafraid, even though no cup receives them. There is streaming from Your lips too in such hours. And what pours from them softly and soundlessly is Your life, which waters those thirsty gardens in which strange springtimes pamper You.

Don't be angry with me, Helene. It was only when I realized how much I myself loved this state that I felt its great danger. We lived with our senses turned elsewhere, Helene. We scarcely ever saw our mothers, and our fathers' rare gestures of tenderness didn't reach us. Shall I tell You what color the walls of my room are? I don't know. Please, go into our empty apartment, take a look and write me. We thought all walls were transparent. In what mistakenness we grew up! Day before yesterday something happened to me. Here, in the bright, hot midday sun, all the small barren roads between the vineyards are blindingly bright—the more so for being totally empty around this time. One walks there constantly flanked by stone walls that reach up all the way over my head (thus Yours, too). One's gaze grows weary from the white dust of the road and leans sleepily against the walls. These also are blinding. But the sun glances off their steepness down onto the path and leaves only its bright trace behind. Besides that they are uneven, rough, more warmly tinted in areas where the plaster has peeled off, and thus one's gaze can hold onto them. There are reddish places on them as if a chrysanthemum had rubbed off there; small slender stubs that protrude from the crevices between the stones lay their shadows down before them, like carpets across which Your eye approaches; but darkest of all are the crevices themselves, like goblets brimful with night. And Your gaze begins to skip from crevice to crevice in order to drink from each. But suddenly the deep blackness recoils, as a wave passes through all the small vessels—and they are empty, so that You find yourself looking into their shallow gray bed. Small rustling animals have borne the darkness away with them: You lost it through too loud a movement. For (only later did I realize it) do You know where my gaze was again and again coming to rest: in eyes. In a thousand watching eyes. In each crevice a small lizard was awake, and the eyes with which it watched me were the blackness inside that space. A thousand lizards were watching me.

And do you know what: all walls are like that. And not just all walls: all things! Whether we cast our glance up when it feels light to us, or whether we let it fall like a hot burden—there is always an eye coming open that catches it, holds it, and gives us back a glance that shines more brightly. And with this new one we go on gazing and from the next thing to which we turn receive another in its place that is yet more beautiful . . . is that not a great good fortune? And the more we gaze, the more splendid the glances we receive in exchange, for each always exceeds the last. Oh Helene, let us gaze into as many eyes as possible!

But don't You feel now that one is forbidden to gaze into realms where there is *no* eye? Do you know that there are blind enemies who drink our eyes out? Until we have no glances left and walk about with empty eyelids. . . . Tear Your eyes from the dream's lips, Helene! Turn them toward the things and the sun and the good people, too, so that they may fill up again with glances. . . . Dearest! If I had You here! If Your parents had only let You come with us, so You could see how changed I am. In my eyes now there are a thousand eyes. If You could gaze into them, You would understand everything and in an instant would have caught up with me. And would kiss me. And would weep. The way I am weeping now, because at this hour my laughing sounds to me too common, and too childish, and above all too loud.

Yours . . .

Easter Monday, 16 April 1900, afternoon

LONGINGS are in error when they weep
for some lost, unreached goal:
for they're really about fairy tales
and crowns with perfect gems
from which not one pearl has fallen.

Longings don't want to be quenched
with a drink from some dull, mundane glass;
they want to be your objects' portrait
and your desires' equipoise.—

Tuesday, 17 April 1900

THE dark beech trees had light conversations
and, while they did, gave us their old
ceremonious reserve to hold,—
as if it were a cloak, whose heavy folds
drop straight down like fates
through the interweave of shapes and stars.

er Maria Rilke, 1896–97

Lou Andreas-Salomé, 1897

Rilke and Lou Andreas-Salomé in
Wolfratshausen, 1897

Paula Becker in Worpswede, 1900

e and Lou Andreas-Salomé with the Russian poet Droshin, at Nisovka, June 1900

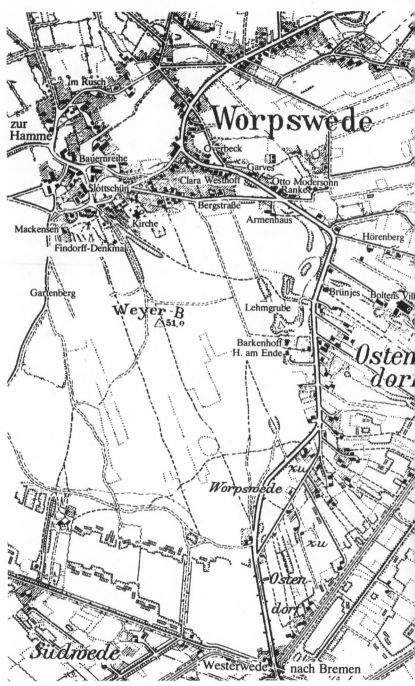

Map of Worpswede and vicinity in 1897

Rilke in Worpswede, 1900

inrich Vogeler in Worpswede, ca. 1900

Heinrich Vogeler and Martha Schröder, ca. 1898

Portrait of Clara Rilke-Westhoff; oil painting by Paula Modersohn, autumn 1905

...e and Clara Rilke-Westhoff, shortly after their marriage in Westerwede, 1901

Entrance gate to "Barkenhoff." Left: Otto Modersohn; right: Paula Modersohn-Becker and Martha Vogeler.

Paula Becker and Otto Modersohn in his studio, 1901

Do you remember that anxiety we felt
as our unaccustomed arms trembled
from that soft, velvet burden:
for we both knew what the danger was:
were our hands to lower just a bit,
we could not but stain those deep hems
with our path's vexatious windings.
But I'm certain no hand of ours dropped
and that we breathlessly gave thanks
when, not long after sunset,
the woods wished to don their cloak again.

Tuesday, 17 April, in the evening

SUDDENLY you see among different hours
an hour that appears the youngest.
Her pace is as if surmounted,
and her smile has exhausted crying.
All her sisters seem to shun her,
and, as they near, they take on features
and you see that they are foreign;
and you step with your richest phrases
before the mother of that *one* hour,
in order to ask her for her bridal child.

24 April 1900, one of the prematurely ripe spring days

SONG:

THE garden outside the windows
is only an image in green
of a much more unbounded garden
in which we're both abloom.

Whatever blessed its senses
as winter covered them
shines and muses and rains
over our year, too.

The garden has its wonts,
just as do you and I:
two shrubs striving upward
soon branch as one.

Added from April 18:

COME along into the tossing meadow;
now the poorest field feels just like you.
A silent blue is leaning quietly
on a light green world.

Even the streets grow landscape-like
and widen in this youthful year;
a miracle—understandable in silence—,
but too wondrous for any word.

Yet all seems almost as always:
what's actual is this shimmering,
and that old fear—a symbol;
as though it had never left us,
so simply, solemnly, and artlessly
Spring makes us whole once more.

> By the little forest lake "Hundekehle," 2 May 1900, evening

HOW deeply the pond by evening light,
framed in forest black, keeps silent;
as if, high overhead, a visage
had just leaned over it.

Solemnly and full of awe it mirrors back
what, forever musing, is awake:
that forehead that makes the cherubims'
clear voices grow dizzy . . .

From a letter. St. Petersburg, 31 July

On the Volga, on this restfully rolling ocean, to be days and nights,
many days and many nights: a broad, broad stream, high, high woods

along the one shore, along the other a deep moorland in which even great cities stand like mere shacks and tents.—One learns all dimensions anew. One discovers: land is huge, water is something huge, and above all the sky is huge. What I have seen until now was no more than an image of land and river and world. Here, however, everything is itself.—I feel as if I had been witness to the creation; a few words for all existences, the things in the measure of God the Father. . . .

Moscow, Stshukin Museum: vis-à-vis the Japanese painting in the room with the translucent ceiling:

May 1900. Added

GODDESS OF GRACE

SHE stands in deep-blue ocean depths
into which many rivers pour
from distances on high.
A gray fish carries her along,
delighted by her weight's lissomeness,
which trickles over his fins.

Out of his gills spews excited
spraying—bubbling rush of breath.
But into her beauty rises
coolly, ushered along in waves,
his forever level feeling.

Worpswede, 1 September 1900

When I read this to you in the America House, do You remember my saying: Yes, everything that has truly been seen *must* become a poem! Oh, I felt so happy saying that. And I still can't believe I was wrong then—although . . .

Both possibilities are equally disheartening. Either I have not *seen* anything since then, have not truly, with my entire being seen, or my seeing is not so closely bound up with creating as I once thought.

For back then there was only pure sound in me: once in Poltava, at evening, when the cabins were so pale and solitary in the coming on of night, once in Saratov among the Cossack houses of the eastern districts, later in the midst of the Volga waters, again when through the course of a long night we felt ourselves journeying farther and farther into the light . . . but I can extract no word from the weave of these sounds, indeed I don't even know if they went with words.

Nonetheless, just outside Kazan in the evening, a song came forth; it began, I seem to remember:

> . . . FROM all others I will absent myself,
> I will build my life stone by stone,
> not from the rubbleheap of rich housefronts,
> from ashlars that still bathe in rivers,
> from mountains that still stand in meadows . . .

But it seemed wrong to express my inner happiness, which was free of everything external, in these words, which had just lost their meaning in the face of mundane reality. So I was glad when my sound died out, and its sense flared up in me again only much later in Moscow, as landscape . . . evening:

> THE horses saunter over with their red yokes
> as if passing under many gateways,
> the evening glows, called to by bell-chimes,—
> and all cabins stand as by the sea . . .

This may have been an echo of Yaroslavl-Kresta.—Then came Droshin, then Novgorod, where on that one morning there was a possibility inside me. . . .

I made nothing of it, as was the case with so many on this trip. Countless poems I failed to hear. I passed over a spring; what wonder now when there is no true summer. Everything that arrived found me locked up. And now, when I open the doors, the roads are long and empty. . . .

But this is *not* the journey's sum. The tremendous is still somewhere inside me. I *did* experience it all, I was surely not just dreaming. If it would only somehow come back to me. I have such a longing for what has passed. I don't want to dwell on it. But I wish I could feel its presence half-instinctively in the things that are around me now. I shall never cease to mourn these losses. Why did I forget that not dying is not the same as being alive, and that not sleeping is still a long way from being awake. To be awake and to be alive are deeds, not states. And I did not *do* them!

Worpswede, 4 September

I give parties. Dr. Hauptmann arrives on the path over the hill with two sisters, one blond and one dark. Herr Modersohn and a strange young man whose speech and manner remind me strongly of Holitscher have joined up with them. We sit in the music room. You remember: white, with white doors, vases painted over them with rose garlands falling gracefully to either side. Old etchings, little amorous garden scenes, delicate portraits. J. J. Rousseau's tomb. Empire chairs, an armchair, just right for the blond sister. Piano pieces by Richard Strauss, Robert Franz, Schubert . . . Later on, since I am asked, I read a few things. First, following the music: the evening with the young men in the dimly lit room. Then poetry, "The Minstrel" included . . .

I still have a strange feeling whenever I recite "The Minstrel." There is always that same sense of coming upon it in the act of speaking it; each successive line takes me by surprise, yet at the same time I feel calmed with its onset, like someone who is being confirmed in his intuition of a great order. The girls loved the song. It was lost on Dr. Hauptmann: he suggested that the last line, "and to where, no one knows," might be omitted. . . . How differently Nikolai Tolstoy understood these lines! How much more as a poet . . .

And later Dr. Hauptmann read. Read maxims, aphorisms, read poetry, too. Everything was prosaic, although even his prose labored to be poetic. Contrived, abstract, all values divorced from their contexts, tottering, propped up by images laboriously wedged in under them. Hauptmann is extremely agitated. He feels a whole host of things that are beautiful, deep, and intimately connected, but when he tries to put these feelings into words, he ties them down to small pretexts, to helpless or banal images, and if one nonetheless recognizes them as feelings, it is due solely to the man's pure and noble being, whose scent has a way of lingering. What an unworldly soul; pampered by solitude, he turns to intimacy far too eagerly in moments of rare sociability, speaks of all he's so filled with, takes delight in the words that readily lend themselves to the never-before-said, and forgets that these words leave him and go off into a world not his own. When he suddenly senses this, he digs his finger into the deep creases that extend from his nostrils down to the corners of his mouth, as if to divert one's gaze from everything else that is happening on his shy face. And at other times he makes awkward attempts to cloak something with his shoulders, something that he feels to be cold and bare. Then suddenly he realizes that it is his soul, and falls silent. And does not sleep that night and the next day is diffident and shy.

In a poem written in free verse he was a poet for the length of five lines. "Over ocean waters . . ." it began. But in the sixth he is already contriving, being led without knowing it by abstract concepts, and trying to drown out that much-hated intellect with something loud. . . . That's how his verses feel.

So often what incites him to poetry is music. Without music he would never—it seems to me—have found verse. But in the harmonies of music he receives already gathered up and ordered what the poet must seek out darkly and obliquely amid the world of things.— And therefore his poetry is: a strongly personal interpretation of music.

Late, sometime around midnight (the candles at the piano had burned low), our conversation became a rapid dialogue between Hauptmann and me. I had shown everyone paintings and icons and finally brought up Kramskoy. I related a few things, and then: Kramskoy had felt for years: Somewhere there's laughing.—And he tried to paint this laughing. He painted it far away and then began embodying it in figures that were closer and closer. And the laughing grew, became broad, broad, enlisted a hundred faces, took possession of poor and rich, kings and mercenaries. Before the laughing seized them, all shapes seemed alike; in it they became individualized. And no amount of figures could sate this laughing's appetite; as a whirlwind lifts columns of sand, it spun itself human being after human being, even though such a myriad of laughers had already been created. And suddenly the painter feels: everyone is laughing. The world itself is laughing. Laughing is the world's voice. And he can no longer counteract with his own person this laughter's huge weight. He must seek someone else to maintain the equilibrium; he must with all his prayers, all his powers of recognition, all his creative strengths conjure up someone who doesn't laugh. And in infinite fear he seeks and waits. And from far away the One who is eternally coming comes. And positions Himself bound among the loosened. And stands . . .

But the world is not laughter. That's not true. It's the figment of misunderstood genius that feels itself ridiculed. The world is good, souls are noble, and to laugh at suffering is an aberration, something reprehensible . . . thus Dr. Hauptmann.

No, good Doctor, the world is not laughter, but it is the great common realm of happenstance whose loudest and readiest voice is the sound of laughing. And to the solitary, to the deeply serious person, such laughter can only mean the masses, who are forever hammering at his aloneness. He *hears* laughing; what goes on behind it may not always be suitable for laughing, may in fact be toil or poverty—but far up above it all there's laughing from a hundred mouths . . .

Dr. Hauptmann later: And being together in lightest laughter is our best communion.

I: Better to be together in solemn seriousness. . . . Lightness is really only meant for one. The moment two people really touch each other, their communing can only be in seriousness. Think of our own good Fidus: the shining before the shined-upon face.

Dr. Hauptmann might well write in his diary one day (a diary by the way in pigskin, whose giant pages could put out the stars with their tempest):

> HALLO! I come here from the hill,
> Good host, a brimming tankard fill!
> My thirst gives me a pain . . .
> And if he has a daughter fine,
> Then let me see his sunlight shine,
> before I'm off again . . .

And it wouldn't be that he actually *means* this, just that he needs to express something real and earthy in lyric fashion. . . .

Two evenings. One in the white music room. People undergoing changes amidst songs and verses. Seriousness, conversations, silence; the candles burning low, shadows passing across foreheads. Solitudes issuing from mutuality, reticences from fellow-feeling. The farewell truly a leave-taking, each from all the others. Black trees, huge shrubs, voices clear in the night, familiar in a special way, and one loses one-self among the stars.—The other evening: harvest festival; not with the common people, that took place yesterday among the . . . ah good Lord, among . . . well, just among those who. But the painters join in. The blond painter in the white dress is there, she who grew so serious yesterday, the sculptress is there with all her dark vitality, which is strength and strength again and frustration that such strength is not more needed. Nothing should be as finished as it is, everything should want to be made more tactile, every hour should welcome being shaped better. . . . Vogeler is there . . . his figure cool and self-composed. His eyes dark, without luster. His high-collared neck with the exquisite cameo, the high velvet waistcoat . . . a por-trait. An infinitely distant ancestral portrait, but this time in a stor-age room and unframed. Everything around is just so much junk. These women with their dancing-fears, these men in their awful Sun-day coats, animated at the table over beer and assuming a grave, al-most unmoving solemnity when they dance. I get to meet Mackensen. Am distracted, had moreover such a curiously distinct picture of him, which naturally is disappointed. . . . Continually I want to say: You have changed, Herr Mackensen, changed indeed . . . and so I say nothing, say nothing to him, say nothing to his brother . . . say nothing.

God, how sad all this is. Granted, there are a few here I would enjoy having by my side so that I could say something to them; but they are like isolated fragments in this welter. I shake hands with some, with others not, I smile and don't smile, rouse myself and stiffen, sit in a corner, smell the beer and breathe the smoke, finally stand up and walk, walk straight into Dr. Hauptmann. He is com-ing diagonally across the room, looking rather bleached out in his bright English overcoat. He sighs with relief when he sees that it's me:

"I feel so diffident today." "So do I." We shake hands warmly and think, yesterday we were not diffident . . . indeed, not yesterday.

A little later I am on my way. The night arches high overhead. Winds race behind me without overtaking me. The dance-music is growing more and more fleeting and inconspicuous, while up in the tent the world had seemed filled with it. . . . But out in the great world it is barely a small voice, and people come, people with much silence in them, and for a single night they turn around a small voice. And the night is outside and it passes and passes inexorably and will never again exist. . . . But the small voice will stand again at the same spot in exactly a year's time, and will not in the least notice that the people who come to it are different by a year, younger or older by a year, and will twirl them, brash and mindless, as though they had experienced nothing, had suffered nothing, and hadn't loved. . . .

But by then Vogeler will be married.

6 September

We walked through the heath together, in the evening wind. And walks in Worpswede always take the same course: for a while two ramble on together, deep in conversations that the wind quickly destroys—then one of them comes to a halt and after a few moments the other. So much is happening. Beneath the vast skies the darkening colorful fields lie flat—wide hilly waves of rustling heather, bordering them stubble-fields and new-mown buckwheat, which with its stalk-red and the yellow of its leaves is like richest silk. And the way all this lies there, so close and strong and real that one can't possibly ignore it or forget it. Every moment something is held up into the vivifying air, a tree, a house, a slowly turning mill, a man with black shoulders, a large cow or a hard-edged, jagged goat that walks into the sky. There are no conversations in which the landscape doesn't take part, from all sides and with a hundred voices. But the other evening we were suddenly walking side by side, oddly oblivious to all movement. And Vogeler said: "There's something else important I still have to tell you; it has to do with why I'm so often not here anymore. Next spring or fall I'm going to be married."—In that moment a sense of infinite partaking filled me. I felt: So everything is fine now!

The struggle is over. "Yes," said V., divining my happiness, "the struggle is over. She is a local girl, a girl of the common people, a strong, simple, lovely girl. First she has to be freed from the way of life here; she's been living in Dresden, alone, and now she's staying with my brothers. We've been meant for each other from the start. We've shared everything—for a long time now, for ever and ever. . . ." What could I say. "I know," I smiled, grateful to be his confidant, "—I knew about a lot of it, and sometimes worried about the whole thing; it could have so easily been ruined by some chance event or local prejudice. Especially that time you came to see me in Berlin, I was afraid . . ."—"Yes, that was the most perilous moment. But now everything is fine."—"Now that I know, I assume you'll be returning to Adiek. I'm just happy that you let me share it all here."— Again landscape. Then V. said: "Of course in all her studies she's . . ." And he had to smile, with me looking so knowledgeable from all eternity.—I was elated. Especially in the last few days I've felt this girl so strongly, as if sometimes she were walking about in the gabled house near evening. And now I know: she has been! All portraits are in praise of her, and for years everything has been fulfillment. Thus these fairy tales in which everything unfolds, thus this festiveness and quietness and absence of yearning. For in all the best fairy tales there is no yearning. All possibilities arch over them, so close that yearning is much too long an arm, much too far-off a hand.

7 September

THE BRIDE

> I have felt her in this house,
> The blond bride, who long languished here.
> All hours sing with her voice
> and all sounds move with her gait.
>
> The objects, which had to serve me daily,
> grew downcast whenever *I* approached,
> and they yearned for someone more intuitive
> with whom their simplicity could commune.

Nothing in the house declared her presence,
yet everything said "it's not for you,"
and when at dusk I wandered through long hallways,
all mirrors begged for *her* soft image.—

Vogeler is back in Adiek. He has told me so much during these days—
not about himself, and not about her either. On the contrary, he has
often been praising other women since he arrived, and celebrating
them quite beautifully. He spoke of Clara Westhoff and then of Frau
V. D. Of the latter he remarked: "She is so much the young girl.
There is an enormous amount in her that her husband doesn't possess at all."—He is a master at characterizing people briefly, through
colors, words, or in snatches of dialogue. He has stories of so many
places: of Bruges and Naples, of Paris and Munich, Düsseldorf and
Amsterdam. He knows everything. He embraces so many things in
this world with an amazingly rich sensibility. He could speak of fleeting encounters and long friendships, of odd characters (Peter Filippi),
of gorgeous women and courageous girls. Of landscapes that stand in
the evenings, of strange days on unknown islands to which he journeyed with beautiful women on small boats heaped with roses. Of
sailors who gather in smoky rooms around the open cauldron, of old
men who had been in America and with trembling voices intone
Negro songs that their light-blond grandchildren and their strong
sons do not understand. Of dancing peasants from the moor and of
the strange ones among them who are full of superstition and foreboding. Of rich fathers and superfluous sons who can't start living, of
notable strangers who pass by, of guests who stay, of pictures and
epistles, of Adiek and his own land. Of its many beauties, only a few
of which I shall have seen, of its sunrises and autumn evenings, of the
light on the snow and the darkness over the deep land in November.
Of life on the mountain. Of the church and its feast days, of death in
the moor. Of old oaks and young birches. Of the eternal wind. Of
spring with its meadows into which countless tulips rise, yellow and
bright red. Of the house that roses embrace ever more tightly, of the
trees in bloom, of a tall fir and a yellow oriole that flew over it. Of the
canals and how the boats approach in them. How the sails stand with
dark shoulders; how the men in the boats greet each other, how much

darker the fields are with their rich sod. Of women bound to the plow, hard and lean in their black dresses and large white sunbonnets. Of drunken gendarmes who sing while all in the room grow pale and frightened and many women weep; for outside a thunderstorm rages, and the thunderstorms are fearsome over the great moor and kill many in their homes. That's why the men keep silent and fill the low vestibule with their smoking, and the women bend down to the children, and many girls stand by the walls and sob. And in the midst of it all the gendarme with the little saber dances and shouts breathlessly during the thunder's pauses: ". . . nothing beats a wooden tiled stove . . ." And many more scenes and many figures. Once he and Clara Westhoff and a young woman drive across the heath in a happy-go-lucky mood. They come to the sea. They board a ship. With the ship-folk they dance strange dances that they can suddenly execute with ease. Dancing barefoot on the burning deck under a vertical sun, in heavy noon. Clara Westhoff finally says: "No, now I have to stop." And her feet are red and full of deep blisters. And now to see the sailors: all that they drag up, water and wads of cotton, a new never-used ship's apothecary, oil and salves and everything mild imaginable. But it was to be otherwise; an old man, hard as nails, his pipe clenched in the left corner of his mouth, steps up, lifts the foot until he has it right up to his old eyes, looks at the thing calmly and objectively, as if it were something completely detached, and declares briefly: "Ayeah, that's got to go," fetches his knife and calmly opens, with a cut of this trusty old knife that serves all purposes, every blister. Supported by sailors, Clara Westhoff returns to the house, and this house becomes the center of concern to twenty men, who against strict order secretly steal away from the ship at night to find out if their dancer can sleep.—A few days later they travel across the strip of unfamiliar sea to the next island, an isolated piece of land to which outsiders scarcely ever find their way. There they live as if in the beyond. And then one day they drive to the end of the island. There is a village there. They travel for a long time through dunes. At last they come to the crossroads where a tall man stands, stands gazing intently into the distance. He must have seen something. With impatient movements he begins to walk rapidly toward whatever it is that is coming this way; but suddenly, as if pulled by the spot on which he had been standing, his gait wavers, pivots, and turns swiftly back to the spot on which he again positions himself, staring out. They watch for a long time from the cart as this strange game gets repeated. Its protagonist is someone who must wait . . . year in, year out. He can't tell anyone what it is he waits for, but he must have known once, and it was no senseless waiting— once. But now so much time has passed that it no longer relates to anything around, and whoever was supposed to come probably died a long time ago. And the whole village has that feeling. Strangely questioning eyes follow them in the streets, and when at last they are sitting exhausted in the inn, out of dark corners of the large smoky room eyes fix on them, and no sooner does someone absentmindedly open a door than an old gray woman rushes to their table with frantic gestures, a question seems to jostle her about, her lips tremble— but once again the mad woman is jerked back, and a door slams shut behind her scream. A moment later she leaps with wide eyes out of yet another door. . . .

They arrive similarly at a seaside resort. Dusty and hot after a long bicycle ride, they want to put up, much to the horror of its German vacationers, at a large hotel festooned with bright lamps shining everywhere. They are met by excuses, and by looks that regard their flushed faces and wrinkled clothes half suspiciously, half in scorn. It is evening—the streets are full of people out for a walk, and they all pause full of curiosity in front of the inn and relish the predicament of these foreigners who are such an affront to them. Then one climbs back onto one's bike and rides out to the darkening, deserted churchyard, and behind the church there begins a great bustle with comb and brush, which is not entirely without effect. From the churchyard one advances on the resort a second time, guiding one's bicycle circumspectly, and this time one is actually allowed to stay.

9 September

Sunday. Evening before last I was with the blond painter.—First I talked about the moods in Worpswede, how heavy they are, how full of sadness; I remarked that one thing here especially has an uncanny effect on me: the strong colors that persist without sun, when there is no radiant light left anywhere. There were all those days with gray sky and soft drizzle: but nothing grew pale or indistinct as a result. On the contrary, all colors became even more intense; the violet of the broad heath-fields took on warm, velvety nuances, and a white goat that was crossing the heath looked as if he were made out of ivory. Completely detached from the leaden sky, the earth went on reveling in its myriad vivid colors, and even its distances didn't disappear in mists. The roof of the large mill stood out against the clouds as a rich dark brown, and its strong arms traced a sharply delineated cross. And whatever had trouble making its effect in the distance seemed to crowd up closer: a cottage, red with green beams and a mossy roof of thatch, a tall chestnut tree on which the light-colored husks were clearly visible in the hanging foliage, a darkening shrub next to its shadowy entrance door, and inside, a single red dahlia, burning with ripeness.

> The reddest roses never showed so red
> as on that evening that was cloaked in rain.
> I thought so long about your softest hair . . .
> The reddest roses never showed so red.
>
> The bushes never darkened quite so green
> as on that evening in that time of rain.
> I thought so long about your gentle dress . . .
> The bushes never darkened quite so green.
>
> The slender birch trunks never stood so white
> as on that evening that was dark with rain;
> and then I saw your hands, their perfect shapes . . .
> The slender birch trunks never stood so white.
>
> The waters mirrored there a land of black
> that very evening I found misting rain;
> and thus in your eyes I recognized myself . . .
> The waters mirrored there a land of black.

"It's true I don't laugh as much since I've been here," said the young blond painter. "And yet I felt homesick in Paris. At first Paris was much too foreign for me, but even after we had grown accustomed to being there, often we would feel a strong yearning for moor and heath when one of the peasants wrote us a postcard or someone sent us the first snowdrop."—"But in the spring there must be cheerful moods even here?"—"Cheerful? Poignant would be more like it. Spring comes so softly, without interruptions or delays, but with such an indescribably bright green. . . ."

Later Clara Westhoff joins us. She relates: "A few evenings ago I walked out into the meadow under the tall chestnut trees. Twilight was settling in. I see: children running, and something dark, bent-over, herding them before it into the house. This dark something interests me. It's night now, I realize, and the chestnut trees are calm. The dark thing suddenly draws something out of itself and changes shape. There is still a high-arched back, but now the head is visible, and it thrusts out toward me and observes me, apparently just as interested as I am. I can feel its looking at me. And from the dark formlessness a bone-thin arm stretches out and manages to reach me, even though I am still quite far away—and as its hand holds me, it says: 'You dun know me and I dun know you in the dark. . . .' For a while I was silent, and the dark something was silent, too. Its words had a curious weight, as if they meant more than they said. Then I quickly cast off my uneasiness and made the old woman's acquaintance.

"On this same farmstead (it's the one where I have my studio) there is another figure. She is small and old-looking, her body lacks contour and drops off sharply on all sides. She has a nervous disorder. Her right arm is bent, and its hand rests across her right hip, its cupped palm turned upward slightly toward the back. One never sees her walking, all she ever does is stand in different spots. She's charged with overseeing the children. She stands at the center of every game, stiff and silent like a post, and gazes vacantly out over what surrounds her . . . Now that I've made friends with her, she'll be my neighbor too." Thus Clara Westhoff. And now I imagine: autumn, everything green goes away. There is only the deep brown of the moor earth, which always appears shadowed by huge, invisible things, black wood on small bridges over canals that stand like black glass. Empty trees. Yellow leaves around their base and eternal wind in them. Birch trunks, indescribably bright, like metal . . . And as a part of all this, the dark old woman with her thin, uncannily long arms. Is that merely autumn? No, it's much more than that. It's Death.

Death in the moor. How easy it must be to meet him here. He needn't possess some particular garb or gait. There need only approach a man, dark the way all are, tall, hard-shouldered, with heavy-hanging hands for grasping. One has been watching him approach on the narrow footpath beside the black canal for some time now. He walks and walks. And one ponders even while he is still far away: How shall I make room for him? On the left the moor is so close that the path that runs hard by its edge ripples and behind one's steps sends little waves over the wilted grass-clumps along the trail. On the other side stands the canal. It would be possible, of course, to press against the nearest birch and let him pass by; then, too, the moor alongside will surely support one for a few more steps; and at worst the canal is barely shoulder deep. . . . But one calculates all these escapes in vain. It will happen otherwise. On a slippery bridge, the width of one board, beneath which an endless canal trembles from some wind, one will come face-to-face with him. There is no struggle; for he is blind and walks on, on, as if no one were there. . . . That's what they'd have to extract from this landscape. If anywhere, this is where a dance of death would arise.

Occasionally they find moor-corpses. During Roman times in these parts there was a punishment for adultery: the naked woman lay down with her face and breasts flat against the black moor, and lying this way she was stamped into it by the feet of heavy farmhands. Years ago they found such a body, perfectly preserved. For a thousand years its outlines had expressed fear and terror without disintegrating. Only under the hands of the discoverers did they decompose. And the dust was buried in the cemetery of Worpswede next to the little church whose bells Clara Westhoff had tolled once to celebrate the evening.

September 10

I give another party. There was a beautiful moment . . . The girls, all in white, came down from the mountain out of the heath. The blond

painter first, smiling beneath a huge Florentine hat. I was just then
standing at the studio window handing in to Frau Freitag a heavy
paint table. The blond painter entitled this scene "The Bout with the
Table." Then I greeted everyone. This time the painter, Frau Bock,
had joined them. While we were still standing in the dark vestibule
growing accustomed to one another, Clara Westhoff arrived. She
wore a dress of white batiste without bodice in the Empire style.
With a high waist lightly gathered beneath the bosom and long
smooth folds. Blowing about her beautiful dark face were the curls of
black hair she had left hanging at either cheek, in keeping with her
dress's style.—The whole house flattered her, everything became
more stylish, seemed to adjust to her, and when upstairs during the
music she leaned back in my large leather chair, she was the mistress
of the house among us. Every time I looked at her this evening she
was beautiful in a different way. Especially in her listening, when
that aspect of her face that is sometimes too strong is bound up in
something unknown. Then the rhythm of restrained, listening life
imprints itself on her figure, softly as among folds. She waits, completely given over, for whatever she is about to experience. . . . That
was the perfect time for reading *The White Princess*. I myself was left
with a strong sense of sound and power at its end, and it was a shame
that Carl Hauptmann had to lunge almost immediately into his the-
orizing, which required of me a response, the whole verbal exchange
needless to say getting nowhere. The girls didn't join in. They had all
taken *The White Princess* to heart.—Earlier the painter's sister had
given a recital of songs. An Italian folk motif: "Senza di te . . . ," a
Handel—and songs of Mignon. I was able to give myself over to
only one piece the entire evening, and that was the Goethe poem
with the great mysterious opening: "Thus let me appear till I become . . ." Dr. Hauptmann had one song with a dreadful text repeated for him over and over, an invocation to Art the
Comfortress—which the singer did sing with beautiful simplicity. The
words began: "Thou noble art, in how many dismal hours . . . , etc."
This song provided Hauptmann with his great breakthrough vis-à-vis
act IV of *Forest People,* which for weeks now he has been writing and
rewriting, cutting and piecing into shape. I had been right: music is
what prompts him. It provides him in concentrated form what he

can't find in nature; all that's left for him to do is unfold what he has heard and pad it out with what his mood at that particular moment affords him. I had been right about something else, too. When around midnight wine had been discovered in Vogeler's cellar, he requested a drinking song from me and repeatedly declared that some day I would realize the hole that gaped in my art, seeing that there was no drinking song in it anywhere. He insisted on singing Dehmel's drinking song, of which however he could not recall a single verse. How awful at the end of an intimate gathering to be looking for wine . . . and finding it made the last hours disconnected and inane. It was touching when the singer-sister sat down beside me, asked me about Leopardi, and with a voice still resonant from singing recited melancholy Italian words from a beautiful poem. But that was only an isolated episode. The others were all dancing; Hauptmann with Fräulein Westhoff. A few whirls about the room . . . waltzes . . . finally Dr. H. stopped, cocked his head pensively toward the left, raised his forefinger, and announced out of breath: "Now I am starting to get dizzy," with which he thanked his lady. I was unbelievably alone. It was as if the words were not coming toward me at all, as if they were whirling at the periphery of those who were laughing. And of course a poem had to be pieced together for Vogeler: jokes, clowning, sickening end of German conviviality. But the ending was beautiful in spite of all, and it was the girls in white who redeemed it. I opened the door to my room, which was growing cool and dark blue like a grotto. I pushed open my window, and then they came to join the miracle and leaned out brightly into the moonlit night, which enveloped their laughter-hot cheeks in cold. And suddenly they all became so poignant in their gazing. Half fully aware, i.e., as painters, half intuitively, i.e., as girls. Initially the mood seizes them, the single note of this misty night with its almost full moon over the three poplar trees, this mood of faintly tarnished silver robs them of their defenses and forces them into the dark, yearning-filled life of girls. . . . Then the artist in them gains control and gazes and gazes, and when the artist has become deep enough in this gazing, they are once more at the threshold of their own being and miracle and glide gently back into their life as girls. That's why they always gaze so long into the landscape. . . . And so they stood at my window, and all those whom I would have only grudgingly allowed into my room a few moments earlier, back when their fun-making had so disfigured them, now brought a mystery inside with what they lived, and I loved them for their beauty, around which my window drew a large, chaste white frame.—

And so I parted warmly from them all. It was long after midnight. The round forecourt with the small urns was steeped in white. Immediately behind it the mist had closed. The trees stood as if in front of a pale silver door in its wall. All were bright and slender. There was no longer a disturbance of footsteps and voices; the silvery world stood, untouched by us, under cool skies, peopled by other beings, and we were not real as long as this lunar fairy tale, with its firmament of stars and forms, endured.

> GIRLS, those are poets, who learn from you
> to *say* what you so complaisantly *are*;
> and through you they learn to live, you far-off ones,
> as the evenings through the great stars
> grow accustomed to eternity . . .
>
> None may ever give herself to the poet,
> even though his gaze begged for a woman;
> for he can only think of you as girls:
> the feeling in your slender wrists
> would break beneath brocade.
>
> Let him be alone in his garden,
> where he greeted you like guests eternal
> on those paths that he wandered daily,
> by those benches that wait steeped in shadows,
> in the chamber where the bright lute hung.
>
> Go . . . it grows dark, his senses seek
> your white guidance no longer,
> and the paths he loves long and empty
> and no whiteness beneath the dark beech trees,—
> and loves especially the silent room.
>
> Your voices he hears move far off
> among people, whom he wearily avoids,

> and his tender memory suffers it
> like foresight, that many gaze on you . . .

It's such an extraordinary experience, and part of what makes girls so wondrous for me: the sense that one must observe them the way one does flowers growing. Not alone, unto themselves; side by side and always blended with the land and with the great celestial connections: with rising and going down, with meadows and beside streams full of trembling images, under rushing rain and in vast evenings that have cleared. Girls can't be seen with less than an entire landscape, for that is their secret: that they are not yet isolated in their solitude, that their faces don't yet employ expressions and form statements with their looks, that beneath the great events of their feeling they are simply shadowed or shone upon, just as the blessed meadows are.—

This really is a fairy tale. I sit in a pure white house of gables that is overgrown everywhere with gardens, among lovely inestimable things, in chambers that are filled with the mood of someone creating. I sit in its dreamy chairs, enjoy its flowers, peruse myself in its mirrors, and its clocks address me as the master of the place. There I dwell in solitude, always waiting, for six days. And on the seventh I receive, in the white hall with its twelve candles standing in tall silver candlesticks, the most sincere men of the region and incredibly beautiful slim girls in white, who, when I ask them, play songs and sing and sit together, in exquisite Empire chairs, and are the most elegant pictures and the richest abundance and the sweetest voices of these whispering rooms. . . .

> THIS has long seemed to me a kind of death:
> this losing of youth's visage;
> onto soft, slender cheeks the mask of man
> clamps down—harsh, bearded, red.
>
> How do they bear this losing of their youth?
> Suddenly one is just another cog—
> no longer young and no longer wondrous
> and yet alone.

No longer is one brotherly with trees,
leaning at one's window, one no longer shines out;
grown men, armed with any sort of pretext,
crowd around the quiet garden bench
where once they happily ignored the youth.

They gauge him by their common measures—
he, who was once for them some odd foreigner;
they put their stupid hat upon his hair,
which for years has been blowing in all breezes.
And he has a hundred images and prayers
that suddenly are withered, without effect.
He must cease bowing in the wind,
and not show anyone
that in his heart all violins
are his sisters.
What has drawn him on
in darkness—
all that's unconscious—
must cease to be.
No longer may the evening
find him alone:
only among like-minded ones.
Yet of those many:
Who muses on things the same as he?
Who stands bowed over God?
Who keeps silent?
Who with all his gestures indicates the sea?
Who dreams of girls as if
of evening hours?
And where
might *that one* be found
who fled from the garish feast of men?
The sheen of dancing girls
is what they love;
to use their wit and come out winners,
to *seize* with all their senses,

is what they crave.
Among them, what should he do
with his dream-endowed
bright serenity,
how should he talk with them
when from each one
he's severed by a hundred wonders.
How should he laugh along
over a sly reply . . .
and after many a cup
wake up with them to morning,
to that daily, thousand-faceted event
that moves him so differently?
No matter how blunt their actions,
he'll stay on among them:
a youth, conducted into manhood.
He'll go about, as they, in current fashions,
in a city suit, with polished shoes,
but in the forests, in a light loden mantle
he'll walk the old trails barefoot.

Manhood, in the form it nears us,
manhood of the weighty daily deed—
this manhood is a disguising
of longings and laces:
a nasty affair.

A growing-similar to everyone,
so that those whose gaze
is on the crowd won't pick us out,
and a concealing of ourselves—
from which we'll feel such rue
in the bride's silent, inquiring eyes.

No, let me quietly go on being
what I perhaps still am,
so that my solitary days may bear me
toward manhood differently.

I still have my first growth of beard,
my tender strength trembles
along my arms' shaft,
barely broken out in bloom.

I don't know what I will become,
nor what I was to be,
I can only replicate the earth's
deep gestures.
I have storm and stillness,
clarity and dusk;
my will is absorbed in growing
and young . . .

11 September

A fine evening at the Overbecks'. The blond painter was with me for
the length of a twilight; I showed her some Russian books, the pictures
of Nadson and Garshin, Droshin's portrait, and other mementos. In
the evening she sat next to me, and there was much conversation between us. The table was nicely set; small chamomiles slanted to one
side framed the simple white runner, which was accented by blue-
and-red-embroidered signatures of guests who had preceded us. Dr.
Hauptmann and I added our names to this roll. Hauptmann was in
rare form, made many cutting remarks regarding the temper of our
time, always in his most charmingly ingenuous way. He told us (as
our conversation turned to uncanny happenings) about a novella by
Kleist. In an old castle once an act of great cruelty was committed:
The first ancestor struck a defenseless old beggar woman, struck her
dead in his rage. Ever since then there can be heard at night, always
at the same hour, a sound, as if someone were getting up from
rustling straw, were lifting himself with moans and groping his way
with a heavy stick into a corner (where the sound vanished). The new
lord of the castle, who refused to believe this rumor, bedded himself
down to sleep in the infamous room, woke at the mystery's hour and
observed everything, just the way they had told it, with horror and
rage.—The next day, still doubting his own senses, he resolved to take
a dog with him. And scarcely had the rustling in the straw begun

again, when the animal started howling hideously with raised hackles and grew so frantic that in a moment of pure terror the lord of the castle set the house on fire. And so the mystery remained, cloaked by the flame's folds, in the stricken night. . . .

Clara Westhoff had come on her bicycle. But she walked almost the whole way back to Westerwede, since while we were talking I had passed by my gate and continued on at her side. It was about two hours past midnight. The skies were gray, quiet, and the landscape could be seen, completely without color, stretching far in the distance. . . . The birch trees stood like candles beside long trails. The only thing whiter was a white cat, which would appear from behind the bushes in silent leaps, then vanish in the mistless meadows. It was a melancholy cat that staged a solitary dance. In the garden everything green was a shade darker. Almost black, the full bushes leaned against the white railing of the forecourt. Around the urns there was depth and air.

And today yet a different kind of morning; bright, with close round clouds that frame pieces of inconceivably deep sky. Movement in high trees. In all the young ones great quiet. Many apples falling. The lawn seems to rise more gently toward the house, which is dark inside with quiet lights on everything silver and a sheen in the glass over the portraits, so that one can scarcely make out what each individual frame encloses.—There are so many days here, none like any other. And yet all differences are like confirmations of one great similarity among these days, which may be no more than this, that I receive them all with the same gratefulness. . . . But one does in fact learn to see something new here. In addition to sky and landscape there is a third, equally vital element: the air. Objects have always seemed to me like arms and extremities, coextensive with the great body of the earth; but here there are many things that are like islands—isolated, bright, washed about on all sides by the always agitated air. It's what makes their shapes so strong.

There is something like selflessness in this way of taking part in nature. I am gradually beginning to comprehend this life that passes through large eyes into eternally waiting souls. This daily attentiveness, alertness, and eagerness of the senses turned outward, this thousandfold seeing and seeing always *away* from oneself. This not-accompanying-oneself in the changing landscape with one's looks, this being only eye, without having to justify over whom.—This purity of life, this always being joyful because something always is happening, not that it has any bearing on one's own personality, but simply that there is motion and change. How large the eyes become here! They want at all times to possess the whole sky. A land for apprenticeship years. One stores up beauty the way one does knowledge and bits of wisdom. One scarcely uses it . . . the time hasn't come yet. One learns. One learns always and from every moment. I also learn.—In how poor a sense do we actually *see* compared with these people! How richly these people must travel! And when once they truly arrive at themselves after this blissful apprenticeship-time, what a wonderful language they must possess, what images for everything experienced! Then they must confide themselves the way landscapes do, as with clouds, winds, things going down. . . .

12 September

Yesterday I was in the old park by the brickworks. First meadows, surrounded by high trees. Individual gnarled apple trees stand amidst the grass, hunched and heavy, glowing with all their apples. In a narrow grass-ravine a densely laden trunk rears up under burdensome branches. On the other side again meadows. In wild-rose hedges goddesses of stone, gray, moss-silver in tone. Then, thickly overgrown, the old gallery in which the picture Vogeler started hangs dimly and mysteriously, as if painted many years ago. At the park's end an alcove of firs and lime trees. In shadows stone lions rest, gazing out into the land. The lioness's head is raised, surveying, and in front of her left curved paw an acacia sprout stands brightly and without fear. Opposite the two animals a long bench without backrest, on which I sat for a long time, watching the garden that from time to time would grow solemn beneath cloud-shadows. My gaze kept returning to a gray stone figure that stood as in a mosaic among the patches of apples, apple leaves, gleams of sunlight, and the intricate tangle of wild roses and old blackberry stems. In a similar thicket there also rose two brown-green juniper trees, and beside them stood a small marble statue of Flora, who could scarcely fend off the encroachments of late summer.—But there was more to come. After supper I walked across the heath. In the sunset everything was clear and simple. But over the moor, darkness and a gray wall of clouds stood as from rain just past. I kept gazing in the direction of the sun, behind which a strong wind was coming up across the heath. Suddenly, however, I noticed a golden line in the eastern skies, like a word that is slowly burning out; but the line kept growing toward the left and forming small golden streaks that again and again expired. As when men at night walk across battlements with torches: for brief intervals the contours brighten. . . . Finally I realized that the moon was drifting from right to left behind this edifice of clouds, allowing whatever silhouette lay across its path to shimmer goldenly in passing light. And occasionally, at thin areas of the cloud-wall, its half-veiled radiance also broke through farther down. Then it seemed to rise, and finally it flew, lifting itself half above the cloud-rim, always from right to left, still bright-golden and metallic, as if it were the helmet crest of some radiant god who stood on a ship behind the clouds.—And in the next instant it hung pale and small in the clear, cold night sky, beneath which the heath lay faintly lit, almost a lighter hue than the immaterial sky. But whenever a cloud passed in front of the moon, the heath bordered velvet-black on the much brighter edge of the sky.— I sat at the edge of the wooden observation tower, my heart overflowing, and said:

> I BLESS you with everything inside me
> that isn't used up in my songs.
> I will dive quietly into your sleeping
> and kiss your eyelids from within . . .

And I uttered many verses that I no longer remember. I had sound for everything and a gratitude I cast out into the uncertain, scarcely daring to turn with it toward a god.

"La nature est pour nous un dictionnaire, nous y cherchons des mots. . . ."

—Delacroix

At parties I usually fare rather badly. I feel in constant alternation between isolation and entering in. Now I see myself deserted by everyone, now again especially well received by some single person. If there is such a one among them who in the midst of it all reaches out with a sensitive remark, then I would prefer to have him all to myself, and if not, well, then the whole affair is unnecessary and ridiculous.

All my involvement, it should be said, in the person closest—that person much too near—requires some mutual third. In all relations with other people, no help nor sign of thanks goes straight from me to him. It is deflected toward someone neutral who passes it on. That's why any two such people can only affect each other by accepting into their relationship, at least for a brief moment, someone both know. (With each other we are like jousters with long spears; near each other we are defenseless no matter what weapons.) We are in intercourse indirectly via a third. And the farther our third is from each of us, the nearer we are in understanding and love.

13 September

Sometimes to someone lonely there comes something that works as a wondrous balm. It is not a sound, not a splendor, not even a voice. It is the smile of long-lost women—a smile that, like the light of perished stars, is still on its way.

15 September

Before noon two days ago Vogeler returned from Adiek. After lunch (as he was packing up etchings), I went to Modersohn's for about two hours. Had excellent discussions with him about being a teacher to someone, about being able to teach anyone, and about the degree of maturity any pupil must have attained before the teacher of an art can reach him. If you desire something from me, please, first be a bowl and beautiful, first be ready to receive and be calm for holding. Don't come to a teacher filled up with foreign things. First live. And when life gives you longings, then come. We are not your fulfiller, we who teach, but we can be a silent confidant of each fulfillment. A certain lady came to Modersohn still searching in all the arts for expression, for an expression of what she cannot clarify in life. But since her capacities in each art have so little direction, they create for her, working in the absence of all discipline, caricatures of what she feels inside her, and so the girl loses heart. Don't seek refuge from your uncertainties in art. Only when for the first time some experience takes hold of you, in this first coalescence of your being, whether from grief and loss or from abundance, then *throw* yourself into art, blindly, eagerly, and with unmitigated confidence. Then you will receive an image in art, an image that makes you who you will be. Will see towering into the sky the figure whose darkening, agitated wave-image you are, will know that you exist somewhere else, eternal and serene, and that only your reflection will vanish when one day you withdraw yourself along with your true being from the deep waters of life.

People who before their first synthesis attempt to find and express themselves in art wind up overmagnifying individual fragments of their being, and become more and more remote from that harmony that is the ground of all art. They suffer from a hypertrophy of that very quality that initially gave them their quickest access to art, they build themselves on inclination and accident, become onesidedly soulful, experts in emotion; whereas once that first coalescence has come about, one's art provides one with a confirmation that is pivotal for one's development and independence; one has the feeling of being a unity vis-à-vis the manifold, and one's task becomes to simplify more and more that manifold, i.e., make it part of oneself. One's growth has a foundation. One's soul lives in all directions. One's eyes are innocently open. One's lips patient and seldom speaking. One's hands at work. One is an artist.

Without doubt there exists somewhere for each person a teacher. And for each person who feels himself a teacher there is surely somewhere a pupil. So speak out, you teachers, when the voice has entered you. Harken then, you listeners, into the night. There will come a time when each mouth will find its way to its destined ear across people and oceans. For we are still in an era of prelude and expectation.

He who keeps silent is wise. But he who speaks does not speak for his present time.

A note on M.'s manner of working. He likes to use plants and animals to study color. Pressed leaves, with their darkness and pale fadedness, give him a feeling for what outlasts coloredness per se, and he learns from them a scale of tones more enduring than the bright upper register of summer. *Its* colors remain more vibrantly alive in the plumage of dead birds. In his studio there is a glass case with various species of stuffed birds—among them every type to be found in the countryside around Worpswede. The rare yellow oriole, the beautiful blue roller, upon whose wings blue and silver hues merge in subtle transitions beside other, red ones. Beautifully feathered ducks, various kinds of snipe, swallows, falcons, hawks, then songbirds, from the small wren upward, and finally waterbirds, birds of evening, and the great solemn birds of night, with their scalloped color-pattern on the broad feathery body of their soft breast. All these beautiful things surround him in the hours when he is unable to view clouds and sky, and prepare him for the long walks out into the moor, during which he makes extremely rigorous studies—of cabins, stretches of heath, cloudy skies, long canals with unsteady catwalks, and especially of trees. Often only a fragment of birch trunk seen at close range against a background of meadow, or the portrait of an entire birch tree posed against the sky. Worked out in a splendidly vivid, almost sculptural manner, with broad, simple strokes that abjure excessive detail. I remember especially a red moor-house around which thin birch trees ripple down on all sides like a white rain, trembling like images of birch trees in water. But in the paintings that originate from these studies, something ineffable must assert itself alongside such sharply grasped certitudes. This M. preserves on small sheets that he dreams at home under his lamp every evening with red and black chalk. These small sheets, each half the size of this page, offer endless riches to the viewer. For they are created from all that exceeds this moderate personality's bounds, and in contrast to the strongly realistic studies are dark and visionary. A vestibule in twilight, a spring morning in the field, a clear evening over the moor, an old woman in a fairy-tale forest (and promptly sitting there on a branch is a large, auspicious bird). . . . All this exists completely and to perfection within the small sheets; filled with the eternity of these simple impressions, they strike one as infinitely large and unforgettable. And if by chance (chance understood in the larger sense) the realism and facticity of the studies should merge in a single painting with those atmospheric values preserved on the small sheets, then something very great must become a work of art.

From M. I went to meet the blond painter heartened and reassured. I sat beside her (she had just put down *Advent*) and gazed into the corner, deepened now by darkening fabric, where the mask of Dante hung; the guitar was propped against a pile of sketches, almost making music with its softly glimmering strings; in front of that the new lily was in bloom, beautiful and slender (even slenderer against the dark background). We never got to Beer-Hofmann's book. We made our way toward each other through conversations and silences. It was a very quiet occurrence, as if the world were turning more softly by several degrees of nuance. It was a shared hour or a shared moment at the edge of that hour when I said: "And there's only one experience I know of that can confirm, apart from all externals, that one is desiring the right thing and living one's own life. When each time one encounters beauty one suddenly feels oneself to be devoutly continuing, across all the intervening years and inner chasms, one's childhood; when one feels that one's present moment would fit exactly against that edge where childhood borders somewhere on confusion and chance, on the pressure of things great. . . . It's the only source of praise and confirmation one can trust. . . . So often lately I've had the feeling of interlocking with that place where I was before all the foreignness and worldliness broke through." And in this confession we were one. Knew ourselves in what is past and what is to come. . . . Had suddenly heard one another—and after many words that were sound only, the great eloquent silence came: the stones spoke. . . .

> SUCH are the hours toward which we wend
> and toward such hours wend for years and years;
> then suddenly a listener is found—
> and all words have meaning.

Then comes the silence we've long awaited,
comes on like the night, arched with great stars:
two people grow as in the same garden,
and that garden is outside time.

And when soon after that the two are severed,
—with the first word each utterly alone—
they will smile and scarcely know each other,
but they will both be greater . . .

Perhaps that is what all communing means: to grow through encounters. On a long road whose end no one could foresee we arrived
at this point of eternity. Surprised and shuddering we gazed at each
other like two people who stand unexpectedly before the gate behind
which God has already arrived. . . .

I hurried away into the heath. And if I had remained alone after
that, I might have entered . . .

But I had to get home. I read the "Annunciation" and the "Last
Judgment" with a glow in my voice. But then I recited several things
unexceptionally, and when after a supper in the inn (we talked about
Johannes Gerdes!) I finally came into my red room, I was tired and
had only dim memories of faded and far-off feelings from which no
bliss could issue any longer. Thus it is that our friends lie on us like
shadows. Sometimes they soothe us with their darkness, but often we
feel only the coldness and weight of these shadows, which are not
shadows of objects, of things at rest, but of shifting, arbitrary, wandering kinds of twilight.

Friends do not ward off our loneliness, they only set bounds to our
solitude.

Friends should be only like dance and music. One should never come
to them deliberately, but always out of some spontaneous need.
Friends should be outcomes. On the way they are hindrances.

On the road to Bremen (yesterday) Vogeler told me several things
about Martha Sch. During his first year in Worpswede, once when he
and Mackensen were lying on the hillside and gazing off into the
landscape Mackensen called over a fourteen-year-old girl. She was

blond and quiet and full of an odd soothingness even then. Mackensen lived at her parents'. . . . . "It was strange then how quickly Mackensen and I got to be friends. . . ." They took long walks together into the moor, would enter one of the cabins, and scarcely were they together there and talking when Martha Sch., simply by busying herself with something, had always somehow made herself an integral part of that interior scene, and her quiet blondness was already inflecting the picture. Before long she entered similarly into Vogeler's pictures. Up till then he had always drawn wild, strange things. Feasts, aftermaths of carousing in the early dawn, and out of the breaking day centaurs leaping in, carrying off sleeping, wine-drunk girls. Suddenly now she simplified him. Made him see the countryside, in which he began to celebrate her dreamily. Thus their coming together coincided with his becoming himself. Martha was there before him. Was a child of the land, a girl of the moor, fending off with many small tendernesses the life she lived, very much alone and suffering from her isolation. And so to rescue her from hostile surroundings he brought her to Dresden, where she learns languages (French and Italian) and weaving and listens to different kinds of music. He is giving her room to mature there, just as he gave her such room back home, while he waited. He is careful not to intrude into her girlhood, she has her dreams and her adorned memories, of which he also is probably a part, more so than of her actual life. In the fall they want to start growing closer and plan to begin cautiously reading French books together, later looking at paintings together, beginning in Holland. . . . "And that will be the hardest part. . . ." Will they grow accustomed to each other's company in gradual stages? Or will some one event unite them? Before a painting, over a book? And must these attempts be carried out through book and painting and cautiously?

You have written me just now: "Tolstoy has fallen seriously ill in Yasnaya Polyana." Perhaps we did bid him farewell. How clearly I see every moment of that day before me! What elation I felt as we drove through the wavy meadows with its trembling bells, journeying through the Russian landscape for the first time, the same way that Gogol and Pushkin journeyed, loudly with jangling harnesses and galloping steeds. And thus into the startled hamlet that was full of eyes in all its weather-beaten doors. And thus out of the hamlet and down the road and up to the two white gate-towers that mark the entrance to the high park. Our passage into its shadows is silent; we're anxious, we feel the weight of what's to come, and wish we could have this park and this day to ourselves without the old man toward whom all this is heading. And then we stand for a while in front of the white house in which everything remains silent, go around past the green oval bench and at last find someone in the courtyard next to the well. He takes our cards. We wait again. A dog comes right up to us, trusting and friendly, as we stand there in front of the small glass door. I bend down to the white dog and as I straighten up again I see behind the glass, vague and distorted by the flaws in the pane, a pair of searching eyes in a small grizzled face. The door opens, lets You in and slams sharply against me, so that I, only after the Count has already greeted You, come in and now also stand before him, feeling awkwardly large beside his slim bright shape.

He leaves us alone with Lev Levovich and withdraws again into his study after this reception. Then I climb the wooden stairs behind You and step into the light-filled room where only the old oil paintings are dark. The table is long, narrow, covered in white, and a large silver-white samovar stands at its upper end. We sit down. There is very little in this large hall whose three windows receive shimmering reflections from the rich green of mighty trees. We inquire about the ancestral paintings. The oldest one is especially interesting. A nun from the time of Alexei Mikhailovich. Apparently painted by an icon maker, she all but replicates the character of St. Sophia in posture, integument, and the strongly conventional expression of her face. Only with her hands did the painter, the observer, come to life in the craftsman, and he painted these exactly, with realistic attention to his subject; in doing so he lost sight of the overall proportions, painted the hands accordingly larger, and now this saintly woman bears the heavy weight of her earthly hands, with which she must be able to raise a very great prayer. And yes, I know, there was one of those fine "portraits" there. A powdered nobleman from the end of the eighteenth century, his clothes and the area around his face—with its black eyebrows and the witty mouth of that talkative era—turned completely dark. The frame made of old, grayed, silver-coated wood, oval and almost unornamented. This painting was oddly beautiful on the bright, cheerful wall of the long hall. Modern works were there as well: a sculpture by Ginsburg and the "Tolstoy" of Prince Trubetskoy. We spoke occasionally, drank coffee, and gazed out often into the sun-drenched day, where strangely nearby a bird snarled and called out *knarr-knarr* with a fierce *r*. We chatted about this bird for a while and finally followed it out into the park. So much was in bloom there. The avenue of old birch trees was shadowy and beautiful, and at the end of it there was a balcony that shook strongly under our steps. We gazed out lovingly onto the landscape, which with its meadows of forget-me-nots was rippling calmly and ripely as if with waves. Far off the train went past, much too distant for the ear, and for the eye no more than a toy. Then we came back slowly along the path, carrying flowers and asking the names of many trees that were old and stately. From the back we walked up to the house again. In the entrance hall the Countess was busily putting books back into a window case, and we had to endure her annoyed welcome and all the displeasure she loudly expressed to someone invisible. What a harrowing half-hour that was in the small room with the walnut furniture! We examined books that lay behind glass and on top of cases, tried to concentrate on various portraits, but were really only listening for the footsteps of the Count, who walked into the entrance-hall. Something had happened: voices grew agitated, a girl wept, the Count consoled, in the midst of it all with complete indifference the Countess's voice booming . . . the sound of footsteps on the stairs, all doors in motion, and the Count walks in. Coldly and courteously he asks You something, his eye is not there with us, only its glance comes toward me and the question: "What do *you* do?" I'm no longer sure, I answered, I seem to recall: "I have written a few things . . ."

16 September

I sent a telegram for the opening of the Secession Stage yesterday: "What is more beautiful than to begin! Each 'Let there be' / is as sacred as that first pronouncement. / And may the shaping gesture from the players' band / ever more beautifully rise." Heinrich Vogeler and my name.—Then I was in the Lilies Studio. Tea was waiting for me. A memorable time together in conversation and silences. The evening came on wondrously; our words touched on many things: on Tolstoy, on death, on Georges Rodenbach and Hauptmann's *Friedensfest,* on life and on the beauty in all experiences, on being able to die and being ready to die, on eternity and why we feel a kinship to something eternal. On so much that extends beyond the moment and beyond us. Everything grew mysterious. The clock struck an hour that chimed on and on and weaved itself loudly into our exchanges.—Her hair was of Florentine gold. Her voice had folds like silk. I had never seen her so soft and slender in her white youthfulness. A large shadow passed through the room . . . first across me, the one talking, across my wandering words, then across her bright shape and across the endless luminous things. We looked over toward the bank of west windows. But there was no one visible there who might have just walked past.—Immediately after that occurrence I got up and went from the blond girl, who with her warm cheeks and her quiet eyes had remained sitting at the table, out into the blond evening, which possessed a wondrous breadth and clarity. Walked in the shadow-colored heath. About my feet I could feel the coolness of the early dew already blowing, while about my cheeks and forehead the warm soft day still lingered. And I felt its departing comforts and remained all eye over every phase of its decline. And when at night I came back across the heath, I said to myself, without knowing of whom I said it:

> HE left home when he was still a child.
> Early on his hands grew tired of play.
> And his parents talked and talked,
> and he left them like a dark good-bye.
> And became a wanderer. His thought was this:
> to leave the solitudes that pampered him
> and join those whose days are drowned in sound,
> to approach someone as one would the sea . . .

How much I learn in watching these two girls, especially the blond painter, who has such brown observant eyes! How much closer now I feel again to everything wondrous and intuitive, as in those days of my "Girls' Songs." How much mysteriousness invests these slender figures when they stand before the evening or when, leaning back in velvet chairs, they listen with all their aspects. Since they are the most receptive, I can be the most giving. My whole life is full of the images with which I can talk to them; everything that I've experienced becomes an expression for what lies deep behind experience. And often I can waken in myself with new material, simple material, those nuances of feeling that had previously been bound up in overly complex concerns. Slowly I place first one word, then another, on the delicate silver balance of their two souls, and take great pains to make each word a precious gem. And they sense that I am somehow presenting them and adorning them with jewelry full of splendor and goodness. And I attempt with my altering words to keep their souls swaying ever so slightly up and down, so that they play, without either pan ever dropping, within the two shores of equilibrium.

> A GIRL, white before the evening hour,
> again and again I feel them both like precious finds;
> it's not *what* they are that so enthralls me:
> the gentle lines of neck and hair
> and how they stand out against the background.
>
> They live so softly in contours only;
> likewise the words they speak toward evening—
> before meadow flowers or orphan boys—
> are all contour . . .

21 September

Then Sunday came. We all gathered in the afternoon around five. Outside there was still evening and color, but in the white hall a faint twilight had already set in, so I lit the piano candles. Fräulein B. played several songs, a great many voices came over us, and never had the time seemed so right for my reading. I began with two "Thoma" poems, recited the "Certosa" and the poem "Music." A beautiful rapport was evident before me, so I decided to read a little from the *Book of the Good Lord*: "The Ghetto of Venice" and "Of One Who Listened to the Stones." I could feel the last piece ring strongly in my heightened voice.

It was the most powerful effect I have ever had on a *group* of people, an effect of isolating each individual and yet somehow gathering them all together in the background. I trembled myself when, in the guise of my voice, that one phrase loomed over me: "Michelangelo, who haunts the stone?" This story now seems to me the best developed of the whole book, since it displays a great figure, and a long shadow cast by that figure, whose fright is that of an entire century.

Slowly, left to myself by the others, who all were dark and full of gratitude, I walked behind our group on the path through the heath. In the inn we sat under black trees at the edge of the light cast by a lamp, so that our faces stood out brightly before a hundred backgrounds. Gradually gaiety overtook everyone. And this gaiety that followed the long silence made me happy, very happy. I was tired, and my voice had lost its clarity. But I felt sheltered, cared for even by the gaiety and kindness of these people and almost spoiled by their gratitude, which was discreet and not threatened by words.

On the way home I said to the blond painter: I far underestimated everything here (I mean everything, people and sky and land) when I thought that I could belong to the past here. Here I have no memories. My eyes won't let themselves close. They follow every movement wide open and dwell in every restful presence. And what an infinite supply of rest and motion there is here! The things here take everyone in their hands with infinite simplicity, and I am always more than willing to be grasped:

> HALF to live unawares, half in fervor
> to set down what one saw, and how, and where.
> To pursue goals and then again become
> a vagrant in the uncertain, blessedly alone.—
> Here these lovely girls live that way:
> half still enthralled, already such enthrallers . . .

I place a great trust in this landscape, and will gladly accept from it path and possibilities for many days. Here I can once again simply go along, become, be someone who changes. On the grand tour it was a great burden to have to be someone who is firm, someone who stands, someone who remains immovable in the face of the profusely fleeting, the always unexpected. . . . In the white hall I read another story and then passages from Loris's *Adventurer.* They suited the mood well. Then we all rose together and went into the Lilies Studio. There a joint effort produced a late-night coffee, and suddenly someone remembered that the goat stabled there needed milking. The kerosene stove was carried outside to serve as lantern, and for a long time we in the room heard nothing but random sounds in the stall, the clanking of a chain and the whispering voices of the excited girls. Then they both came back hot and with tangled hair, suppressed laughter in their dark voices, and the blond one brought over a stone bowl to those of us at the table. We all looked into it and fell silent. The milk was black. Even though we were all startled, none dared voice his discovery, and everyone rationalized: all right then, it's night. I've never milked a goat at night before. From dusk on their milk must darken, and now, two hours after midnight, it is still jet-black. No use pondering it now. Each will have to cope with this phenomenon on his own. Tomorrow . . . And we all drank from the black milk of this twilight goat and grew oddly alert from this mysterious libation. At around three o'clock, Heinrich, his brother Franz, Clara Westhoff and I stood in front of the entrance to Barkenhoff. But only Heinrich went home. In the white hall he found a forgotten candle, burnt deep into the gilt-wood candle holder that a moment later would have caught fire. But we went on. At Clara Westhoff's there is a bower of dense grapevines, and the darkness beneath it was so thick now that the starry night out before it grew deeper, and one could discern the window-crosses of a distant cabin. What one sees, by the way, when one gazes out from this vine-bower, is only one last cabin—otherwise nothing but fields and moorland with darkly mirroring canals. We stood close together, three not very sociable people who happen to view a night and feel that to be something festive. There is something inexpressibly mysterious about for once not being transported by some conveyance from light to light, about walking across the dark mountain into the different day as a wanderer and awake, not lying down, asleep. That way one does not find oneself suddenly before the completed morning, not knowing what clouds it overcame and which were the last stars it stepped across to reach earth. The slender morning towers like a statue; but whoever was awake remembers also the night, that beautiful black column on which it stands.—We were like all who are alone in nights, playthings and looking glass for the few clear sounds of this deserted hour. Only when we went into the bower did we pass by the open windows of the living room, and then we heard quite clearly the clock inside ticking with all the importance of clocks left to themselves deep in night. Then we felt that steady swinging no longer, turned around outward as we were into the night that had no ending anywhere, the way one no longer hears one's own heartbeat in the closeness of someone else's heart. Out there was a dog, a cock, and an evil, sharp-voiced animal that was killing something somewhere in a ditch or on a tree. We lit the lamp in the living room and sat by it for a long time. Franz fell asleep. Then we decided to walk over to the studio and break open the door, since the people who had the key were sleeping. Now added to the night's voices was the barking of the heavy sculptor's hammer that sprang so fiercely at the lock that the entire night seemed to be splintering outward in radiant slivers around the dark door. Involuntarily our feeling followed the sound of each blow right up to the threshold of silence, and perhaps aroused by the relentlessness of this hammer, Clara Westhoff, with a gesture of fending-off, suddenly placed her hand on the lock, directly under the next blow. The studio was open just in time to see inside in the light of a trembling lantern the blood of a helpless hand, over which the right moved back and forth as if to smooth out the pain that seemed to build up again and again in the left. Now we were suddenly with someone hurt, and there was nothing but different objects in the room: washbasins and water buckets and hand towels. The wound streamed a while longer into the water, then settled down, and the pain, which rose and fell in her pulsings like a fountain, mounted in smaller columns just a little above her wrist. And we talked and talked. At first to keep the pain from becoming loud, then because it had grown quiet. When we finally went into the studio, all that remained to us of this incident was a shared sensation of a shared concern and a fright in which we had seen ourselves, and we understood that danger is always the thing closest and that it is important never to be safe, never to be invulnerable and like iron. That we have a thousand gates behind which our blood harkens, ready to rush out jubilantly toward the one who uses all things as an ax and pushes steep battering rams against our walls. And that this treason of our blood, which feels itself imprisoned inside us, makes us strong and mighty, so that we make use without knowing it of all the hostility that presses within us like someone who feels himself unjustly held.

In the studio there was a small statuette in its early stages, representing a boy sitting on the ground; the one leg is pushed high up under the chin, and the clasped hands reach out around the other. A tremendous assurance was expressed in the stretch of this figure's spine, in the bare-boned angularity of this boyish back, which does however already show a degree of completion where the arms join, as if the latter had been doing man's work for years. Clara Westhoff talked about Klinger. About the misgivings with which he accepted her, and about his efforts to represent to her everything she strove for as hideously difficult for a young girl; how he again and again forgets all his admonitions and warms toward her. How he finally presents her with a piece of marble, out of which in her studio she chisels a hand. And how he, conquered by her strong, grappling will, finally grows sympathetic, becomes almost a teacher. How then later she was in Paris with the great Rodin. How much she learned there with Rodin. Later in the conversation I expressed my own feelings about Rodin, and it was good to get certain things into words for the first time. One thing especially seems to me of utmost importance to him: that his works do not look out, do not from some point turn toward one personally as if to make conversation, but remain always an artwork—that is to say, something not really present and at hand but at every moment creatable. More than any other work, the statue, which has no background, stands there exposed among people— they can walk around it, look at it, and touch it from all sides. And this happens in every case without restraint whenever the sculpture is open somewhere toward the outside, when it, feeling its lack of surroundings, turns toward people as toward supplementations. . . . A human being can never be fraternal next to a work of art, and the thing created falls off drastically the moment it makes contact with one of its viewers. The moment it views him. The moment it looks out of itself, out beyond the orbit of its own laws, upon whomever just then happens to be standing opposite it. It gives up its solitude, its sacred being-stone that distinguishes it from fleeting forms and errant gestures. And this is one of the most superb qualities of Rodin's sculptures—that they always remain within this untransgressable magic circle toward which one may approach, and from whose border one gazes toward the work of art as toward something near that becomes feelable from far away. All that can pass from the work to its viewer is longing; works of art are not our neighbors. They are to us like images in a well; we cannot approach them beyond a certain angle without obscuring with our own selves the very thing we have come to view.—There were only a few other works in the studio; a plaster cast of an old woman. Clara Westhoff's first sculpted work. When we stepped out of the studio, our eyes had to adjust to an increase of light: the day must have just finished dawning. The things all around were still trembling, and the air was like water in a beaker that had been filled a moment earlier and was gradually leveling out. . . . We (Franz and I) walked along next to the white birch trunks, silently headed toward the broad, rising heath. Up above a man was cutting heather. The dark colors of his coat and hair stood out smoothly and vividly against the rough darkness of the heather, which extended in a wet, uniform expanse all the way to the young forest. I went home alone then and had breakfast. Half an hour later we were seated on the high yellow excursion coach that traveled swiftly on under the rustling of the trees. We drove for four hours all the way to Adiek. The moor ends, clumps of bushes begin, great stands of trees lay the little shadows of early noon down beside them into the bright green swells of meadowland. Then comes a stretch of fir woods, occasional brickworks on the left and on the right of the road, and then small wilted heather begins to spread across everything, looking from a distance like many old folded hands. I had the sensation that the land was journeying toward sadness, and the coming days would provide many confirmations of this feeling. In front of the farmhouse where the brothers live, the breeding-works stands like a small factory in a vacuum, while tall old trees darken around the house, which with its whiteness and its green beams and its thatch roof is the very epitome of the peasant style. In the evening we walked across megalithic graves out to the Oste brook, which makes its way darkly under bushes bent forward, and for a while we stood and watched the water, which like a delicate piece of weaving bore heavy colors as if playing some game. During these hours we found several prehistoric burial sites, hills with heather, some protected by a surrounding ditch and now angrily defended by bushes with thorns. We emerged from the heath's darkness into the scarcely bearable fertilized meadows, which are bright green and still full of moss and wash back under one's footsteps with a rolling slurp. This meadowland is still not quite usable, and, higher up, wide stretches of heath have only just been broken so that pine seedlings may be planted there. The ground, which holds a rich supply of stones of all kinds, had to be dug up with a plow that reaches down seventy-five centimeters, due to one extremely hard brown stone that remains all but unbreakable underground yet deteriorates quite rapidly on the earth's surface once the atmosphere begins to act on it. Atop its dark-brown remains lie various colorful and exotic forms of flint, basalt, quartz, and sandstone, and amidst its scattered pieces the first pine shoots are already coming up, as if with bright green plumage; forests of future years occasionally fill the wind already with rustling as it rolls to and fro in this unfounded space. Everything still has to come into being here. That is sad beyond words. And in order to feel the joy of this coming-into-being, one would have to visit here for a much longer time. I tried to ask about everything in order to acquire this feeling, I inspected, as well as my ignorant eyes were able, the chicken coops and the incubators and learned any number of things from the two brothers, things that have wider application. Almost all observations confined to a small area can, if they are only undertaken seriously and diligently enough, be understood as a symbol for something larger, as images for vast processes and relations that configure themselves a thousand times within smaller dimensions.—But in spite of everything I could not shake my uneasiness, and when I was alone I was filled with homesickness for Worpswede, for its high, rapturous skies beneath which the shadows of so many images and gestures and objects also are constantly moving. I watched the evening hours go by without the accustomed dear conversations. Outside the barn door the dogs chased each other and made great leaps into the darkness and came creeping up as if pretending to be strangers. . . . And at night an apple tree stood outside my window. And although the night was dreary and windless, often two, three pieces of fruit dropped heavily into the grass. I lay in bed, looked at the window obscured by the garden, and listened. There was a sound—like a waiting horse stamping impatiently on the turf. . . . And I knew that I wanted to ride, ride out. . . .

The next day we visited the old church in Heeslingen, which with its broad buttresses resembles a gigantic stone-heap. The arches grow somewhat sharper toward the middle, the cruciform vaults are irregular and grottolike. Under the roof the surfaces of the three vaults lie like three mountains, gray and barren, like a threefold Golgotha whose crosses have collapsed. The same day we visited Hans Müller-Brauel, that fortunate discoverer of so many pagan graves. Stone weapons, urns, rings fill his cases. Just as a water-diviner listens to the ground for some secret rushing, so every shining that is cloaked in darkness reveals itself to him, and all buried pasts have become for him bell-chimes swaying at the end of shafts as in the tops of towers turned upside down.

The evening passed during a walk through meadows and across heath. The house held the same meaning for me. A solitary house amidst dark trees, into which one is brought after a fall, bleeding, with fading memories, in order to die quickly and without preparation. . . . Strong rain the next afternoon. Path through wild parkland. Tall juniper with harplike branches, juniper walls around small darknesses, wilting fern-stretches, and tall juniper embraced by long-stemmed rosebushes, completely suffused by them and intertwined by their rich tendrils. But all that without liberation and far away, barely reachable with the tips of a feeling.

> THUS must you understand the hours:
> grow and seldom be afraid.—
> Be instead a sound:
> then you'll glide across all chords.

26 September

Saturday afternoon we drove to Bremen in coaches. The broad, comfortable barouche was full of flowers we had brought with us. Red dahlias with light shimmering through at their edges, sunflowers, even larger than usual, and in the side pockets of the roof, gillyflowers. On the way Clara Westhoff, breathless, overtook us. She was riding to the Oberneuland country estate on her bicycle, and with dark eyes and trembling lips spoke a few brief, choppy words into our coach. I waved after her for a long time. Throughout the trip I held the wreath of heather she had wound for Hauptmann. For Clara had told me: "It really should be yours in honor of yesterday. . . ." (I had read my drama *Beginners* to great effect.) Oh, and so much could be said about that evening also and about the previous afternoon and about everything later on, about the incomparable Hamburg days that were so full of brightness, happiness, and comradeship for us seven. Where should I begin? Where is the starting-thread in this dark-colored weave of experiences and memories? So I rode holding Clara Westhoff's large heather wreath, and across from me the blond painter sat with a wonderful Parisian hat (light black straw, cut high at the crown, with a wide, deep-sloped brim on which dark red, slightly tired roses lay unemphatically, as if some solitary hand had casually set them aside). In her lively brown eyes I saw much of the agitated, wandering land toward which my back was turned, and her open gaze presented me with all the feeling that connected her with this land. Even as I write this I can feel again her eyes, whose dark cores were so smooth and hard, slowly unfolding, how like ripening roses they grew soft and warm in their opening and held gentle shadows and delicate lights as on the tips and curves of small petals leaning back one upon the other.—And so I sat across from these eyes in the red velvety barouche and carried Clara's large heather wreath. Around the curve of the branches that she had forced into a circle the simple reverent power of her sculptor's hands still played. Thus I savored the strength of the one girl with my propped-up hands, and out of the dear face of the other something gentle came toward me from which all humility takes heart. I still have to set down here what Clara told me Thursday, as night approached, on the quiet forecourt behind the white urns. Shortly into the year she came to Paris. Confused by the city, she arrived outside in Joinville at the house of a family from Bremen that lives out there under odd circumstances. Always near the mother somewhere is a vindictive, embittered girl. The second daughter plays the piano for a living. The son married a dubious stranger from Switzerland who has filthy tattered clothes and ill-kempt hair.

He lives in the adjacent villa. These villas are small white country houses along the Marne. In the placid river their smooth white facades (the style is called Louis XVI there) alternate with reflections of poplars that in reality rise into the open sky. Small gardens fill the forecourts; fragrance crowds into the diminutive rooms, whose clocks tick more loudly than need be, as if they, too, were aware of the mother's deafness.—With all the unaccustomed noises of the day-long journey and the rushed-through city echoing in her, Clara Westhoff entered. Almost furtively, the mother welcomed the guest with a pale voice—quietly, with solemn tenderness, the way one receives a child coming home with a fever. Her talking didn't touch on what was near at hand. She had no feeling for the life that circulated in the words of those around her. She spoke the way a thing would speak. Spoke of the great woe that hadn't come to her out of words. Her life, which she had never heard named by someone else, received all its images and expressions from her own way of talking . Shunned by the others' words, this fate was a garden with overgrown and neglected paths, and when she voiced it, startled birds seemed to rise out of its wilderness and circle her softly talking face, so that the latter would become alternately shadowed and clear. The one daughter walked in coldly, with evil eyes, upon this hour of first confiding. When she offered her hands she seemed to take something out of Clara's, for Clara's own felt eerily empty afterward. And later on the brother arrived full of disdain for everything. And so the small house filled up with utterly distant and estranged people, who during the time the guest was present could only with great effort reconcile themselves to a mode of life together. Amidst the flurry of sharp words the quiet, solitary mother sat untouched, and she was full of hollow sounds and things far in the past, an island with its own trees, completely windless. Clara sat and looked across at her large watchful eyes, on which one's gaze could rest without causing them to waver. The small rooms grew quieter and quieter, and when two clocks—one right after the other—struck a long hour, they retired. They slept together in the small house. The mother on one side of the large living room, next to the other wall Clara and the daughter. They had exchanged a few words and gone to bed. The mother had kissed Clara's brow and then, apparently while falling asleep, had uttered something no one understood. But later, when the two girls were about to put out the light, she was lying there again with open, watchful eyes, and occasionally the blanket would veil a thin, slow movement of her sleepless body. Clara wanted to go to sleep. But in the bed next to the window the embittered daughter sat up and started talking loudly, without any thought of her voice, about the small everyday miseries, about the mother and her quirks, about the brother's insolence in bringing into the family this dirty slut with holes under her sleeves, and about her wretched lesson-giving, with whose wages so incredibly much had to be paid for and bought. And about the neighbors and about an elegant courtesan who lived across the way and in her own little houseboat traveled the Marne at night—and again and again about the mother. . . . All her words passed over the hearing of the waking woman as over murky water, passed, without making a reflection, over her deadened ear. But Clara sat in her bed shuddering and again and again looked over toward the mother, who quietly, with open, watchful eyes, gazed into the darkness which was for her sadness only, but sadness without voice. . . . And Clara sat feeling increasingly guilty about her own hearing. And her feeling wandered about lost in the haunting, angry voice, searching for a way out.—Clara stayed with this family for a time, mainly out of concern for the quiet, isolated mother, but also hoping that her presence there might draw them all into a more peaceful relation. She was with them even on Christmas, at the brother's, that is. Whose wife felt that they were all obliged to be festive. And since no means occurred to these people by which festiveness might best be achieved, they sat for many hours around the increasingly cluttered table and stuffed themselves until their heavy heads turned red. On this same late evening we spent outside in the garden, Clara told me many other things about Paris, about the luminous springlike gaiety of its environs, and about the delicate pale evenings along the Marne and in Vélizy. Later in her studio I read my "Last Judgment." Then the two of us were with Modersohn at his house, where after a time others arrived also, and this bounteous day concluded with my read-

ing the "Dream" fragment from *George's Death* in the blond painter's
studio.

All other incidents take place in Hamburg and on the way there.
We arrived, eight of us, in Hamburg. We waited for Dr. Hauptmann
to join us in the Café de l'Europe, ate lunch with him, and then separated. Franz Vogeler went with Clara Westhoff to Hannover Station,
the blond painter and I waited for Milly Becker at the Cloister Gate.
The time until Hauptmann's premiere passed with conversations between any two of us punctuating a kind of shared dreariness. It took
that evening's performance of his play *Breite* to unite us. We children
of the heath had been so affected by the city that our initial es-
trangement made us sad and uneasy. Only the blond painter, Clara,
and I remained in high spirits, and the three of us together were alert
to every happening. A funeral procession went by, darkening by turns
each of the high windows of the café. A coach, black with strange
barbs on its roof, behind it men in knee stockings, flat three-cornered
hats, and tailcoats. And in its wake swift carriages again and slowly
trotting horse-cabs with lean black coachmen. Unfortunately we were
separated at Hauptmann's premiere; I sat in one of the balconies with
Heinrich Vogeler and Fritz Mackensen. Milly Becker waved up a
greeting, and occasionally we made contact with the blond painter,
agreeing, across many people, that the theater is not such a good
thing. The play was nicely performed. Everything fit together rea-
sonably well, and only the act with the wedding feast lagged badly.
After just the second act Hauptmann was called on stage, and following the fifth he was presented with our large heather wreath. We
congratulated the author warmly and all repaired to a small dining
room at Kempinski's. In addition to Worpswedeans and Haupt-
manns, a state's attorney, a critic of the worst kind from Berlin, the
actor Otto and his wife, and also Fräulein Galafé, the play's heroine,
with her (not the heroine's) mother. I sat next to Frau Bock, at quite
some distance from Dr. Hauptmann and from the other Worpswedeans. Over dessert (Otto and the critic had already performed
their piece of flattery) I spoke a few tremendously simple words as the
company of strangers followed me in amazement. I began, deliberately circumventing the form of a toast, by saying: "Dear Doctor
Hauptmann!" And merely related how the noises and clatter of the

sprawling city had estranged us and how it had taken the salutory impression of his play, along with seeing Dr. Hauptmann again—which had brought back so many hours spent together in Worpswede—to free us from this excess of confusion and alienation here. And that three phrases above all remained with me after the play. And that these three phrases conjoined would yield an intimate connectedness, the image of an inner evolution. Filled with landscape and viewing everything through landscape, I approached the play now on this same path: When Father Jakob shoulders his load in the freezing morning to resume wandering with his pack, he says to the maid who is telling him about the young woman's loneliness and desperation: "It hurts me to have to take to my icy way with this thought in mind." That was landscape for me. I saw him step out: a morning just beginning; and as he walks, the first on a path not yet trodden, everything becomes still, the wind hangs in the heavy fir branches, and falling snow seems suspended in the glass-gray air. And not one movement, not one progress toward day—only the man walking heavily under his load and under his fearful thought that grows louder and louder over the rigid, clamped-up world that still seems so far away from morning.—But this old man's path leads to the second phrase: "Everything takes us." The old man wanders defenseless, nothing but a brain for this cruel wicked thought that wants to be thought by someone.—Everything takes us. The good and that for which we have no name. But as we are continually being gripped by all that asserts its might above us and above the things, we begin to trust more and more the hands that do this to us every day and in all the nights in which we lie awake by ourselves or dream deeply. And some day the knowledge will come to us, when we have just given something its shape, that even with the darkest thing we say we do not mean Death, not Death at all, but Life. And the young woman does not die. Her face turns to stone. But her hands, which were already stretched down toward the water, toward that water which is unfathomably deep, rise back into life. That is the beauty in her. And then, reaching out past all her despair, all her parting from what her longing had hoped for, her hands find the phrase that her tired lips repeat stiffly and still not fully understanding: "Come to work!". . . That is like resurrection. When the hardened hands of someone desperate, of someone helpless or forsaken, leave the cramplike clasp in which they fed each other's flames and come to work, side by side, as if neither had knowledge of the other, then they, the superfluous, un-requited, all-too-many, have become necessary to a thing. The things have remembered those whom all had forgotten, and what they have prepared is like a bath from which the hands will rise warmly and as if transfigured.—I feel oddly confused and clear these days. I find a land and people, find them as if they had been expecting me. What shall I do: Come to work!

THE
WORPSWEDE
DIARY

DESTINIES are (I feel this daily)
much more than chance, a little less than fate;
are—air, felt by a wingbeat,
evenings experienced by a rose . . .

ON THE MORNING AFTER HAUPTMANN'S PREMIERE I
brought the girls an armful of red roses, and they drank them almost
all empty on this city day that passed so quickly. We toured Hamburg
on a high four-horse excursion coach and followed that with a trip
through the harbor. Each of us held one of my roses, with which to
find one another again if some one of us got lost in ruminations.
Nothing much caught my attention. All the avenues along the Alster
were still familiar from that winter, I could even remember individual houses, and with certain gardens the only thing new to me was
their late-summer appearance. I thought up a new kind of caress: to
place a rose ever so lightly on a closed eye, until its coolness can
scarcely be felt any longer and only the softness of its petal still rests
on the lid like sleep before daybreak.
Fragment: By the time Death arrived along with morning, her

rich, many-sided life had wholly entered her face. Finding it there Death tore it away, leaving her cool, youthful body untouched. But his quick grasp ripped back out of her crowded face as out of soft clay, leaving behind there features that were long and sharp, almost as if extruded. George couldn't bear to view this trenchant chin and this gaunt nose against whose ridge the shadow bordered so harshly. He went outside, with angry looks broke off two hard red rosebuds that had become frosted and misty in the autumn air, paced about in the garden with the two heavy blossoms, and then without thinking came back into the room to be with his dead beloved. It tortured him that her last gaze still stared darkly from her open eyes. With a trembling hand he pulled her wide white lids down over her eyes and placed on each a hard heavy rose. Now at last he could gaze calmly on her dead countenance. And the longer he gazed, the more he felt that the wave of yet another life had surged up to the edge of her features and was slowly receding again toward the inside. He even remembered having greeted, in some of his sweetest hours with her, this life that now lay on her brow and about her mouth that was past suffering, and he knew that this was her sacredest life, the one into whose confidence he had scarcely entered, the one he knew of only as if from songs and rumors.—She had died. But Death had not drawn *this* life out of her. He had been diverted by all that rich everydayness in her loosened visage; that's what he had torn away from her along with the soft lines of her profile. But the other life was still inside her. A short while ago it had washed up to the edge of her disfigured mouth, and now it was slowly retreating, flowing soundlessly toward the inside and pooling somewhere over her shattered heart. And with infinite yearning George longed to possess this life that had escaped Death. Surely he was the one person who had a right to it, the heir of her flowers and books and her soft garments that were still full of the scent of last summer's sun and the swaying lines of her graceful body—he alone could be the heir also of this life that would soon be beyond the reach of his mournful eye. He didn't know how he might hold on to this warmth that was receding so inexorably from these cheeks, how he might grasp it, with what he might take it. He reached for the dead girl's hand, which lay empty and open on the blanket like a shell after its fruit has been extracted. A quiet, impassive cold had entered it, and it already had the feel of a thing that had lain all night in dew only to become quickly cold and dry in the strong early wind. Then suddenly a shadow stirred in the dead girl's face. George watched, tense with expectancy. For a long time nothing moved—then the left rose quivered. And George could see: it had grown much larger. The tip into which the many petals whorled had opened out, and the calyx below had been lifted as if by an intake of breath. And the rose over the right eye was growing also. And while the gaunt, jagged countenance was settling into death, the roses were resting more and more fully and warmly over the departed eyes.— And when this soundless day had yielded to evening, George carried two large red roses to the window in his trembling hand. As in two chalices that shook from their own weight, he carried her life, that overabundance of her life that had never been bestowed even on him.

And yet another fragment: She lived the life of the others almost indifferently on the secluded farmstead. She spent the solitudes in which she grew and changed in a wild-rose bower that everyone had forgotten, and this setting may have been a great inducement to the daily dreams of her soul. Then visitors came, among them George. And her entire life was channeled away from the abandoned bower and continued among girls who were all alike and upon wide meadows that shimmered with light dresses. Then she learned to walk down the long avenues at George's side, the avenues of evening that lead so wondrously far, much farther than all the paths of day. And at the end of one of those avenues, at the place where it unexpectedly hit the wall, she learned to say good-bye. Or rather didn't learn. He had gone and summer had left with him. How then was one to summon up the strength for autumn days? For a week she walked past them all. Still she hadn't wept. But one morning she found herself before the rose bower. In that instant she felt the whole depth and loyalty of the life she had possessed *before* George. And she yearned for those long unvarying girls' days and felt that she had not become a stranger to them. And she entered. A spiderweb tore away from the narrow entrance and clung tremblingly to her pale cheeks, which it embraced with the feeling of a veil. And with her face covered this way, she, the returner, gazed into the dark bower, inside of which everything was still the same. . . .

EVERYTHING felt: in plastic shapes and actions
it becomes infinitely large and light.
I'll not rest until I've reached that one goal:
to find images for my transformations.
The spontaneous song no longer will suffice.
I must venture now with all my strength
to make visible for those outside
what barely happens in a premonition.—

Monday afternoon we were in the private art collection of the banker Behrens. I saw there first of all a very strong Böcklin, sleeping huntress beside an outcrop of rock, two brown fauns observing her. A large, broad movement runs throughout this rich-hued painting. The two fauns, one old and one young, press with lascivious intentness against the gray-green, mossy boulder in front of which the unsuspecting body of the goddess, just slightly veiled, reclines on a dark blue mantle, her wonderful sleeping feet clad in red calfskin shoes. This gesture of pressing-against and gazing-on seems to repeat itself everywhere in clouds and trees; a frightful anticipation thrills through the whole wonderfully balanced painting. I walked past much else that was there, and it was not until the last room that I received deep impressions again—from an *Evening* by Daubigny and from two paintings by Corot (not to forget Stevens's *Lady*, who stands clad in a light dress and squeezes a lemon into a glass with her arms stretched out in front of her).—The *Evening* by Daubigny was bold in its use of color: a house, a mill perhaps, stands beside a calm, clear duck pond. Trees clump in the right foreground, and toward the back bushes crowd in darkening masses, far into the distance, against a sky that has remained golden and infinite behind the setting sun. Corot: house, with a path trailing by. Autumn. Slender empty trees whose soft branches gather around the trunks like fog. A far-off figure of green and brown with white headcover in the background. Toward the front a brown ploughed field with harrow, two white horses standing in front of it. Especially this latter area perfectly rounded and finished, calm in the light that is silvery and delicate over the painting's whole expanse. The second is a girl at a well. Painted as if it were an interior, incredibly intimate in feeling. And these colors! A reddish, coppery-bright skirt, over it an apron, green, the green that darkens in the plumage of small birds, and complementing it this delicate, slightly brownish fleshtone. When they were all standing in front of the Böcklin and talking, talking about this painting of the huntress and about various other works, I was still sitting in front of Corot's *Girl.* I feel as though I am only just now learning how to look at paintings. Have I perhaps until now been viewing many a work novelistically, or responding primarily to its lyric qualities, which I have sometimes (as, for instance, often with Leistikow) taken to be painterly values? But the pleasure in some small detail within the painting, in some portion of a foot, for instance, or in a fabric fold that stands in especially subtle relation to its surroundings: this way of looking was foreign to me before my intercourse with these rigorous and excellent painter-people, who get so unbelievably close to their pictures. Two things are certain: I must learn as much as I can from these people, must be attentive and alert and more grateful toward all surroundings. And a second thing: after Christmas I must go to Paris no matter what, must look at paintings, visit Rodin, and catch up with so infinitely many things to which I have become a stranger in my solitude. The Russian journey with its daily losses remains for me such painful evidence that my eyes haven't ripened yet: they don't understand how to take in, how to hold, nor how to let go; burdened with tormenting images, they walk past things of beauty and toward disappointments. And if I can learn from people, then surely it is from these people, who are so much like landscape themselves that their nearbyness doesn't frighten me away, only broadly touches me with images from which I draw sustenance. And how they love me here. How good our time together was in Hamburg. How they responded to me as a counselor and helper. How requisite I was to them. And how I grew strong enough under the shelter of their trust to be everything they needed, to be their happiest one and the liveliest one among them. All strengths rise in me. All life gathers in my voice. I say everything richly. My words are as if laced with dark stones. I speak often of things that are eternal, and I feel: "Of great things you should speak greatly or remain silent," and sometimes I can see from their reaction: I *have* spoken greatly. O that such speaking might not seem arrogance—that it might sound like humility and like thankfulness! But there are days when I cannot speak of myself without naming God, the solitary God in whose shadow my words darken and shine.

PRAYER

AND again my deep life rushes louder,
as if it moved now between steeper banks.
Things seem ever more akin to me,
all images more intensely seen.
I've grown more at ease with the nameless,—
with my senses, as with birds, I reach
into the windy heavens from the oak,
and into the small ponds' broken-off day
my feeling sinks, as if on heavy fishes.

On Monday a whole host of other things took place in Hamburg. After the Behrens Gallery we were in the café, where our talk turned to the study of works of art. I maintained that it is the artist who is best equipped to fill the role of unbiased observer, since even those works of art that don't appeal to him directly can by their technique— or better, by the way they express themselves—compel his appreciation. To value a Böcklin and at the same time recognize what is significant in a Toorop requires a great breadth of judgment, a very mature sensibility. I'm convinced that all true works of art are related via certain traits, and that on the basis of those traits one feels instinctively that a painting either is or isn't a work of art. With works of art that touch you closely, you'll probably never even think of the artist; you'll simply grasp them happily for what they are; with those that feel more remote from your experience, you'll probably want to inquire about the artist, so that something in his personality might reduce the work's distance from you. But of course this broader judiciousness doesn't mean that you have to take seriously painters like Sichel who only casually venture into painting, while all the time their sensibilities are being quite nicely fulfilled by everyday life and are not *compelled* into any art. One must, however, try to be fair to *all* artists, even at the risk of forfeiting standards of judgment—but only to all *artists,* i.e., people whose life would be nothing without their creative work. And these are not really so difficult to distinguish from the others as one might think.—

Later we all decided to attend an evening performance of *The Magic Flute.* On the way we bought books from a street vendor. I purchased a very fine edition of J. J. Rousseau's *Confessions* and one of *Émile*—seven small blue-gray volumes with three excellent copperplate prints in *Émile.*—There was much drollery in the theater. The comic people whom Schikaneder, that wretched scribbler of the libretto, has inserted into Mozart's music stand around with unbelievable oafishness in this luminous shimmering pavilion of his rich harmonious sound. The music this evening was something infinitely soothing. It spread delicate veils across those thoughts that were not taken up with Papageno, and the notes settled like rose petals on our mirroring emotion. As for everything on the stage, it came off as grotesquely comic. These characters sang like human beings, and then they stood opposite each other and chattered vehement phrases in the manner of birds who blurt out in a single hour everything they have ever been taught to say.

After the theater Dr. Hauptmann joined us for a late supper. We were all tired, and yet even this hour was buoyed by a spirited good mood. A lightly aromatic Chinese tea was served, to whose scent the breathing of nearby roses (we were never without roses during these days) was like quiet accompaniment. There was much random chatting, and in the midst of it Modersohn recounted: "It's very difficult to bring joy into the life of animals. This is the way I do it with spiders: I take the sack of eggs away from a running spider who is having trouble carrying it about. Immediately she starts scurrying back and forth in bewilderment and growing more and more agitated. I quietly place her sack ('Did you put something into it?'—I interjected) back in front of her. She is baffled, stops, thinks: 'I've never been *here* before'; but then, trembling with happiness, she picks it up, shoulders it, and runs away smiling." Thus into the humdrum life of a spider some new, strong emotion has suddenly entered, and this no doubt has an extraordinarily ennobling effect on a spider's character. Contribution to the improvement of the spider for a life filled with joy. I will never forget how Modersohn looked as he told this story—his eyes so wide that one could almost read in them how the animal was running and coming to a stop, his hands miming enthusiastically how the joyful spider threw her sack over her shoulder. There was much more discussion about this matter. I have forgotten it all. It was half past midnight when we walked back along the Alster. Four hours earlier I had stood there with Clara Westhoff. It is a strange sensation to leave the tumult of the city and after only a few steps come to this black water, into which the lamps that frame it so spaciously sink their light like golden ladders. Occasionally a small steamer chugs crossways through this smooth blackness like a thick bundle of lamps, and a bit later a loaded barge, mysterious and heavy, cuts through the light-reflexes on the water, and the figure of its oarsman stands out sharply against this brightness and then merges again with the night and the nocturnal waters. And out of the black water suddenly a beautiful swan came swimming toward us, approaching close to the edge of the walled quay. It remained perfectly motionless in its soundless gliding—only the scarcely perceptible current that flowed toward it slipped the flat folds of its waves under the swan's broad breast and rocked it up and down, so that it looked from the front as if it were bowing. It came closer to us on the black water, lifted its head quietly, searched for us with its feeling. . . . "As if it wanted to say something . . ." (I heard Clara Westhoff's quiet observant voice). Then another swan glided up, with its curved neck leaning back in such a way that it was nearly resting on its feathers, and its two hinged wings held up almost like the side walls of a loge. It remained this way, swayed gently up and down, as if delighting in a caress it were procuring for itself with its cool, evening plumes. And the first swan was still looking up toward us. We both had that feeling one sometimes gets with fairy tales when something happens in them: "This means something, one mustn't forget this, this will occur again later. . . ." Were we only deluding ourselves?

The next day we all had breakfast together, and while the rest walked to the Kunsthalle I went to meet Hauptmann and we joined them there later. All of us were attracted to quite different paintings. Vogeler was most taken by a Böcklin of '78. It depicts the pale, tearful, upturned head of a Mary Magdalene, a head whose skin is painted like faded silk, hair like falling, brightly minted gold, tears like crystals, and which strikes one with these color-textures completely divorced from all warmth and sensuality as nevertheless infinitely sinful-sensual—its flesh still flesh, its hair still softer and gentler than silk even though it rings so metallic in its fall. And the whole thing looks as if it had been put down in a single hour onto some black, disordered background, onto some other painting that perhaps showed Lady Sin herself when she still laughed and openly displayed her ardor. For ardor is hidden within this painting, it burns under the coolness of these colors, and somewhere beneath this devotion to the daily death there is a haughtiness, a pride in this new, gray beloved whose skull rests palely beside her pallid breasts.

Hauptmann accompanied us to the train station. On our way I went on at length to Vogeler and Clara Westhoff about the theater. About how as a group we should try out a number of things together. About many things that I will keep forgetting until one day I will have simply done them. About the importance of objects. About trying sometime to set down a milieu with such precision that the objects' boundaries will constitute the figure's contour. That the figure needs to emerge from deep within the stage and not be inserted into the stage from without. About appropriate timing. That certain scenes, love scenes, for example, are always being played (and also written) at the tempo of reality, while writing a letter or sleeping always transpires much more rapidly on the stage than in real life. That one needs material that is cognate to the stage, material that manifests even quietness as something visible from far away. Subject matter that bends and reerects its figures, lifts their hands and makes them slack, alters their steps and the heaviness of their pace, rather than situations in which everything significant takes place at the corners of the mouth. And much more of this sort of thing.—Clara Westhoff got off at Oberneuland and asked the others to show me the country house and the large garden, the summer residence of her family. She told me that this garden is where her whole life had unfolded; all her life as a child transpired there, and the entire city winter was like a breath held in, a waiting for the time when among trees and flowers the reality that had been broken off so sharply with the move to the city would resume. Even in its darkening treetops this garden has retained everything the child entrusted to it: what she gave a small seed to carry now rests high on the wind-blown branches of a young birch. Clara especially remembers the first time when as a young girl she was granted her wish and allowed to stay in the country for an entire year. Now she felt that grown-up's prerogative of experiencing everything the trees and creeks underwent, of witnessing not just the sunniness, the things that are easily bearable and fill one with happiness, but also what was sad and solemn in nature, as if she were now an adult being initiated into a whole range of relations and shown everything that might frighten and shatter a child. She received every fall and winter day with an impatient waiting,— but even during that year she was learning that there was *only* beauty—the fading of autumn, its growing vast and golden was beautiful, the coming-on of winter with its broad expanses and simple contours was beautiful, every storm and every sorrow in the landscape was beautiful, and the beauty of its rare solemn gestures stood out all the more clearly on the bright, blue-shadowed snow. Whereupon I remarked that it seems to me an auspicious sign of progress that the seasons no longer stand behind us as happy and sad backgrounds that succeed one another with dispassionate regularity. That we perceive sad springtimes and blissful autumn days full of richness and joy, that summer days can be grave and bleak and unbounded, and that winter can touch our emotions like the pellucid ring of a triangle, like silver on damask, like roses nestled against a young girl's cheek. . . . This is what enables us to live more peacefully and in a deeper agreement with nature, i.e., more intuitively. If behind our sadness a shimmering springtime flickers and moves about in high clouds, then our sadness will be more heartfelt, and our feeling dons purple robes when it forms wreaths out of falling leaves and expends all the colors of October without any thought of what their dying means.—

Tuesday evening we arrived back in Worpswede by mail coach. Beautiful, still, starry night, festive and so apt for a homecoming. It was at that moment that I decided to stay in Worpswede. Already I can feel how with each day the solitude grows deeper, how this country abandoned by colors and shadows keeps growing vaster and vaster and becoming more and more a backdrop for wind-tossed trees in a storm. I want to remain in this storm and feel all the tremors of being so deeply moved. I want to have autumn. I want to cover myself over with winter and not betray my presence with any color. I want to remain snowed in for the sake of a coming springtime so that what is germinating inside me might not rise prematurely from the furrows.

29 September

Yesterday morning the construction workers looked for water on our property. They did this with a green forked oak wand. The one searching holds it by its branched end, the single piece pointed upward, and in this position walks forward attentively until the upper part of the wand begins to descend against his chest. If it descends strongly and quickly, then a great deal of water is quite near, often only two or three meters below the surface. But for all that, yesterday's search proved futile. I saved the wand. Since it failed in this attempt, all its strength still resides in it unused, and I may want to steer it above the earth some day when I am thirsty. I walked out into the moor beside a long canal with the hot morning sun above me. The mood was robust and colorful. After coffee Vogeler brought down his old sketchbook, and I was touched to be shown something so personal. It contains various compositions from his Düsseldorf period: centaurs and fauns, a profile of Napoleon, a Dutch landscape, and then suddenly an exquisitely drawn rose branch extending across a page, and under it in the left corner without emphasis "Worpswede." This is Vogeler's true beginning. The fairy-tale ease and simplicity, the effortless reexperiencing of everything amorous in the mode of fairy tale, swans on very dark ponds, strange long-snouted animals and dragons, snakes stretching toward large crowns, and knights guarding the heart of a forest in which a childlike maiden feeds a tame black bird. The canals, the birch tree avenues, the huts, the church by Weyer Mountain—everything that is part of the landscape picked up instantly and expended in fantasy. From the mood of gusts and clouds, from the woods and waterways, the call to fairy-tale sounds out, and the oldest kings come and the most youthful girls, and the knight comes, iron head-to-foot and shining darkly under the ancient trees. Bright meadows unfold, springtimes play with easily moved shapes, and an old woman sits before autumn—an evil woman around whom all the leaves are falling. Winter is on its way. Great shining angels who do not even leave prints in the snow but are as tall as the skies will bend toward hearkening shepherds and sing to them of the young girl's child in Bethlehem. Many angels, successors to that one who stood before Mary with his round full lute, singing her the message and caressing her with his approaching voice. Many angels, many announcing ones, will stand in the skies and will be clarity and splendor in these skies. And down below, next to their feet, there will be trees and people. People bent over and massive dark trees. And the voice of the angels will not come to the ears of these people who are bent down in their burdens. It will surround them like wind and will rip their clothes open over their hearts. And will make them stagger and cast them down and raise them up again. And will move them as they have never before been moved, will roil them like oceans and fill them like chasms. Will seize them and take them away from herds and homelands and will let them stand solitary on islands and bloom there and bear fruit on distant isles. And will transport them into great fears of dying on heaving ships and in huts over which thunderstorms rage. And will rescue them from the edge of the daily deaths and will keep them from perishing so that there might be eyes beneath whose gaze the young girl's golden child can unfold. And will guide their eyes to this sight. And place their face before a countenance. And guide their hands before a princely needfulness and their feet over soft radiant straw. And will receive them after all their wandering with balsam and mountain crystal. And will extinguish their dust so that their garments will become clear again. And will order their confusion and sunder it and transform the staff, warm from their hands, into a fruit tree and into a shade tree above the world's cradle.

> ONE of them bowed to the crown-blond woman,
> and sanctified her gentleness with speech,
> and the many angels, with their silken cones
> rustling around them, came in his wake.
> Followed him to flocks and sleepy shepherds,
> while the landscape lay in dusk's repose.
> "Help us find the way, for now we've lost it!"

they chanted to these strange humans.
And the shepherds had risen from their sleep,
and the dark herds swayed heavily,—
and behind them the angels came closely,
increasing and in pleated garments.

This particular sketch was so strongly visual, as was "On the Flight to Egypt." Disposed before a deep, clear evening, the following group: donkey, husband, mother and child.

AFTER a long day on narrow trails
with anxious looks back toward the town,
all apprehension has been discarded,
since everywhere, with twilight's grace,
the vastness has been transformed.
How could such golden light contain a foe,
what seam could interrupt such bliss?
All is robe about her sweetness,
and all is radiance about her head.
The watchman with the lance still stands
alert near mother, child, and beast,
yet he's holding it so gently now, as though
he were planting in all that splendor
the first shadow over her . . .

Later I was with the blond painter, who welcomed me like an old friend. We had not seen each other since Hamburg, and so there was much to catch up on. She mentioned Clara Westhoff's new statuette, for which I already had such strong feelings from that long night when I had seen it in near dawn. Apropos of that work our friend remarked: "It often moves me to watch how Clara Westhoff, whose instincts as a sculptor are so strong and monumental, will cup a flower in her hands, a single flower, or apply to some one small object all the kindness and fullness of her broad being—how she'll gather all her senses around one small word so that it almost collapses under the weight of love. Watching this makes me melancholy. Watching how she contracts herself, withdraws herself from her own dimensions, and with all her love comes over a thing to whose small-ness she must first accustom herself! How she leads all her senses, the way one would children, out of the deep mountain forests in which they have scattered and teaches them to stand on a shaded meadow around a small pale flower and sing. . . ." You blessed girl, you see such things in your friend and see them and say them beautifully. And don't know what greatness and good fortune it is to become so selfless and dedicated in the context of another's life. As you speak these things, I am your auditor, your pupil, and become *your* teacher, now, in turn, as I teach you how good and sacred you are. Do you un-derstand?

> OTHERS must travel long paths
> to reach the dark poets,
> must always be asking someone
> if he has seen one of them singing
> or placing hands on strings.
> Girls alone never ask
> which bridge leads to images.
> Only smile, more brightly
> than strings of pearl
> before bowls of fine silver.
> From their lives every door opens
> into a poet—
> and into the world.

"I've also," the blond painter told me, "been reading in Beer-Hofmann. And he appeals to me much more now than back then when you read him aloud. I have to proceed very, very slowly from page to page. These broad images cause me a certain strain, and it al-ways takes me awhile to get used to them. I'm like someone who must constantly keep her eyes held open." "Perhaps," I rejoined, "but one should also enjoy this book the way in one's tiredness one takes in those richly embroidered silk fabrics that are full of images: by clos-ing one's eyes and fingering the beautiful silk and the figures that rip-ple through it like waves. It's the same with this book: sometimes one needs to take it in with one's feeling. And besides, there are any number of other poets who are more suitable for lingering over a book with open eyes—Jacobsen, for instance. All his images come from reality and bring it near: they transform it into close, familiar feelings one can have in direct connection with his plot. But with Beer-Hofmann, all feelings are expressed through actions and circumstances that occupy no particular place and time, that either veer away from the book's progress or have nothing at all to do with its unfolding. With Jacobsen everything is absorbed into the novel's central strand; whereas Beer-Hofmann hasn't been able to complete a full novel yet because his 'plot' begins and ends in the infinite. That's also why its borders to the left and right are so uncertain. But for all that, Beer-Hofmann's book has more actual life in it than Jacobsen's or, for that matter (since though we've not been referring to any specific novel by Jacobsen, we're both thinking of *Marie Grubbe*), than Jacobsen's works in general. Jacobsen had nothing in the way of experience, had no great love, no defining adventure, no moment of worldly insight—had only a childhood. A great, immensely colorful childhood in which he found everything his soul needed to dress itself in imagined guises. He conjured up the whole plague-ridden atmosphere of Bergamo from this childhood, conjured up the sufferings of Frau Fönss and the graceful Page's Song. The sorrows of Niels Lyhne and the whole great epoch of Marie Grubbe were already fully limned in this childhood, and both rose before him with such overpowering rightness and fullness that space would have had to be made for these figures in Denmark's past had one not known about them from history. He didn't reconstruct a past era using documents and old chronicles: he *created* an era and gave greatness and violence, kindness and brightness and splendor to those who filled it with their destinies and dreams, their disappointments and yearnings. He created an era and the style of that era. He fashioned costumes and movements that in their own particular garments take place differently than in our overcoats. But in his case the soul still had the option of a broad plot and could thus unfold through its temporal and psychological unities; it didn't rise toward itself in images. It filled one great picture with all the grace of which it was capable. It rose over particular people and transformed an epoch when it set. And came again and again, and there were days and nights for the figures upon which it shone, many days and many nights within the orbit of his sunny soul. Beer-Hofmann's soul is too open and agitated for that. It doesn't know quiet courses over fabricated destinies. As into different suits of armor it climbs now into this, now into that figure, leads it into battle or to the extremes of a feast and then abandons it after its first flash of splendor, its first show of beauty: for in the wake of beauty there is nothing but decline. And there is nothing out beyond beauty. Beauty is closure, the final vista. . . ."

As we were still talking this way, a very young painter, Fräulein Reyländer (who everyone insists is the most talented of all the young women here) came to say good-bye. Half an hour earlier she had decided to go to Paris; now she was gazing out into the deep evening with sad eyes, regretting her decision but still resolved to leave in twelve hours. A child still, with overly quiet eyes, full cheeks, and indifferent lips that dropped stunted words, all of them heavy with disdain. The blond painter was full of solicitude and encouragement, even offered pieces of furniture that she said were still being kept for her in Paris, was in everything she said and did all kindness toward this ungrateful and somewhat petulant child. Observing this I said to her when we were alone again: "You are the very soul of kindness. . . . This is the second time I have said that to you. When I shall have said it for the third time, it will be irrevocable."— "O there are many I treat much less . . ."—"And precisely that is kindness. Treating gently those you've chosen. For kindness is, as are all those qualities we call virtues, not something simply given, working its effects blindly, but one's own store of life opened to someone else's needfulness. Someone who is kind without distinguishing, is simply kind; but someone who bestows her kindness on those few she's chosen is doing so much more. . . . Are you still choosing?" Then it was twilight and farewell. The evening is always huge when I step out of this house. The moon's slim beginning stands bright as glass in a sky the yellow of amber. The woods are black, and their coolness needs no wind to make its way across the path and into the meadows that border on the waters. The fallen leaves have opened the trees there a little more, and all space has widened. The objects stand out against the plain in soft contours, like many islands in dark glimmering air.

1 October 1900

SONG

MY father was a banished king
from across the sea.
Once an envoy came to him,—
in his cloak he was a panther
and his sword was steel . . .

My father was, as he always was,
without crown and ermine,
around him the room lost luster
the way it always did.
His hands trembled
and were pale and empty,—
into walls without paintings
he blankly gazed.

My mother walked in the garden
and wandered all white through the green,
and felt for stirrings of the wind
that heralds evening's glow.
I dreamed that she would call me,
but she walked alone,
let me from the edge of the steps
hear fading hoofbeats
and run back into the house.

"Father! The foreign messenger?"
"He's off again in the wind . . ."
"What did he want?"—"He recognized
your blond hair, my child."—
"Father, his clothes!
How his mantle flowed from him,
all the gems and armor-plate
on his shoulders, breast, and horse!
He was a voice inside iron,
he was a man made out of night,—

but what he brought here
was a narrow crown.
With each step it rang
against his massive sword,
the pearl in its midst
must have cost many lives.
From furious grasping
that hoop is bent
that had so often fallen:

It is a child's crown;
because kings lack them . . .
Let my hair have it.
Sometimes I'll put it on
in nights pale with shame,
and then I'll tell you, Father,
where the envoy came from—
What it is like there,
if the city is all stone
or if in wind-blown tents
they yet await me."

My father was sorely aggrieved
and knew but little rest.
He listened to me with darkened
brow for nights on end.
The ring rested in my hair,
and I spoke up close and softly
so as not to wake my mother—
who thought about the same things
when she, all white, walked
distantly through dark gardens
before thick twilight masses . . .

THE Sunday was a silken gray,
the land soft and wide
like background for a woman
dressed all in green.

Only child-voices were awake
at some far-off game
into which rain sometimes,
sifting gently through branches, fell . . .

In the afternoon Fritz Mackensen arrived with his brother, unexpectedly. After him our guests. Also the singer of our Sundays. We
stood for a moment in the studio, then set out on the path over the
hill. The sky was a single soft sheet of gray, with a few bright rips and
fissures that scattered light over the land in a way that made it deep
and broad in all directions. The distances were like biblical landscapes with their mountains, stands of trees, and watercourses. . . . Of
simple contour, not some particular region, simply: the earth. The
earth over which the nations were scattered like dust in a storm. The
earth which is too vast for man, which expands under his wandering
into the heavens and out beyond days and nights and which on the
other side of the oceans always begins anew and grows, this strange
biblical earth, the earth which God still holds in his hand and which
is thus without beginning and foreseeable end. The heath stood there
dark and insensible, the trembling grass soft like Japanese silk, the
harvested buckwheat field a metallic red, the plowed land black and
heavy. The wind was broad. And the bright dresses and white movements of the girls had all colors for their backdrop, and for a moment
Clara Westhoff's light, reed-green slenderness stood out against the
landscape with gray twilight air surrounding it, so ineffably pure and
great that we all grew solitary and each was completely held in awe
by this sight and given up to pure gazing. I could scarcely find my
way back to the others again, so forcefully had that impression severed me from all connections, removed me from human beings and
set me down in the object world, where the things mutely endure one
another's presence. After that encounter I continued walking some
distance behind the others, who (with the exception of Mackensen)
were supportive of my being alone; and having dropped back like
that, I began to experience them as more and more image-like, more
and more beautiful, more and more like landscape. Now they were
walking two by two. The men, scarcely distinguishable from the gray
sky, only Vogeler black with his round high collar and his beret. Beside

him a slender figure in white. Just ahead between two slopes there was a gorge across which the winding trail, as if indulging in some game snakes play, led downward and upward. And the figures simply let it take them along with it; the ones on this side still climbing down, while the others beyond were already negotiating the soft round declivity on the farther side, all of them lost in thought, oblivious to one another, striding more firmly and solemnly against the wind's resistance. This is how that rich wandering and aimless strolling of human beings—such as one sees on the winding paths in the background of old devotional paintings—entered the landscape. And I thought to myself that in the foreground of this image, too, there must surely be towering some quiet figure whose shoulders stand calmly and colorfully before our wanderings, that we are in the background of a Madonna and are small and moved to praise her rich, peaceful stature.

2 October

A YOUNG king from the North was
vanquished in the Ukraine.
He hated springtime and golden hair
and harps and what they say.
He rode a gray stallion,—
his eye gazed grayly
and had never dreamt of splendor
at any woman's feet.
None was to his eyes fair,
none had ever won from him a kiss;
and when an anger seized him,
he ripped a crescent-shaped tiara
out of the softest hair.
And when a sadness came over him
he forced a young girl's will
and found out whose ring she wore
and to whom she'd given hers,—
and hounded her betrothed to death

with a hundred hunting dogs.
And he forsook his gray country,
which was devoid of voice,
and rode into a fierce resistance
and fought for love of danger
until the Miracle vanquished him:
as if in dream his hand went
from coat of mail to coat of mail
and there was no sword in it;
he had been wakened into gazing:
the lovely battle coaxed and wheedled
at his sense's fixity.
He sat on horseback: no gesture
anywhere around escaped him.
Now link to link on silver spoke,
and voice was in every object
and hanging as if in bell-chimes
was each bright object's soul.
And the great wind was different, too:
it *sprang* into the flags,
out of roaring funnels, breathlessly,
a trumpet blast took hold of it
and sang and sang and sang . . .
And drums kept going back and forth.
The blond boy was wounded,
and as he bled he beat
the marching drum, the marching drum,
and bore it into black masses
as into waiting graves.
There many a mountain was still clenched
as if the earth were not yet old
and were just now putting forth its forms:
the iron stood fixed like basalt,
the mightily moved pile
swayed like an evening's forest
before a red sun's ambuscade.

The darkness steamed, a stifling gloom;
was it noon or deep in night?
The battle outweighed time,—
and over storm and trees there arched:
the great vanity of iron
and the grandiosity of blood.
From clouds there formed in foreign garb
a swarm of far-off provinces,—
and as the iron broke out laughing:
the twilight battle glittered
from some prince in silver mail.
The flags streamed like joys,
and all hands had in their gestures
a royal extravagance,—
from far-off burning buildings
the stars caught fire . . .
And night fell, and the battle ebbed softly
back like an exhausted sea
that bore many an unknown dead ashore,
and all the dead were stone.
Cautiously the gray horse stepped
(by great fists fended off)
through men who died in rage,
and it trod on flat, black grass.
He who sat on the gray horse
saw down below on the wet colors
endless silver like shattered glass.
Saw iron wilt, saw helmets drink,
saw swords rise out of armor-seams,
dying hands he saw gesturing
with some last remnant of brocade.
And saw it not.

        And the echoes of that din,
that battle-noise cast far and wide like dust,
he pursued on horse as if enraptured,
with his cheeks hot with passion
and with the eyes of lovers . . .

3 October

YOU pale child, each evening the singer
shall stand darkly among your things
and bring you, over his voice's bridge,
legends that ring out in the blood,
and a harp, filled with his moving hands.

Not out of time comes what he tells you,
it is lifted as out of tapestries;
such figures have never known existence,—
and what never existed he calls life.
And today he has picked for you this song:

You blond child of nobles and out of women
who stood alone in the white hall,—
all, almost, were afraid to aid your making,
knowing one day they would gaze on you from portraits:
on your eyes, with their serious brows,
on your hands, bright and slim.

You have from them pearls and richest turquoise,
from these women who stand in paintings
as though they stood alone in evening meadows,—
you have from them pearls and richest turquoise
and rings with obscured devices
and silks, which waft faded fragrance.

You bear the gems from their waistbands
past the high window into the hours' brilliance,
and in the silk of soft bridal garments
your small books are bound,
and there inside, written very large and with rich,
round letters, you, mighty over lands,
have come upon your name.

And it's as if the past owned everything.
They have—as if your coming were annulled—
on all goblets placed their lips,
toward all pleasures whipped their feeling,

and on no grief gazed painlessly;
so that now you stand here
and feel ashamed . . .

You pale child, yours also is a life,—
the singer comes to tell you that you *are,*
and that you are more than a dream of the forest,
more than the blessedness of sunshine
that many a gray day forgets.
Your life is so inexpressibly your own
because it is laden with so many.

Don't you feel how all the many pasts
grow light, when you live awhile,
and how they prepare you for amazement,—
companion each feeling with images;
and how whole epochs seem only a sign
for some lovely gesture that you raise.—

This is the sense of all that once existed:
that it does not *remain,* heaped up in all its weight,
that, woven into us, by magic,
it *returns*—to our hands
and to our hair
and most of all to our feeling.
Thus were these women as of ivory
by many roses redly shone upon,
thus the weary mien of kings grew dark,
thus sallow mouths of princes turned to stone
and were unmoved by orphans and by weepers,
thus boys resonated like violins
and died for the heavy hair of women;
thus virgins for whom the world was wild
dedicated themselves to the Madonna.
Thus lutes and mandolins grew loud
in some unknown player's greater span,
into warm velvet slipped the polished blade,—
destinies accrued from faith and fortune,

farewells sobbed in evening arbors,
and over hundreds of black iron helmets
the battle on the plain pitched like a ship.
Thus cities grew slowly great
and collapsed back like waves in oceans,
thus the swift birdstrength of the iron spear
hurled itself toward high-rewarded goals,
thus children dressed themselves for garden pastimes,—
and thus things trivial and difficult took place
only to give you for each nascent day
a thousand great similes and likenesses,
by which you prodigiously may grow.

Past upon past has been planted in you,
in order out of you, like gardens, to arise.
You pale child, you enrich the singer
with your fate, whose praises he may sing:
thus a vast garden-party is mirrored
with many lights in the astonished pond.
In the dark poet each thing quietly
repeats itself—a star, a house, a forest—
and many things he wants to celebrate
are all around your moving form.

These days so rich with gifts scarcely leave me time to insert here a few things from last Sunday. When everyone else was already sitting together in the yellow room, I walked the whole distance to my house in order to meet the two girls who had gone home beforehand. As we stepped out of the clear night into the half-bright vestibule, there was already singing up above. We stopped at the edge of the stairs, unseen as yet in this darkness by anyone, and the singing wafted down toward us as toward things and surrounded us with shadow and tenderness. Finally, after the third song, we left this stillness in which the singing had sought us out so quietly, walked up into the bright, bright white music room and stood before the faces of the others, who seemed remote and strange to us. There was much playing, and many of the pieces were beautiful. Especially a Beethoven, with the words "In questa tomba oscura lascia mi riposar," was grand and pure, and in the wake of that my "Sketch for a Last Judgment" resounded with a wonderful strength. When it had ended, everyone remained silent. The girls grew incredibly beautiful as they lingered in the shadow of my words amidst so much light, musing with all the lines of their white figures, like streaks of brightness that fall from skies onto a pool of dark water. . . . Later in the evening I stepped out among them in my red tunic with red shoes and remained with them for the rest of the evening in my Russian shirt with the Kazan boots. Attired thus I accompanied them all down into the vestibule, where someone remarked that we would not be convening for two Sundays. We all stood next to each other feeling the same sadness. Until it occurred to us that our shared Sundays must be special indeed if the thought of having to do without them can cause such distress. And we all felt how beautiful it was and how fortunate we were to have one another's company. Now everyone was out on the dark forecourt, whose bordering walls curved softly and whitely around the night. And suddenly—or is the wind deceiving me?—voices, soft, increasing, not like commencing voices, voices setting out, but like voices in the midst of a song that is always in progress, and that only to those who grow very quiet inside will suddenly make itself audible, and I hear: "Praise be to God on high . . ." And then I knew that this song, that was rising as if on many steps, is always present, and that we become aware of it when we view singing profiles before starry nights. And we lingered a bit longer in the amiable living room of this dear house before which the voices had risen like fountains, above and beyond the high poplar trees into the deep, spacious vaulting of the night.

On Monday evening we visited Clara Westhoff in her studio. There was a new small sculpture: two children, one of them standing, the other kneeling, propping herself up with her hands. At Vogeler's suggestion Clara arranged the two more intimately, so that out of their juxtaposition they grew into a charming pair. Absorbed in the exacting proportions of the individual figures, Clara had not yet felt the need to consider how the two child-forms interacted. And then again, perhaps their stark juxtaposition had all along been her hands' intent. . . . But we marveled again at the statuette of the sitting boy, which, especially when seen from the front, is an exquisite piece of work. The left knee, around which the wreath of the arms stretches, is gently drawn up, while the right, more acutely bent, peaks directly under the extended chin, for which it serves as prop. This building-up toward the head has something incredibly monumental about it. It is conceived directly in the spirit of the stone, this arrangement of the limbs that feels almost like a formation in slate and at the same time functions architectonically as a strong pedestal for the head. Later on we sat across the hall in Clara's room, and the rain outside spoke of the leaves of the bower, which we could feel nearby with its mysterious framelike darkness. We discussed Fritz Mackensen's presence yesterday at our Sunday. About the danger created for our circle by each expansion. "Yes," I said, "in the first place, simply because every close group is grounded in exclusion and a certain shared bias, so that its harmony will be broken one way or another whenever a new element enters. The moment that happens fifty people might just as well be added. Once an harmonious group has filled itself out, it should never be lifted out of its tonic element, for when that happens it will be open to all sounds and accidents, and there will no longer be any rationale for excluding anyone at all. The group's like-mindedness, which made everything one could want seem available, will suddenly appear as poverty, as accident, as one possible form of closeness among a whole host of others. But for the most part I'm persuaded that it's very hard *not* to be aware when your presence makes you one too many; the more difficult thing is not immediately to show the one you've imposed on that you understand what he's feeling and finding a way out that allows you to exit quickly and with minimum ado. But when someone truly doesn't understand, he needs to be taken under his arms from either side and led away like a drunkard or a lunatic. For a circle of friends that has closed its ranks is a sanctuary. Let us guard our sanctuary."—Then Clara went with us to supper. She told me (Vogeler had gone to the post office) about those days preceding her Paris journey, in November of last year. At her father's request she postponed the trip to do a bust of his mother. Out of the fantastic, faraway regions to which her dark eyes had already accustomed themselves, her gaze had to turn around and come back and adjust itself to the close face of a solemn old woman and walk every day on wearisome paths across its furrows and wrinkled folds. Snug, silent rooms with cautiously commencing clocks attend all the feelings she now has regarding this time; locked up in a hushed old house, it seems without connection to any prior time or to the colorful Paris days that came later. There is always the refined, cautiously withdrawn woman sitting patiently in her chair, talking quietly and growing fond of Clara, trying, almost embarrassed, to conceal her hands behind their unaccustomed gestures of tenderness, and moreover constantly pulling them in like drawbridges, so that at any moment she could suddenly become isolated again, sitting apart from the things, unreachable from any of them, inaccessible, a long life behind many walls. Clara arrived one morning to find her talking about what had already been a long day, about the host of things she had already seen to throughout the house, about all the ordering and commending or upbraiding she had done that day. Then when she sat and spoke of a tree in front of the high windows of the glassed-in veranda, a tree that for her was nothing more than a sign of autumn, Clara felt strongly that she mustn't turn around and look at this tree, which for her meant freedom and an entire countryside and great sunsets and wandering storms. For she was yearning for Worpswede and the friendships there and things foreign and far away. And every day she modeled the face of the old woman, walked about patiently with small, hesitant steps on the overgrown paths of a receding life, which was in its own way mysterious also, full of wonders and verities, and which came to exert a kind of power over her. In this manner she completed the bust. And it was not until December that she traveled to Paris.

Later, when we were sitting in the living room, I began talking about Tolstoy, recounted for the first time the entire episode of our visit to Yasnaya, including many details that had only recently become clear to me, then talked about the fear of death, about the first great incursion by the consciousness of death, which is at the same time the first moment of heightened, all-inclusive personal life. Talked about that process of becoming solitary that is necessary so that one may cease being solitary, and about how this development sometimes, crowded into the few hours of a dying person, can come about with great force and violence. And characterized Tolstoy as someone who turned life into a dragon so that he could become the hero to do battle with it. Later on I read. We left together. The night was full of vague blackish colors, unglistening, with stars in distant skies that seemed to belong to a different world. At night light burns in many cabins. From far away yellow lamps stab out of uncurtained windows, strike you in the middle of your face and wound you with their bright tip.

4 October

Yesterday was a fine evening in the studio with the lilies. I read some things from my work, and following that there were good conversations.

PRAYER

I SPOKE of You as of my secret sharer
to whom my life knows many paths,
I named You: the one all children know,
the one all strings are stretched across,
the one for whom I'm dark and still.

I named You the neighbor of my nights
and all my evenings' deep secrecy,—
and You're the one none could conceive
had You not been thought out from eternity.
You're the one in whom I've never erred,
the one I entered like a well-known house.
Your growing now goes on beyond me:
You are Becoming's essence, all-evolving.

"When you were first here I so often marveled that you used the name God (Dr. Hauptmann also pronounced it often) and that you were able to use it so beautifully. I myself was totally without that word. It's true I never felt any great need for it either. There were times, earlier, when I believed: he is in the wind, but for the most part I didn't experience him as a unified personality at all. I knew only aspects of God. And many of those aspects were horrifying. For even

death was only a component of his being. And he seemed to me unjust in the extreme. He tolerated unspeakable things, permitted cruelty and grief, and was massively indifferent. And that there are many
miracles, and that I myself partook of several, several good and powerful ones, changed none of that. I also lacked the intellectual distance
to take all miracles, which worked so variously and at such great remove from one another, and sum them up into a single, emanating
will—and even if I could I would have known no name for this unity,
since 'God' meant nothing to me. All the same it would be com-
forting to believe in a personality around whom all circles close, a
mountain of power before whom all people and all countries of all
people lie open. . . ." And later on: "No, it would all be foreign doctrine, for me God will always be 'she,' Nature. The bringing-one
who has life and gives it freely . . ."

But I argued on his behalf. That his shortcomings, his injustice,
and the deficiencies of his power were all matters of his development. That he is not finished yet. "When was there time for him to
have *become?* Man needed him so urgently that he experienced and
envisioned him from the very beginning as *being.* Man needed him
complete and said: God is. Now he must get back to his becoming.
And it falls to us to help him do so. With us he grows, with our joys
he evolves, and our sadnesses bring forth the shadows in his countenance. Whatever we do bears on him once we have found ourselves.
And you shouldn't picture him over the crowd. The crowd wasn't his
wish, he wanted to be borne by many individuals. In the crowd each
person is so small that he can't lend his hand to God's building. But
the individual who walks straight up to him looks into his face and
rises confidently to his shoulder. And is powerful with respect to
him. And is critical for God. And this most gives me the heart for life:
that I must be great in order to benefit his greatness, that I must
simplify myself in order not to complicate him, and that somewhere
my seriousness connects with the seriousness in his being. . . . But
whenever I hear myself pronounce on all this, I feel that I'm not just
living a life toward him, for the very reason that I'm talking about
him. Those who pray to him don't talk about him. Perhaps I am
more than someone whose vocation is to pray. Perhaps I've been
called on to be some sort of priest, perhaps I'm meant to cut myself

off from the others and then from time to time walk up to a single person, ceremoniously, as out of golden doors. But if that's the case the only ones who will ever see me are those who live near golden doors."

"For young people (I said in a different context) Christ is a great danger, the all-too-near, the coverer of God. They grow accustomed to seeking the divine with human means and measures. They pamper themselves with the human and later freeze to death in the bleak summit-air of eternity. They wander back and forth between Christ, the Marys, and the saints: they are adrift among figures and voices. They become disillusioned with the half-akin that does not astonish them, does not cause them terror, does not rip them out of their daily lives. They learn to content themselves, when to know God they would have to grow immodest."

Once, by a southern sea, I was approached by a young philosopher whose God, reachable on very safe paths, sat in the midst of peaceful, clockwork systems, and he spoke to me of this transparent God with full, youthful enthusiasm. And asked, since he had little knowledge of other areas: "How is it in modern art, do they believe in God?" I was startled. What could I answer? At a loss, I glanced out onto the dark, heavy sea. And felt its greatness. And felt the great beauty of my Florentine days and all the goodness of the countryside in which I lived. And was surrounded by goodness. And said with great intensity: Yes, we know that nothing can be accomplished without him. That's what I said—before I had found him; my voice was oddly festive as it bore this strange confession I had yet to grasp. Only much later did I realize that this hour by the evening sea already contained everything I have since been living and learning each day how to live better. It is like a remote, perhaps already deceased mother of my feeling, and I still know exactly what she looked like, and that she was beautiful.

And earlier I said, directly after the "Song": "There comes a time when every past sheds its heaviness, when blood affects us like brilliance and sadness like ebony. And the darker and more colorful our various pasts were, the richer the images will be by which our quotidian life redeems itself. And that holds true as much for the course of history as for an individual life. All cruelty and force becomes brilliance among grandchildren. All heirs bear deceased fates like jewelry. Dead eyes full of lament have been transfigured into precious stones, the gesture of a great leave-taking repeats itself, scarcely noticed, in an inconspicuous fluttering of their garments. . . ."

[Here at least one sheet of the diary has been torn out. As a result, the first two stanzas of the following poem, which appears in its entirety in the 1902 *Book of Images* as "Solemn Hour," are missing. It is impossible to know how much else has been ripped out of this place in the diary. The last dated entry before the torn portion is 4 October. On 5 October Rilke left Worpswede in early dawn for Berlin, without explanations and without good-byes, and did not return even for a visit until his marriage in 1901. His only gesture of farewell was to leave Paula an evasive note and a notebook of his poems. The verses that follow the gap in the diary seem to issue from the solitude of Berlin, and the next dated entry is 21 October.]

> WHOEVER walks now anywhere out in the world,
> walks without cause in the world,
> walks toward me.
> Whoever dies now anywhere out in the world,
> dies without cause in the world,
> looks at me.
>
> I AM growing more alone.
> The landscape is enlarging.
> The slim trees are condensing into clumps,
> the house nearby is dwindling, like something far off.
> Soon I will be as if the first of all.
> The flames serve me like things scarcely tamed,
> and my creeks don't speak of people,—
> and the flower that I pluck
> smiles at me like a veiled woman.
> Dew is like cool noble stone,
> and wind like my garment,
> and evening-sheen like
> my hair, which has grown long;

and what I speak of
erects itself around me,
grows similar to things: quiet, weighty, real.
And my silences are the ocean
that carries ships and also crushes them.
And what I saw belonged to me,
and if you feel I'm vanishing,
it's because my life enshadows me.
Before you possessed me,
I didn't exist. But I remain now
when you no longer see me.
Not in the words I write down;
I live on
in all that decays,
blows away . . . :
I am growing more alone.

IN the faded forest there is a birdcall
that seems meaningless in this faded forest.
And yet the round birdcall rests
in this interim that shaped it,
wide as a sky upon the faded forest.
Pliantly everything makes room in the cry,
the whole land seems to lie in it soundlessly,
the great wind seems to nestle up inside;
and the moment, which wants to go on,
has, pale and silent, as if it knew things
for which anyone would have to die,—
risen out of it.

I AM a picture.
Don't expect me to talk.
I am a picture. And even the slightest
gesture is hard for me.
My life is: the stillness of final form.
I am gesture's beginning and end.
I am so old

that I can't grow older.
People sometimes stand next to me at night
and hold the lamp up to my face
and know only: It isn't me.
In the corner my heraldic beast rises,
my sleek, steep greyhound.
And over all of that the heavy helmet's
closed visor enforces silence.

Sunday, 21 October 1900

I KNOW you're all listening: a voice is wafting,
and Sunday-evening fills your white hall.
The silence here that presses on my solitary brows
turns wilted and gray. I would like to hear
you listening again for a sound-prayer.
Beethoven spoke . . . My senses are still trembling,
and all the darkness in me reverberates.
We were children, earliest embarkings of life,
and sat there quietly, our heads lowered:
Beethoven spoke.
We rose out of childhood with amazing speed
into a ripeness, a rich surrounding,
all things grew exalted, life was a share,
and we were wider than the grave
and hale,—
even our cares were almost motherly—
Beethoven spoke.
I am alone. This house is loud and full
of one of those Sundays that hates me blindly.
But I'm gripped so tenderly by the sense
that at this very hour some guest
is singing in the white hall before your joy.
And the awareness that evening has turned to sound
wraps softly round my shoulders, like damask,
and I feel rich rings upon my fingers.

O HOW everything is far off
and long deceased.
I think now, that the star
whose beam reached me
has been dead for a thousand years.
I think now, that in the boat
that slipped past
I heard something fearful being said.
Inside the house a clock
just struck.
Inside what house?
I would like to step out of my heart
and be under the great sky.
I would like to pray.
And one of all those stars must
surely still exist.
I think now, that I know
which one alone
has lasted,—
which one like a white city
stands at its light's end in the skies . . .

KINGS in legends are like
mountains at evening, dazzle
those to whom they turn.
The belts that gird their loins
have cost countries and lives.
Their richly gloved hands hold,
slender and naked, the sword.

Sunday, 28 October 1900

I AM there with you, you Sunday-evening ones.
My life is lustrous and aglow.
I'm speaking, yes; but unlike other times

now each word drifts away from me,
and the silence in me rises up and blooms . . .

For that's what songs are: lovely silentness of many
emanating from the one as if in beams.
The one who plays the violin is always solitary,
and amidst the others, the slender player
is the very heart of silence, is its pulsing hush.

I am with you both, you soft attentive ones.
You are the pillars of my solitude.
I am with you: Let me remain unnamed
so that I can be with you as I am, far off . . .
Thus gardens reaching into distances
sometimes bear the words of the far-off woods
along their quiet, darkening avenues . . .
And you're so near around my feeling. It's not
delusion. This evening-hour is so like
those hours of yours with the white background.
Such varied silences ring out around me.
Music! Music! Orderer of sounds,
collect what is scattered in the great hour,
lure lost pearls onto strings.

In every thing there is a captive.
Go forth, music, to each thing, and lead
out of each thing's every door
those for so long frightened: the figures.
In pairs, hand in hand
they follow you, and walk to those measures
with which we scoop the lucid hours,—
walk like kings with brows crowned in laurel
out of our rooms that had forgotten us.

I am with you, you listeners to that sound
which always is, for which we sometimes are.
We grew fearless of every diminution:
Music is onset. Soul of song,

from many things you shape *one* structure,
within which you ascend into those many things;
out of all women you make *one* woman
and you link girls together, as rings of silver
form cool chains that bind the spring.
And you give young men a feeling to discover
and a region where the world enlarges,
and old men, almost blind now to the world,
remain alive as long as they can lean on you.
And grown men longed for you.

I am with you. Within your circle one is
peaceful the way one is with trees and brothers.
I scarcely know this calm even from dreams;
this unconcern with what one might have missed,
and this savoring of what one knows.
Simple existence, receptive to the heavens—
like ponds that are always open,
recounting more richly what the breezes live,
and, forever placid, over all chasms
transporting days and the winds of evening.

I am with you. Am blessed to have you both,
you who are as sisters of my soul;
for my soul wears a young girl's dress,
and her hair is silken to the touch.
Only rarely do I glimpse her cool hands,
for she dwells far off behind many walls,
as in a tower she stands, not yet set free by me,
scarcely knowing that one day I will come.

But I go through the winds of the earth
always up to that looming wall
behind which in uncomprehended sadness
my soul stands. You know her more intimately,
you've been so much closer than I,
you are my bride's sisters.

Be good to her.
Give my blond sister your love.
Speak to her softly in the rising moon.
Tell her of you. Tell her of me.

Lines on Heinrich Vogeler's picture with the knight:

KNIGHT, WORLD, AND HEATH

AS if it were being borne by dark voices
the heath opens out before the knight.
And he stops, and he hears his heart beating,
beating at the doors of new days
that as yet he can scarcely comprehend.
Of vast days not to be ridden round,
and of goals only to be attained in dream;
suddenly the world is played for him
by a thousand hands upon a thousand strings.

All things are but two: living and oblivion,
but how many things these two comprise!
Living means: to be blind things' visage,
now transfigured and now in tears.
For the immoveable to venture out,
for the root-bound to take one's steps,
to lead everything forever errant
and to understand what remains too mute . . .
Dying means: to ride out on black earth,
to bear arms that rest gleamingly,
on a heavy horse to make a heavy gesture
beneath the dark armor-plate . . .
To wake one's Mother with this gesture
and hide oneself in warm arms—
(in the roots there's just enough room)
and—to extrude a tree from one's heart,
a great red tree
with wind roiling in its branches:
such is Death.

31 October 1900

THE SKIFF

. . . AND one fixed in place, and one passing by,
and all night seems made for just these two.
The skiff with its one old man glides this way,
the other stands tall, heavy as after work,
and the one in the skiff—the old one—drifts off,
and the one who looks at him sleepily is
                                    who knows who.
One who comprehends this drift toward sleep,
one in whose hands all things ripen,
(even if they're but a day out of their seed)
one who stands near all cradles
and near all the yellow housefronts
behind which in the many softly lit bedrows
those who've been given up lie sick.
And he doesn't forsake those growing old,
those who see only *nearby* things
and now, groped at by the *nearby* word,
only understand connection and coincidence;
and he takes the lost by the hand
and leads them all the way out to the edge
of the very last forest—and on the wall
he hangs those who have lost God
like limp clothes soaked
with black water out of stagnant ponds.

But sometimes those *alive* in life,
those who watch and work their wills, wave
to him, and call him into their vicinity:
and he stands there beside Strength like a brother.
Sometimes he's used thus by the truly rich—
those who surround themselves with all they're moved by,
and who in long hours, deep, unique,
survive *that one* who out of long-buried corpses
guides startled warmth up into the winds.

He who, positioned at life's farthest point,
stands like a watchman above a city
and surveys all that shimmers, falls, and fades
while the evening winds circle him beseechingly:
for in his hands he has those bells
whose ringing will summon all to prayer.

7 November

ON RECEIVING THE GRAPES FROM WESTERWEDE

. . . Now I know why that summer night
through which we walked and watched together
grew so hushed in the vine-leaf bower:
then this sweetness was entering the grapes.

That's when all things fear to stir;
in such hours, where ever so subtle doors
lead into ever so secret darknesses,
all winds are hesitant to blow,
the clocks tremble when they have to strike,
the waters whisper in the meadowbrooks,—
else what is gentlest will hold back in the sap . . .
That's why the far-off barking and that strange
animal's evil screams so frightened us;
we had made ourselves guards at every mouth,
so all trees would think they were alone,
unwatched, and far from man's intrusion:
for then the sweetness was entering the grapes.

That's why it seemed so portentous
when the dark blood issued from Your hand
as those unrelenting hammer-blows
were causing the deep silence to quake.
Then Your blood, afraid for that kindred other
(which through the trunks was rising toward the fruit),
out of Your hand came forth to us and pleaded
for all fruit, until the hammer ceased.

And while we, close in the lamplight, pale,
sat ministering to that injured hand

that trembled and slowly from the bowl's edge
bled down into the cool water,
the great silence outdoors healed over;
now the dog slept, the evil animal was assuaged,
and we late-wakers had survived a wound.

Then the sweetness began to move again—
behind the saps that were crowding upward
it rose on, still sometimes hesitant . . .
The berries filled out . . . the clusters clung
more heavily to the strong tendrils.

FRAGMENTS FROM BROKEN-OFF DAYS:

Like birds that get used to walking
and grow heavier and heavier, as in free-fall:
the earth sucks out of their long claws
the brave memory of every
great thing that happens high up,
and turns them almost into leaves that cling
thickly to the ground, —like plants that,
scarcely growing upward, cringe into the soil,
sink lightly and softly and wetly
into black clods and sicken there lifelessly,—
like mad children, like a face
in a coffin, like happy hands that
grow hesitant, because in the full chalice
things are mirrored that are not near,
like calls for help that in the evening wind
collide with many dark huge chimes,
like house plants that have dried for days,
like streets that are ill-famed, like curls
in which all jewels have grown blind,
like early morning in April
facing the hospital's many windows:
the sick press up against the hall's seam
and gaze: the grace of a new light
makes all the streets springtimelike and wide;
they see only the bright majesty

that makes each house young and full of laughter,—
and don't know that all night long
a storm has ripped the garments from the skies,
a storm of waters sent from where the world is still frozen,
a storm that even now roars through the streets
and removes all burdens from the things' shoulders,
that something outside is huge and incensed,
that outside Power stalks, a fist
that would strangle each one of the sick
in the midst of this brilliance, which they behold
and thrill to and believe in with racing hearts.

Like long nights in faded bowers
that have been ripped open on all sides
and are much too large to sit inside
with someone loved and weep together,
like naked girls, approaching over stones,
like drunkards in a birch grove,
like words that mean nothing definite
and yet fly, penetrate the ear, continue on
into the brain and secretly among the nerve-branches
through every limb try out leap after leap,
like old men who curse their race
and then die, so that the harm imposed
can never be annulled,
like full roses, artfully brought up
in the blue hothouse where the breezes lied,
and then from the exhilaration in great curves
strewn out upon the scattered snow,
like an earth that cannot orbit
because too many dead weigh on its feeling,
like a man killed and buried
whose hands are warding off roots,
like one of the tall, slim, red
midsummer flowers, which unredeemed
dies suddenly in its favorite meadow-wind
because below its root hits turquoise

in the earring of a corpse
and stops . . .

And many a day's hours were like that.
As though my likeness, clay-gray, lay somewhere
in hands that tortured it dementedly.
I felt the sharp pricks of their playing.
As though a long rain fell on me
in which all things slowly changed.

IN THE MUSIC HALL

ALL my fear was put to rest like a child.
A longing came forth in the violins,
and it carried something infinitely craved.
And as if the listeners didn't exist
it strode through all those concert-aisles
and I felt: making straight for me.

And I leaned there in the last row,
and my silence brought forth voices, screams,
and scaled them like someone fleeing,
and it came following with so sure a stride,
and strode as long as the violins sang,
and stopped as soon as the last one ceased.

Again I was behind a hundred doors,
and all of them had swung tightly shut,
and I could scarcely remember
which one opened. But behind them all
was the Strongest. And there was a sound within
like someone playing with pearl necklaces.

Saturday, 10 November 1900

MEMORY OF THE SINDING CONCERT

Give me music! What made me wake?
Whoever you are, of whom I was just thinking,
Give me music! Play! It is night.

And each burgeoning accord has room
to grow as great as a huge tree
that has been growing and roiling for centuries.—
I don't know when my whole life listens,
I don't know by whom my whole life is played.
I believe many names have been switched,
I believe I held different things
and let go of different things than I supposed.
I no longer know exactly why I wept,
and when my laughter came, what summoned it—
I no longer know. With what hand I created,
in what mountain my marble dwells sadly,
what image it is prepared to be, and when;—
used by whomever and repaid by whomever
I, far from the others, mused days on end
on the identity of what survives—
whether it's a phrase that doesn't perish,
or a silence written on foreheads
as on pedestals of basalt?
Whether one has to say it or paint it,
or whether it's just part of life?
Whether it resembles happiness or grief,
and whether that fairy tale we tell,
our life's frame, doesn't wish to teach us
to select quietly and seriously
from all we love that one thing most eternal—
that doesn't insecurely survive just us
and two generations of offspring,
that, no longer contested and striven for,
woven into the great connections,
remains a quiet thread in quiet fabric
on the soft armrests of the eternal.
For what those who sought eternity
willed us as enduring legacy
and what centuries have bid us honor
and what we gladly honored, was at heart
only a drawn-out deathbed hour

of old, old, farewell-bidding thoughts.
Did my senses drink music?
Was the night silent?
Is someone awake somewhere who plays,
does someone *play* the night?
Was I thinking of a girl?
Did I have a picture in my hand?
Was I there by myself?
The air is heavy
with words. Was I conversing? With what other?
Were many urging me?—
And who was that one person
who kept silent?

Go to sleep now, you of whom I was thinking,
whoever you are.
There is already much too much night now
in whatever you know.

Saturday, 10 November 1900

Maeterlinck, *The Death of Tintagiles:* The performance last night at
the Secession Stage left me with the following impression: From
dreams we have learned that feelings are large and spacious. Often
under the shelter of sleep actions take place that according to the rule
of nature would have to rest in separate regions of feeling, and which
in reality could only be played out in successive, shifting scenes. But
in a dream everything takes place on *one* stage, *one* feeling stretches
out far as a sky and remains arched over all events, now overclouded,
now clear, however strange and lost they may be in this atmosphere.
Thus, for instance, in a world constituted by fear, one comes to feel
joys and moments of happiness that can strike one as infinitely moving in their naive unprotectedness, in their attitude of children and
girls who walk up to lions with smiles and blandishments. And con-
versely, the dream can give us a single expansive mood of sun and
blissfulness in which sadnesses nonetheless exist, rise up like weeping
birches and bend away from the open skies with a hundred branches
and ripple down through the winds with quiet lament. In the same

way Maeterlinck's drama, with all its events and circumstances, with its tenderness and longing and infinitely fragile happiness, has been shaped inside *one* feeling, inside this great gray fear that manifests itself as the eternal vis-à-vis all events, that is already in existence when the curtain rises and that doesn't cease with the desperate curse of Ygraine.—One doesn't notice at first how opposed this play is to all we are accustomed to finding in modern dramaturgy. Now, with the displacement of the center of gravity from the external plot as such to the region of the soul, an agitated flight of feelings behind which nothing broad or permanent arises has become the dominant impression. Working their effects through contrast, separate and apparently unconnected feelings seen only in profile race across insecure humans as across swaying bridges. As a result we experience only "feelings in movement"—the weight and value of each single feeling count for nothing at all. Whereas if one feeling (as in this case, fear) exists prior to all the rest and endures uninterrupted, not only are we led to reexperience this feeling in its almost forgotten greatness, but the other altering feelings of the plot, standing out for a time against this unalterable background, are presented to us as if for the first time and conveyed in their deep primary significance. That is a progress toward clarity, toward simplicity, and thus also toward dramatic effectiveness. In place of ineffable emotional nuances whose complexity and remoteness could at best serve as stimulants for a pampered few, we rediscover the means to represent simple feelings as something great, i.e., of employing the stage to unify a mass of people, rather than to differentiate individuals in the name of a more refined enjoyment. (Wherever this didn't succeed yesterday, it was because the select audience expected exactly the latter effect and wasn't open to the impact of the scenes sufficiently to be taken up into the former mode.) But a new (and at first unsettling) power did emanate from the feelings, and at least one person in the audience found himself possessed by the odd idea that there may be space for an entire plot in a single fear. The words, too, worked in this new and powerful way. Like colors from the full spectrum striking eyes that have been coddled with mild, whispering, intermediate hues. Utterly simple, everyday words had the sound of words that had never been used before. Caresses shone and curses grew in the air like avalanches. Everything that occurred became large, and everything large became visible over a wide expanse. And what effect could be more appropriate to the stage and more to be desired than that?

Wednesday. Letter.

BLESSING THE BRIDE

IT'S so strange: to be young and to bless.
And yet I crave to do just that.
To meet You at the edge of the words
and with my hands, which leaf
through faraway books . . .
in Your hands to find twilight rest.

This is the hour when hands converse:
the day's work echoes in them,
they tremble softly and live the reality
of thoughts one's lips only spoke;
and were piano keys beneath them, the air
would rise, laden with sound, toward the night,
and if they dwelt at the edge of a cradle
the child within would waken smiling,—
with huge eyes, as if it knew the secret
of what gives each spring its might.
And now my hands are in Yours,
they listen to what your blood whispers,
they invent a kindly countenance
to match these hands that are in Your own.
A wise one, that does life honor,
a quiet one, that hears soft murmurings,
a deep one, which, behind its rustling beard,
remains as calm as behind oak-crowns
through which a storm speaks, a very quiet house
in which You wouldn't fear to dwell.

As You can see, my hands are so much *more*
than I am in this hour when I bless.
When I first raised them, both were empty,

and I felt, with a crippling fear,
ashamed of my light, empty hands—
then someone, close beside You, placed
such splendid things into these poor vessels
that they have almost grown too heavy
and almost shine too brightly,
so overladen with such great splendor.

So take now what someone overrich
discreetly passed me at the last moment,—
clothed me so that I'm like an equal
among trees: the winds are growing softer
and rustle inside me, and I bless You.
I bless You in that blessing way
one witnesses at twilight during spring:
after days that whisper, shiver, rain,
a silence comes, simply, the way a song comes.
The trees know already what is preparing,
the fields, soothed, drift toward sleep,
the tight skies have widened
so that the earth will have room for greatness.
No word is soft enough to say it,
no dream is deep enough to stage it,
and the chests of all fairy tales are empty,
since everyone now wears the clothes
that else in scented darkness lie unused . . .

Wednesday late.

SUDDENLY I know so much about fountains,
those incomprehensible trees of glass.
I could speak as though of my own tears,
which I, gripped by such fantastic dreaming,
once spent lavishly and then forgot.

Could I forget that heavens reach hands
toward many things and into this commotion?
Did I not always see unrivaled greatness
in the ascent of old parks before the soft

expectant evenings, in pale songs
that arose from unknown girls
and overflowed the melody
and grew real and seemed they must be
mirrored in the opened ponds?
I must only remember all those times
that fountains came alive in me,—
then I, too, feel the weight of the plunge,
in which I glimpsed again the waters,
and know of branches that bent downward,
of voices that burned with small flames,
of ponds that, feeble-minded and shunted off,
only repeated their sharp-edged banks;
of evening skies, that from charred western forests
shrank back totally bewildered,
arched differently, darkened, and acted
as though this were not the world they had supposed . . .

Could I forget that star next to star grows hard
and shuts itself against its neighbor globe?
That worlds in space only recognize each other
as if through tears? Perhaps we are *above,*
woven into the skies of other beings
who gaze up toward us at evening. Perhaps their
poets praise us; perhaps many of them
pray up toward us; perhaps we are the aim
of strange curses that never reach us,
neighbors of a god whom they envision
in our heights when they weep alone,
whom they believe in and whom they lose,
and whose picture, like a gleam from their
seeking lamps, fleeting and then gone,
passes over our scattered faces . . .

14 November

I WOULD like to sing someone to sleep,
to sit beside someone and be there.
I would like to rock you and sing softly

and go with you to and from sleep.
I would like to be the one in the house
who knew: The night was cold.
And I would like to listen in and listen out
on you, on the world, on the woods.
The clocks call to one another softly
and one sees to the bottom of time.
And down below one last, strange man walks past
and rouses a strange dog.
And after that comes silence.
I have laid my eyes upon you wide;
they hold you gently, and they let you go
when something stirs in the dark.
Often you wake—alone . . .
then I would like to sing you softly mine
and kiss you and sing you asleep
and know where you are . . .
("To Say to Someone Going to Sleep")

15 November 1900

I HAVE no paternal house
and have never lost one, either;
my mother birthed me out
into the world.
So here I stand now in the world and go
ever deeper into this world,
and have my fortune and have my woe,
and have each one alone.
And am the heir of many a man.
With three branches my lineage bloomed
on seven forest castles
and grew tired of its coat of arms,
already much too old,—
and what they left me and what I acquire
to add to the old possession
is homeless.

In my hands and in my lap
I am forced to hold it, until I die.
For whatever I put away
into the world—
falls;
as if I'd placed it
on a wave.

15 November 1900

IN HOURS when I am full of images,
then young people should be all around me,
then my feeling moves—as the wine's fragrance,
risen from the slopes, enters the village
and pulls yearningly toward the huts.

I don't live the life that's deep inside me,
and I waver in old used-up gestures,
but I can waken that *one* thing
in those youths on life's threshold.
I can move, incite them with a rose.
I can free them from chance, which still
clings to me, which makes me tired and heavy,
for no one in my childhood touched me,
no one enticed me to the miracles
that grant one the awareness of a world.

Mine never was that life inside me.
I carry its soft melody
carefully in the brimful violins,
so that I can sometimes tip my chalice
down toward young lips. And I imbue them
with that drink whose scent alone
I may enjoy, with the hope
that for those full of thirst
I can prepare a feast with my ripe wine.

17 November 1900

STRINGS are bridges. Bridges stretched
only where unknown
chasms plunge between slopes.
But only sounds
walk safely across string-playing.

We stand behind at the chasm's edge, alone;
winds and waters rush between
and blur
with their wild raging
those beckonings and calls of the turned-back sounds
that can no longer see us . . .

Rodin: The thing that makes his sculpture so isolated, makes it as a work of art so like a fortress—guarded, militant, aloof, attainable only by a miracle (and only by such who feel wings) is this: that it has almost entirely freed itself from dependence on environment and background, has come to a stop before its own stone as if hesitating, poised on the lips of the mountain range as its first articulation. (One recalls similar effects: in Upper Italy, where karst and apennine grow together, sometimes a pine tree rises at the edge of a barren rock, slenderly, praying with outstretched arms.) The way the soft, fragrant fruit pulls away from the rind with the entire rich aroma of its flesh, which is warm and pulsing from hidden summers: so these enlivened figures emerge from the hard stone. Like an idea from the massive forehead that conceived it, like the beloved from the dark, musty house in which much confusion is heaped: childhoods of parents and ancestors, fears of deathbed hours, small moments of happiness that in the tired smiling of old mirrors again and again rise to the surface, and the lamenting sound of songs that were begun and then, broken into by a weeping, never played to the end: all of that remains behind her, compressed into a shapeless mass whose weight almost shatters the wedged-in windows, and she steps out in front of it, bright and slender, and all things past seem to have happened only in order to emphasize with their darkness at this one moment the poignant contours of her beautiful body. Separated from the stone from which they had freed themselves, all works of sculpture stood there homeless and orphaned, wards of their random environment, dependent on the wall that was shoved behind them, penetrated by the light under their bent arms and lifted knees, propped against nothing and related to nothing nearby. But Rodin's sculptures remain within all that intimacy of their primal element, retain a hundred relationships to the stone, their great, gigantic past. They are infinitely aristocratic with the millennia behind them to which close kinship binds them, yet at the same time are fully congruent with the contemporary aversion to hero worship, never working as exaggerations of the individual but rather as fragments of great connections and relations in which each limb is assigned a specific role. (Even in the case of the monument for Honoré de Balzac, this grandiose figure in its indescribable pride does not function as the representation of a hero. The cyclone of will and imagination lifts up the column of this mantle on whose froth-crowned rim the brilliant head rests, moved, as it were, by the graceful, delicate caprice of this creative whirlwind.) Drama and sculpture have in common the effort *not* to provide any hero around whom actions or characters revolve, rather to present movements and figures in such a way that they can intimate the great center to which they refer (but which always lies outside their periphery). Hauptmann's *Weavers,* Meunier's *Monument to Labor,* Bartholomé's *Sepulcher,* and Rodin's *Burghers of Calais* are all alike in this sense. And it is good when drama and sculpture occasionally glance each other's way. They, more than any other two arts, are conducive of parallels. Both are meant to be simple and effective over a wide reach. This only as an aside.

For sculpture one other requirement is crucial: that the work of art come to an end within itself. With painting there can never be a gazing-out-of-the-picture, insofar as before the figure in question the space of the picture is always extendable (foreground), to the same degree that it is behind that same figure, so that the figure's gaze always remains within the picture and is separated from the observer as if by a nonconductive vacuum. Sculpture, which exists in the same atmosphere as the observer, must achieve its "looking away" more strongly and on its own. I.e., it must be entirely centered on itself. This, too, Rodin has achieved to perfection; with groups the gazes always exist in relation to one another, neither with individuals nor with public figures are there eyes that are not operative, i.e., *bound,* within the work of art. No viewer (not even the most conceited one) will be able to claim that a portrait bust of Rodin's, for instance Rochefort or Falguiére—or, least of all, the inspired Balzac—has looked at him!

20 November

Shouldn't the tale be written of the person who hurls himself into the most perilous adventures, for fear he might die of some laughable triviality? Or the story of the person who waits constantly for some one particular fate, so that everything he encounters on the presumed way to this fate completely passes him by? Or the novel whose protagonist is the past itself? To display through a character how the past is now the wave that carries and now the tide that smashes? This alternating lightness and heaviness of things past—shouldn't that sooner or later be given form? Embodied in the life of an artist, the life of a prince, and the existence endured by an anonymous poor civil servant. The novel-trilogy *Times Past,* in three volumes. Volume One: *The Civil Servant.* Volume Two: *Prince or King.* Volume Three: *The Artist.* Plans! But with so little serious intent! Designs, but so weakly willed; what sense does it make, day in, day out.—Or that poem with the horseman in the moonlit night? Or a drama, composed for instance—in accordance with the newly devised style—within a single feeling, within longing? Can you not imagine a drama that unfolds within longing? Would people afflicted have to act in such a drama, or should this drama, fitted into the space of a longing, consist in precisely the characters' *not* acting? Can a drama of the *non*acting be conceived? A drama of the paralyzed? But through what should it work its liberation and toward what solution should it lead? I would like to inscribe a drama into the space of longing. It would have to be called: *The Blind Woman.* Suddenly it is in my mind's eye and I see the poignant slender figure of a young girl whose feeling has emerged entirely onto the surface of her body, where it blooms. Infinite fragrances about her limbs. At her young breasts feeling opens as with roses, hard, full roses—her fingers, groping, extend out into invisible lilies. . . . And the drama would have to have a completely unmystical, un-Maeterlinckian effect. Mustn't be about love. Simply about longing, would have to be made of longing, the way there are things made entirely of silk.—Or the drama *Fire!* It has been on my mind for years now. A night that suddenly turns bright, more than bright. (How paltry our phrase "bright as day"! Why not "bright as hell"?) Fire! A gouge through the night, a red gouge, a wound. And the blood that streams from this wound streams over everyone, the blood of this night. And they thought the night had reptile's blood, cold blood or none at all. But now its warm life streams wildly over those abruptly wakened. What? Fire! Ho! A theater is burning, a barn, ten barns, a powder magazine, a refinery, a church, the cathedral, a ballroom where there was a masked ball, a forest—the world, the world is burning. . . . Worldfire. But the drama is merely called *Fire!*—as though it were not the world at all. And one beholds these bright, shined-upon faces whose features are almost rinsed off by the light and great shadows that repeat all terrified movements in huge, huge proportions on perpendicular walls. A drama, shaped inside terror. Something visible over a wide expanse and easily grasped by thousands.

Clara writes today about a black ivy wreath, and what she recounts is again a work of art. The way she speaks of this heavy black wreath that she took down unsuspectingly from the gable of her house and brought in out of the gray November air and that then became so monstrously earnest in the room, a thing unto itself, suddenly one thing more, and a thing that seems to grow constantly heavier, drinking up as it were all the grief in the air of the room and in the early twilight. And all this shall lie then on the thin wooden coffin of the poor girl who died in the South, in the hands of the sun. The black wreath may cause the coffin to cave in, and then its long tendrils will creep up along the white shroud and grow into the folded hands and grow into the soft, never-loved hair and grow into the heart that, full of congealed blood, has also become black and dulled and in the twilight of the dead girl will scarcely be distinguishable from the heartlike leaves of the ivy. . . . And through the empty corridors of the blood the ivy will make its way, leaf by leaf on its long tendrils, like nuns who lead themselves along a single rope and pilgrimage to the dead heart, whose doors are lightly ajar.

I would like to write a requiem around this image.

REQUIEM

> AN hour since, now, there is more on earth
> by one thing. More by a wreath.
> Earlier it was light leaves. I turned it.
> And now this ivy is oddly heavy
> and full of darkness, as if it drank
> future nights out of my things.
> Now I almost dread this next night
> alone with this wreath that I fashioned,
> not suspecting that something enters existence
> when the tendrils coil around the hoop,—
> wholly needing to grasp just this:
> that something can be no more. As if astray
> in never-entered thoughts, where marvelous things stand,
> which somehow I must have seen before.

> Downstream drift flowers that children tore off in play; out of their open fingers fell one, then another, until the bouquet had lost all shape. Until the little they brought home was only fit to burn; then of course the whole night, when they all think one is asleep, one could weep for the broken flowers.

> Gretel, from earliest beginning
> you were doomed to die in freshest youth,
> die fair.
> Long before you were doomed to live.
> For that the Lord placed ahead of you a sister
> and then a brother,
> so that ahead of you would be two near, two pure ones,
> who would show dying to you,
> show you your own,—
> your dying.

Your sister and brother were devised
only so that you might grow accustomed to it
and by means of two deathbed hours
make peace with that third
that for millennia has threatened you.
For your death
lives came into being.
Hands, which bound blossoms,
eyes, which felt roses redly
and mankind massively,
were made and again destroyed
and twice the act of dying was performed,
until, aimed at you yourself,
it stepped from the extinguished stage.
Was its coming-near fearful, dearest playmate?
Was it your enemy?
Did you weep yourself to its heart?
Did it tear you out of the burning pillows
into the flickering night
in which no one in the whole house slept?
What did it look like?
You must know . . .

It was why you journeyed home.
You know
how the almond trees flower
and that lakes are blue.
Much that exists only in the feelings
of a woman who has experienced first love,
you know. To you Nature whispered
in the South's late-fading days
beauty so infinite
that only the blissful lips
of blissful pairs can speak it—two together
with *one* world and *one* voice . . .
More subtly you've sensed it all,
the way a flower does, not tempted by the blood.

O how the infinitely grim
touched your infinite humility!
Your letters arrived from the South
as if written by the hands of the sun . . . orphaned.
Finally you yourself came home
in the wake of your tired, beseeching letters.
For you were not happy in all that brilliance,
every color lay on you like guilt.
And you lived in impatience,
for you knew: This is not the *whole*.
Life is only a part . . . of what?
Life is only a note . . . in what?
Life has meaning only bound up with many
occurrences in infinite space,
life is only the dream of a dream,—
and wakefulness is elsewhere.
So you let it go.
With greatness you let it go.
And we always thought you small.
Yours was so little: a smile, a small one,
a bit melancholy always,
pale blond hair and a small room
that since your sister's death seemed huge to you.
As if all else were just your dress
it now seems to me, you silent playmate.
But how emphatically
you *were*. And we knew it sometimes,
when at twilight you walked into the room,
knew sometimes: now one must pray;
a multitude has entered,
a multitude that follows you,
because you know the path.
And you had to have known it
and did know it
yesterday . . .
youngest of the sisters.

Look here.
This wreath is so heavy,
and they will lay it down on you,
this heavy wreath.
Can your coffin bear it?
When it breaks
under the black weight,
into the folds of your dress
there will creep:
ivy.
Far up it twines,
it twines all around you,
and the sap that stirs in its tendrils
excites you with its rushing.
So chaste are you.
But you are closed no longer,
you are stretched out long and lax.
Your body's doors are left ajar,
and wetly the ivy enters,
like rows
of nuns
who guide themselves
along a black rope,
because it is dark in you, you font.
In the empty corridors
of your blood they press on
toward your heart;
where once your gentle sorrows
met up with pale joys and remembrances,
they wander as if in prayer,
into your heart, which, completely silent,
darkened, to all stands open.

But this wreath is heavy
only in the light,
only among the living, here with me.

And its weight
will cease
when I place it by you;
the earth is full of equipoise.
Your earth.
The wreath is heavy from my eyes, which hang on it,
heavy from the walking
I did for it;
fears of everyone who saw it
cling to it.
Take it, for it's been yours
since the moment it was finished,
take it away from me.
Let me be by myself. It is like a guest;
I'm almost ashamed to have it.
Are you afraid, too, Gretel?
You can no longer walk now,
can no longer stand by me in the room,
do your feet hurt you?
Then remain where all are as one now,
they will bring it to you tomorrow, my child,
through the leaf-stripped avenue.
They will bring it to you, wait with good cheer,
they will bring you that and more,
even if tomorrow it storms and rages,
the flowers will scarcely be affected.
They will bring them to you. It is your right
to have them as your very own, my child,
and even if tomorrow they are black and spoiled
and have long since perished.

Don't be frightened, you won't distinguish
any longer what rises from what sets,
all colors are closed, all sounds are empty,
and you won't even be aware
who brings you all those flowers.

Now you know that other thing, which repels us
whenever in darkness we grasp it,
from what you desired, you've been released
into something that you have.
Among us you were small of stature,
perhaps now you are a full-grown forest
with winds and voices in your boughs.
Believe me, playmate, no violence was done to you,
your death was old already
when your life began;
therefore he ravaged it,
lest it outlive him.

Did something hover round me?
Did nightwind enter?
I didn't tremble.
I am steadfast and alone.
What did I bring about today?

(evening, 20 November)

I brought ivy at evening and turned it
and twisted it together, until it utterly
obeyed. It still gleams with black light.
And my strength
spirals in the wreath.

22 November

Perhaps all the great democrats and anarchists arose from disillusionment with kings and longing for genuine nobility. (After reading the memoirs of Prince Peter Kropotkin.)

Every day is the beginning of life. Every life is the beginning of eternity.

In the night of 25 November

Every lineage that runs its entire course, that is like a string of coral beads that doesn't break in the hands of time and anger and accident and doesn't scatter, fall apart, roll away—would have to stand between two poets and have kings at the high point of its arc. Between the first poet, the blind old man, the Boian, he who sings the remotest pasts on a few knowing strings, and the second poet, the youthful one who has the old man and the kings and the wondrously beautiful women as forebears and whose eyes are large and in whose brightness futures lie spread out like valleys across which morning and springtimes are coming. And when the last of the lineage, who dies young, young in the face of eternity—which he announces in place of life, which finds him according to *its* great measures young . . . when this latter puts down the lute, then his free right hand reaches again for the first singer, the ancient blind one, the one long past, the inaugural one, toward whom the circle of the lineage rounds to a close, and from the hand of the last one, who leads the old man, the essences of a thousand lives, pure and ennobled, enter the spacious soul of the ancient poet. And what for centuries long was life fills him with legends, with past epochs, with rumors and runes and gigantic races. His eyebrows arch over his eternally lifeless lids: he has opened his eyes, which gaze within. His beard tears apart like spiderwebs in the wind of the first word that pushes open his rusted lips. And his hands grow out of his garment like awakening dragons and plunge into the strings, as if they were animals accustomed to living in waves. And again there is outset. Again everything that was is legend, again everything that will be is life. Again God is Father. And again there is future and eternity. Amen.

FRAGMENT

THE STRANGER:

   You aren't afraid to speak of it?

THE BLIND WOMAN:

   No.

   It's so far away. *That* was someone else. Who saw back then, who lived aloud and looking, who died.

THE STRANGER:

   . . . and died a hard death?

THE BLIND WOMAN:

Dying is cruel to the unsuspecting.

One must be strong even when something foreign dies.

THE STRANGER:

She wasn't part of you?

THE BLIND WOMAN:

Not anymore.

Death severs even the child from its mother.

But it was terrible in those first days.

My whole body was a wound. The world

that blooms and ripens in external things

had been torn out of me with its roots,

with my heart (it seemed), and I lay

like churned-up earth and drank

the cold raining of my tears,

which out of dead eyes ceaselessly

and softly streamed, the way the clouds fall,

when God has died, from empty heavens.

And my hearing was huge and open to everything.

I heard things that had not been audible.

Time, which flowed over my covers,

silence, as it bumped against thinnest crystal,—

and next to me, close to my hand,

the breathing of a large white rose.

And over and over I thought: *night* and *night*

and believed I saw a bright strip

that would widen like a day;

and believed I neared the morning

that had long been resting in my hands.

I woke my mother when sleep was slowly

falling down off my dark face,

I called out to her: "Come quickly!

Bring light!"

And listened. For a while it was silent,—

and I felt my pillows turn to stone;

then I saw something that seemed to flicker:

it was my mother's woeful weeping,

about which I no longer wish to think.
"Bring light!" "Bring light!" I often screamed it dreaming.
Space has caved in. Take the space
off my face and off my breast.
You must lift it up, lift it up high,
must give it back to the stars.
I can't live like this, with the sky upon me.
But is it you there, Mother,
or someone else? Who is that on the other side?
Who stands behind the curtain? Winter.
Mother? Storm, Mother? Night, tell me!
Or else Day? . . . Day!
Without me. How can it be day *without* me?
Am I missed nowhere?
Does no one ask about me?
Are we entirely forgotten?
We? . . . But *you're* there.
You still have everything, no?
All things still busily attend your sight,
caring for its every need.
When your eyes rest,
and no matter how tired they were,—
they can still rise again.
Mine are silent.
My flowers will lose their colors.
My mirrors will freeze over.
The lines in my book will run together,
my birds will flutter in the narrow side-streets
and hurt themselves on unknown windows;
nothing is bound up with me anymore.
I've been abandoned by everyone.
I am an island.

THE STRANGER:

And I have come across the sea.

THE BLIND WOMAN:

You've come *here?*

THE STRANGER:

Where?

THE BLIND WOMAN:
  The island . . .
THE STRANGER:
  I am still in the skiff.
  I have lightly docked it
  next to you. It is rocking gently,
  its flag is blowing landward.
THE BLIND WOMAN:
  I am an island. Utterly alone . . . *(pause)*
THE STRANGER:
  You spoke of the other woman, now speak of yourself,
  you say you are an island . . .
THE BLIND WOMAN:
  I am rich.
  At first, when the old paths were still
  in my nerves, well marked
  from so much use:
  then I suffered, too.
  Everything in my heart went away.
  I didn't know at first where to search.
  But then I found them all there;
  all my feelings, all that I am,
  stood together and thronged and screamed
  at the walled-up eyes, which refused to move.
  All my led-astray feelings . . .
  I don't know if they'd stood thus for years.
  But I remember the weeks
  when they all came back broken
  and recognized no one.
  That's when the path to my eyes grew over . . .
  I no longer know where it is.
  Now everything walks about within me;
  secure and carefree like convalescents
  my feelings walk, enjoying the stroll
  through my body's dark house.
  A few like to read
  about memories;
  but the young ones

all look out.
For wherever they step to my edge,
my garment is of glass.
My brow sees, my hand reads
poems in other hands,
my foot talks with the stones it treads,
my voice flies out with every bird
over the daily walls.
I no longer have to do without now,
all colors are translated
into sound and scent.
And they ring infinitely sweet
like chords.
Why should I need a book?
The wind leafs through the trees,
and I know what passes there for words,
and sometimes repeat them softly.
And Death, who plucks eyes like flowers,
doesn't find my eyes . . .
(in my face,
which blossoms toward the inside . . .)

FRAGMENTS

I

THE way old royal houses are intertwined
with all thrones in their vicinity,
we're anciently related to every Power,
even when we're tired, fearful, and cast out.
Infinitely many things pertain to us
that occur far away, to others:
a foreign girl, weighed down by sadness,
in an evening hour a song arose,
the night was mute, and a wall-clock struck
in a room beside a dead mother . . .
We feel all that and live through it
and grow heavy from it and feel a lightness

when that has passed which likens us
to distant destiny, its song and day and death.

II
YOU sang: We saw
your voice
open up for us,
the deep silver minework of your soul.
The secluded room grew dark.
You were silent, a little out of breath.
We felt a greatness,—
still hearing what you sang.
Memories of things never experienced
filled us. And when we begged you: Sing,
we meant: Bestow on us times past,
place ancestors behind us, royal epochs,
create generations that flourish,
women in white and an abode in green
and a slim man in black clothes
and a park, a castle, and a battle,
a frenzied wrestling for a slender flag,
and evenings, figures by the alcove,
the white country house of a courtesan,
quietly repeated in a nearby pond,—
and a pounding at doors and hearts
by fleeting gleams from gold and crystal,
jasmine and roses, scents of summer weeks.
And outside the windows: night and nightingale.
And then again storm and downfall and decay.
Typhus wards, infirmaries, nurses
who teach strange men to accept their dying,
more strange men who fight death off,
torn between fear and longing,
feverish foreheads that distort the world,
greyhounds and great lords,
and everything as close as yesterday
and as distant as never yet:

such was your song.
You sang us epochs.
And with senses as yet unnamed,
and of which no one knows where they dwell,
we received longings
and sensations
we shall never lose.
We shall make gestures
that we have never made before.
And shall rest heavily
from struggles that weren't real.
But what is reality,
must it coincide with time?
The world is real.
And everything is world
that moves us, to great feelings or to fear:
desire and solitude, death and song.

26 November

Today L. said after Helene's visit, during which there was also a conversation about Alma's fate,—very beautifully she said: this is why we need God: so there will be an audience for those events and destinies that no one sees because they never become visible as stage-plays (nor as mood pieces either). Thus he has reserved the best portion for himself, since in these things nowhere spoken of, ungrasped by any gaze, stores of strength have built up, reserves of goodness and greatness that mean more than anything that blares from loud heroic deeds. Things without end are being endured, things without name are being suffered, and this at heart is what we need to experience in order to assess life and its values properly. That is a very fine observation, it seems to me. Only the first part seems to me not quite right, a confusion of identities. We don't really need God at all for this, since I know of a person whose best and deepest-seated faculties include finding, viewing, and loving that which doesn't put itself on show.

26 November

Today the photographs of Clara's statuettes arrived. Even now the sitting boy with the drawn-in knees still takes me by surprise with the simplicity and magnitude of his posture. One could imagine him quite gigantic. He is Clara Westhoff through and through; likewise everything quiet and soft that she says: it could be sung by choirs and received by vast countrysides. And this is the sculpturesque that is part of her, it facilitates her art and yet derives its impetus from her daily life.

Once this book comes to an end . . . what then? I have such a strong feeling of being on the brink of new things and yet I am powerless to say where what doesn't yet exist might come from and what it might be. . . .

I am reading A. A. Ivanov's letters now and trying to imagine my way back from them to their author. A quill, a hand, alas, a painter's hand tied down by thoughts and distractions, by worries, commiseration, and concern. That's as far as I get. I can't see the face. It's as if veiled or averted. The path to this face is a long one—so much so that for the most part I will probably talk about the one until I shall have come upon the other. . . .

Feighin has written concerning Tolstoy, and I received from Gertrud Eysoldt dear rich words about my book *In Celebration of Myself:* "I will take these songs along with me like a traveling minstrel, and I shall extend them to many people as a greeting from you."

29 November

I've asked Gertrud Eysoldt to visit me one evening and hear me recite a few of the songs. So that she can convey them as something she knows from "hearsay."—In addition I'm continuing to read in Ivanov's notebooks, which are becoming wilder and wilder, like gardens whose owner is beginning to slide into poverty. As early as 1845 he is someone threatened by despair. Someone whose hands will soon ache and whose eyes will soon fail. Money, which is such a constant concern, evaporates in his generous, considerate hands, and time weighs him down with a load of pasts that cripple him. And all this year after year!

Especially for you:

1. Пѣсня.

> Вечеръ. У моря сидѣла
> дѣвочка, какъ мать сидитъ
> у ребенка. Она пѣла,
> и теперь она слышитъ
> свое сонное дыханіе;
> видѣвъ миръ и упованіе
> улыбается она . . .
> не улыбка—это сіяніе,
> праэдникъ своего лица.
>
> Дитя будетъ, точно море
> трогать даль и небеса,
> гордость твое или горе—
> шопотъ или тишина.
> Берегъ его только энаешь,
> и сидѣть тебѣ и ждать . . .
> то и пѣсню эапѣваешь,
> и ничѣмъ не помогаешь
> ему жить и быть и спать.

1ST SONG

[Evening. A little girl sat at the sea's edge, with a mother at her side. The child sang, and now the mother hears its sleepy breathing. She sees its peace and confidence, and she smiles. It is not a smile—it is a radiance, her face's festival.
The child becomes, like the sea, the distance, and calmness fills the sky, and of its pride or pain, whispering or silence—you know only the shore and must sit there waiting. And so you, too, sing a song and help it through nothingness to life, to long existence, to sleep.]

This first Russian poem came to me quite unexpectedly today in the woods. You're reading it here in its initial version.

2. Пѣсня.

Я иду, иду и все еще кругомъ
родина твоя, вѣтреная даль,
я иду, иду и я эабылъ о томъ,
что прежде другихъ краевъ эналъ.

И какъ теперь далеко отъ меня
болыпіе дни у южнаго моря,—
сладкія ночи майскаго заката;
тамъ пусто все и весело—и вотъ:
темнѣетъ Богъ . . . страдающій народъ
пришёлъ къ нему и бралъ его какъ брата.

2ND SONG

[I walk, walk, and your homeland is still everywhere around
me, this wintry far-offness, I walk, walk, and have forgotten
that I ever knew another country.
And how far off from me now are the great days by the southern sea, and the sweet night of May sunsets; there everything is
emptiness and merriment—and here: God darkens . . . The
suffering folk came to him and took him in like a brother.]

1 December 1900

Today I saw Gerhart Hauptmann for the first time. He and Vogeler
were invited to Lou's. Grete M. was with Hauptmann. It was a beautiful evening. Hauptmann's face is extremely distinguished—no experience has left petty or vague traces behind, the past lies there in
great lines and has become quiet and no longer changes. At the corners of the mouth and about the eyelids tiredness has set in. But the
eyes beneath are clear and dreamy, the way quiet ponds are under
cloudshadows, and the slightly downward-bent mouth executes the
most complicated movements of his phrases with a supple ease. There
is something quiet, simple, and infinitely gentle about his manner,
and the way it controls the actions and gestures of his tall slender figure is oddly moving. He is like a vessel for something holy and invi-
olate that has preserved itself deep inside him, untouched by fame

and restlessness, and that waits for stretches of solitude and simplicity before it speaks. Before it expresses itself with this mouth that is so infinitely mouth, this mouth cut for simple, weighty words. Before it says things that will perhaps not be marveled at but instead mix with the crowd and mingle with the people, unnoticed by many and yet to all those who are alert and listening a joy.—And he has borne his fame long enough, the daily fame, the being-famous that can no longer be silenced. The voice in the room next door. But he had found many friends, and now he has given them his fame to bear, and hundreds hold and carry what for so long rested on him alone. And his shoulders, relieved of their weight, can move freely again with each new breath, and his figure slowly stands up, the way a flower rises after too strong a rain. . . .

There was a conversation about the death of animals, about the ailing of some small defenseless rabbit or bird that one doesn't know how to help. I remarked that I always thought it unfair to accustom an animal to oneself, to persuade it, as it were, to enter into exchanges and friendship. It gradually gives in to trust, and the very moment it lacks the smallest something, we cannot but betray this trust, since we have no way of knowing the reason for the animal's distress or the meaning of its wishes. What can we give it? We can train it to be close to us, coddle it with our own habits, i.e., play with it. The truly serious things that happen to it are beyond our help and involvement—has anyone really managed to share in the fate of his favorite pet like its friend and brother? We incur a guilt, a host of unredeemed pledges, and a perpetual failure: that is our portion in this exchange. And with people: there both parties bear equally this incapacity, and that makes their relationships more serious and deeper perhaps than a complete understanding of each other would allow.

2 December

On sculptures. There are sculptures that bear within themselves, that have inhaled and radiate, the surroundings in which they were conceived or the region from which they were raised. The space in which a statue stands is its foreign country—its own surroundings it bears within itself, and its eye and the expression on its face pertain to these surroundings hidden and folded up within its form. There are figures that radiate crampedness, crowdedness, close interiors, and others that have doubtless been conceived and imagined in open vistas, in a plain, before the sky. Viewed rightly, such works always have this realm of "ownness" around them, this inner homeland—not the chance space in which they have been set down, and not the blank wall against which they stand out.

Sculptures that have no such milieu within themselves, though, actually do stand among the people, cordoned off by no holy circle and not differentiated from things of usage and everyday—are paperweights, no matter how hard they strain to be a thousand times lifesize and past even that.

5 December 1900

In the city, amidst the bustle at Josty's, I called upon that solitary nightmood and wrote a little Russian poem, which didn't use the feeling up completely but did waken it for the first time. I have in mind that trip on the peasant cart from Novinki to the village and back. Let its name be:

ПОЖАРЪ

Бѣлая усадьба спала,
да телѣга уѣхала
въ ночь, куда-то, знаетъ Богъ.
Домикъ, одинокъ, закрылся,
садъ шумѣлъ и шевелился,
послѣ дождя спать не могъ.

Парень смотрѣлъ ночь и нивы,
то летѣлъ, не торопясь,
между нами молчаливый
неоконченный разсказъ.

Вдругъ онъ замолкъ: даль сгорѣла.
Вѣдь и небосклонъ горитъ.
Парень думалъ: трудно жить!
Почему спасенія нѣтъ?

Земля къ небесамъ глядѣла,
Какъ бы жаждала отвѣтъ.

CONFLAGRATION

[The white manor was asleep, and the peasant cart had driven off into the night, on its way someplace, God knows where. The solitary house had locked itself up, the garden tossed and turned: it couldn't sleep after the rain.

The boy looked out into the night and fields; and between the two a conversation went on, silent and unresolved.

Suddenly he felt: Fire far-off! Even the sky aflame! And thought to himself: Life is hard! Is there no salvation? The earth gazed at the sky as if it longed for an answer.]

6 December 1900

УТРО

И помнишь ты, какъ розы молодыя,
когда ихъ видишь утромъ раньше всѣхъ,—
все наше близко, дали голубыя,
и никому не нужно грѣхъ.

Вотъ первый день, и мы вставали
изъ руки Божья, гдѣ мы спали—
какъ долго, не могу сказать;
все былое былина стало,
и то было—очень мало,
и мы теперь должны начать.
Что будеть? Ты не безпокойся,

да отъ погибели не бойся,
вѣдь даже смерть только предлогъ;
что еще хочешь за отвѣта?
Да будуть ночи полны лѣта
и дни сіяющаго свѣта,
и будемъ мы и будеть Богъ.

MORNING

[And recall how young roses look when you behold them in early morning, before anyone else—all that is ours is near, the distances blue, nothing bent toward sin.

This is the very first morning, and we rose from God's hand where we were sleeping—for how long I don't know. Everything past became legend, and what has happened is such a small amount, and now we must begin. What will transpire? Don't concern yourself and don't fear perishing; even death is only a pretext. Do you want some other answer? Let our nights be full of summer and our days be full of radiant light, and we shall be and God shall be.]

Night. 6 December on St. Nicholas's Day

Родился–бы я простымъ мужикомъ,
то жилъ–бы съ большимъ, просторнымъ лицомъ:
въ моихъ чертахъ не доносилъ–бы я,
что думать трудно и чего нельзя
сказать. . . .
И только руки наполнились–бы
любовью моéю и моимъ терпѣніемъ,—
но днемъ работой–то закрылись–бы
ночь запирала–бъ ихъ моленіемъ;
никто кругомъ не бы узналъ кто я.
Я постарѣлъ и моя голова
плавала на грудѝ внизъ да съ теченіемъ.
Какъ будто мягче, кажется она.
Я понималъ, что близко день разлуки
и я открылъ какъ книгу мои руки
и оба клалъ на щеки, ротъ и лобъ.—
Пустыя сниму ихъ, кладу ихъ въ гробъ,
но на моемъ лицѣ узнаютъ внуки
все, что я былъ . . . но всетаки не я . . .
Въ этихъ чертахъ и радости и муки
огромныя и сильнѣе меня: . . .
да это вѣчное лицо труда.

[Had I been born a simple peasant, I would live with a broad, open face: my features would not contort from what is hard to think and impossible to say. And my hands would be filled only with love and patience—but by day they would close around work, at night they would fold into prayer; no one in my vicinity would know who I am. I have grown old, and my head drifts down on my breast's current; it seems to be slowing. I can tell that the day of parting is near, and I open my hands like a book and place them both on my cheeks, my mouth, my brow. I take them down empty, place them in the coffin, yet on my face my grandchildren will know all that I've been . . . and yet it's not me. The joys and hardships in these features are greater and stronger than I. It is the eternal face of labor.]

Noon on 7 December

СТАРИКЪ

Все на поляхъ; избушка, ужъ привыкъ
къ этому одиночеству, дыхаетъ,
и лаская, какъ няня потушаетъ
плачущаго ребенка тихій крикъ.
На печкѣ, какъ бы спалъ, лежалъ старикъ,
думалъ о томъ, чего теперь ужъ нѣтъ,
и говорилъ-бы, былъ-бы какъ поэтъ;
но онъ молчитъ. Дастъ миръ ему Господь.

И между сердца своего—и ротъ
пространство, море . . . ужъ темнѣетъ кровь
и милая, красавица любовь
идетъ въ груди болып' тысячи годовъ
и не нашла себѣ губы, и вновь
она узнала, что спасенія нѣтъ,
что бѣдная толпа усталыхъ словъ
чужая мимо проходила въ свѣтъ.

OLD MAN

[Everyone is in the field; the hut, already used to this solitude, breathes a sigh and quiets the soft crying of the weeping child tenderly, like a nursemaid. Over the stove the old man lies as if asleep, thinks about what now exists no more, and were he to talk, he would be as a poet. But he keeps silent. May God grant him peace.

And between his heart and his mouth there is that space, the sea ... Already his blood is turning dark, and that sweet, noble love has moved about in his breast for more than a thousand years and has found no lips for itself, and it understood again that there is no salvation, that the poor flock of tired words passed by like a stranger into the light.]

13 December, at night

It is an infinite humiliation to enroll here the names of the last several days; but for just that reason I shall do so and do so briefly.

If every death (like every life) has been allotted a certain portion of time, then days like the last ones will have to be counted up and deducted from its sum. For they are days spent beneath the earth, days in dampness and decay. But that's so Christian a strategem: to turn everything unbearable into consolation, it's the oldest philosophy in Christendom—and deep down I can't subscribe to it. I fear that such days don't belong to Death, just as they don't belong to Life. They belong ... O in-between land, if an in-between Spirit presides over you, an in-between God, then they belong to him, this concealed uncanny one. For this is what he wants. Such stretches of hopelessness, such gaspings of the soul. And should they once *not* recede, not come to an end, not cast away, not suddenly become untrue: if one had to name all this "I," this unspeakably disconnected, helplessly isolated consciousness that, cut off from the voices of silence, falls into itself as into an empty well, as into the depths of a pool that contains stagnant water and animals gestating in muck. What is one then? Who knows how many afflicted with this in-between existence live in lunatic asylums and die there. And it is so frighteningly easy to die in this state. It is dying itself. The growing indifferent and the balancing with the weight of one's own inertia an opposite pan full of doubts and putrescences. What good are the efforts one makes ever more sluggishly, ever more wearily, ever more laboriously, like voices of opposition growing fainter—won over by disgust? One's will is there . . . but it is like a piece of conduit that has hit rock. One tries: uprisings, ascents, one wants to get moving, one stands for a while, and it all comes to this: one lies down, lies down and is content to lift one's head just high enough to see what is standing nearby—people and things. One becomes ever so humble, humble to the point of baseness. Humble like a dog with a guilty conscience. Flat, without feeling and filled only with fear, fear of everything that does and does not happen, of what exists and of any change in what one can scarcely bear. Out of distrust one flatters. Crawls before every accident of the day, receives it like a guest one has been expecting for weeks, praises it, is disappointed by its scowl, seeks to hide the disappointment, seeks to erase it inside oneself, to deny it to oneself, deceives oneself, while one has already been deceived as it is, digs oneself deeper and deeper into confusions and lunacy, has dreams, wakens, wishes for an inheritance, a prince's title, fame, poverty and omnipotence, all at the same time, judges the value of everything now like a child by its golden glitter, now like a whore by profit and pleasure and night—is invaded by everything that happens, is screamed at by all the trivialities and obscenities of the day as by drunken gendarmes, takes up with a riffraff of ideas, drinks, gets drunk on muck, rolls around on stones, goes soiled in the company of cherished memories, drips dirt on consecrated pathways, takes things that piety has kept untouched into one's sticky, sweaty, swollen hands, makes everything common, held in common, common fiat. Pasts fall into impure fire, futures consume themselves in the womb of ill-used hours, put up a struggle, die. And only the unspeakable happens. Deluge and sin's malediction. And this again and again. And afterward living on again, undisturbed and not astonished? And not to think about the fact that it will all lie before you again the very moment you have overcome it . . . (no, not so proud a word as "overcome"), that the very moment it has grown shallow, has been left behind, and you start to feel the sand drying beneath your feet, it rises again and grows warm. God presides over Life and over Death. But he has no dominion over the in-between land, it exists in spite of his power and presence, has no space, no time, no eternity. Has only heartbeats of unspeakably sorrowful hearts suspended high up and frightened, unaware of one another, deprived of all relations and connections, switched off, without meaning, their beating possessing as little truth and reality as the royal proclamation delivered by a lunatic in a straitjacket before crassly laughing guards and frightened inmates . . . This had to be written as a sign for myself. God help me.   Midnight

13 December

PRAYER

> NIGHT, silent night, into which are woven
> purely white things, red, brightly mottled things,
> scattered colors, which are raised up
> into *one* darkness, *one* silence, —include me
> also in the weft of that rich variety
> that you acquire and persuade. Do my senses
> really still play too much with light?
> Will my face not always stand out
> as an anomaly in the world
> of objects? Judge by my hands:
> Do they not rest there like tool and thing?
> Is not the ring on my left hand
> simply there, and does not the light
> lie the same way, full of trust, over them,—
> as if they were brightly lit paths
> that branch no differently in darkness?
> If I really need say: what I shall
> call my life will always be:
> broad nights, not tired, full of gestures,
> early mornings bathed in sun
> and daytime hours close to earth
> and in relationship to shape and stone.
> A craft sufficient to fill the hands
> and One who keeps me veiled
> so that I can be unnoticed and alone
> and far apart and his and mine.
> And simple fare: greens and meal and bread,

and unassuming sleep, dreamsoft, close to death,
and good exhaustion, and after sunset,
to end each day, a prayer,
like a hill on which the soul stands
after its long labor, through day and vale.
And not one prayer like any other;
each one new, distilled from each new day,
imbued with new objects,
rich in some new degree of love,
the day's fruit, which, without wind, grasped
only by its own fully ripened weight,
breaks off and falls and falls
until God stretches out beneath it
like a rolling meadowland . . .
there it drops softly . . .

After many incredibly heavy and vague days, today I experienced an hour of sunshine in the woods.

On the evening of 14 December

Sometimes I remember in exact detail things and epochs that never existed. I see every gesture of people who never lived a life and feel the swaying cadence of their never-spoken words. And a never-smiled smiling shines. Those who were never born die. And those who never died lie with their hands folded, repeated in beautiful stone, on long level sarcophagi in the halflight of churches no one built. Bells that never rang, that are still uncast metal and undiscovered ore in mountains, ring. Will ring: for what never existed is what is on its way, on its way over us, something in the future, new. And perhaps I'm remembering distant futures when what never existed rises up in me and speaks.

On the evening of 19 December 1900

Today was the dress rehearsal of Gerhart Hauptmann's *Michael Kramer.* I sat with Lou all alone in the dark auditorium of the German Theater and waited. Churned up, furrowed open in my inmost being, I was like a plowed field, and when the great gesture of the sower extended out over me, I felt a sharp pang as the single seed dropped onto my bared heart. It was a day of conception, painful and solemn, the first of days crowding in the future that without the hurt and beauty of this inaugural one could not come.—The papers gave out that *Michael Kramer* is an "artist-drama," but it is much more than the drama of a man skilled in some particular craft, it is the drama of a human being, and even that is too imprecise and not sufficiently encompassing: it is hard to know what to call this play whose dramatic intensities increase so far beyond its theatrical frame, totally without regard for the stage's strength and proper measure. I know of no experience in the theater that I could set beside it. Sooner or later a drama like *Michael Kramer* had to arrive as a high point in the evolution of the modern drama, but just a few hours ago I would have sworn that this victory is far in the distance and would have thought that at least thirty years of delay, error, and anticipation separate us from this rich, beautiful hour, when what is deep and vital becomes visible on the stage in a way that it has never been shown before and yet in the only way it really *can* be shown. But today I will attempt only a very brief record of the most salient features of this play. We are introduced first to the nondescript mother of the Kramer family and the astute, serious daughter, Michaeline, the daughter of the father, and the two are discussing a third person about whom both are concerned (each in her own way)—Arnold, the son, the only son, the mother's son, a problem son, as one soon sees. We aren't informed directly about his life yet, but we learn that he stayed out again last night, and that it was close to morning before he came home. Michaeline, who is on her own and even helps support the family, withdraws from the strained conversation with her mother and prepares to leave to supervise her pupils' lessons. But at the last moment a visitor arrives, the painter Lachmann, a former student of her father's and her friend from a time when life had not yet approached the young girl so seriously, with such specific and exacting demands. This Lachmann brings his wife along, a chatty, insignificant little thing, the visible sign of that great resignation with which he has taken upon himself ordinary life in its smallness and almost comic mediocrity, in order at least to bear something—out of duty, out of diligence, out of habit. He has gone downhill or perhaps simply never rose. But in his own heart there *have* been heights and elevations in his life, there have been futures and promises, success and great happiness awaited him back then when he apprenticed under Michael Kramer and shared many unexpressed and openly spoken things with the latter's daughter, who was woven wondrously for him into everything that was on its way. But what was on its way never came and didn't reciprocate when Lachmann approached it. Perhaps he never seriously gave it a try—who's to know? And it doesn't really matter now, now that nothing in his life will ever change again, now that he is starting to turn gray and always, whenever he tries yet once more to enthuse over the future, winds up speaking half-smilingly about memories, about things long past that are paradoxically closer to the active and pragmatic Michaeline than to him. Over the conversations of these two people there hovers, untouched by the drama's events, a single mood; it is a reuniting full of resignation (a shared path in the rain), during which the two speak in an oddly clipped, elliptical fashion, presuming with a melancholy pleasure everything that they never actually said to each other, and yet that must have been the truth once, since now it will never be true again. Circumstances always conspire to surround the conversations of these two with commotion and restlessness, as if life would really rather not grant time for such talks that lead backward and are useless for anything new. With the superiority of someone who has made his renunciation, Lachmann can turn everything into a topic of conversation, and expired wishes and words look almost as if they had existed and were real—as if even today one could continue building on them, could erect factual life on them, if one had not long ago given up just this intention. Lachmann is the most insignificant human being in the play. He is a mediocre person with solid ambitions, his understanding is more a readiness to understand, his enthusiasm the seconding of someone else's enthusiasm, his strength the feeling of a duty, and his art the expression of that feeling. He is a student of Michael Kramer's, and Kramer nowhere says whether he thought Lachmann had talent; Arnold, the son, despises him. But Lachmann still feels that he owes almost everything to his former teacher, that his apprenticeship with Michael Kramer was his preparation for life, that he came to know seriousness there—that stern, quiet seriousness of someone creating, that inexpressible something that is etched more clearly on foreheads and hands than in words, the result of solitude that in turn makes one solitary and teaches one how to live in solitude. And so we learn that Michael Kramer, who scorns the title of professor, comes to his feeling for art and talent via life, and that he tries to help his students travel this long and arduous road on their own, a road on which most of them never actually reach art. Art, then, is for the painter Kramer one manifestation of life among others, to be sure the richest and most sublime one. He does not want to place material that in the hands of chosen ones can achieve immortality into hands that have not yet immersed themselves in life, have not yet bled and trembled and prayed. He is unpersuaded that before that happens anything great can come from them. Thus he is all the more stunned by the effortless, radiant sketches of his son, Arnold, whom, when the latter was born to him, he offered up with the feeling: "Not *myself*—but *him;* I won't reach it, *perhaps he will."* And this son grew up, disfigured by a hunchback, in the strange notions of the misshapen, grew up with the father in him, with this feeling: "First to be a part of life, first to *have* life." But life shuts itself off from him, the repulsive one, all doors slam in his face, and what should have been a quick victory becomes a long struggle, and what could have under different circumstances been a great struggle becomes a daily rout at the hands of an ever more insignificant enemy. Finally he tries to beg his way toward life by turning to the waitress Liese, from whose lips he must hear that he is nothing, has nothing, means nothing, will be nothing. . . . And all that is true. And yet somewhere he is still something, somewhere there is something proud, something quiet that has never begged, that remains there untouched by all humiliation, that does not grow, does not develop—but does not disappear either. But it has already retreated so far into his unconscious that he can't talk about it and has to lie and boast and translate this something of his he can't name into other possessions that people can grasp. Into money, into influence, into recognition. . . . He lacks all that, but people do grasp that this is what power is, and, indeed, power truly is within him. All his lies become symbols for it. He has a whole set of lies for each different person, and since we almost always see him in the company of one person only, we come to know him from various sides of his denial. He closes himself off most fiercely against his father; in icy vehemence, as if he were that part of the old man that is sick and hurts, he clamps himself up inside and lashes out. The gripping scene between father and son is still not the catastrophe; terrible as the effect of Arnold's callous denials are, over against the open, amicable, utterly unselfish nature of the old man—in the end he leaves, goes out unimpeded into his old life, into his final disgrace, failing, melancholy, fear, and death. But even *that* is not a catastrophe—there is no catastrophe in this play. For a time it seems that there is. Arnold has been found dead. Michaeline wakens the old man around one at night, and for a while, through the course of a few hours, the death he perceives is the catastrophe, the death of his child and a shameful death. And he rebels and quarrels and like an idolater tears at his god's face. Until they bring the boy to him; he stays alone in his studio with him, night after night, and then the day comes when the great grief that has been sitting silently beside him takes him into its hands and begins to work on him, and we watch how he changes in the hands of this grief. His words are not words, they are features of a deep face, purifying themselves, growing toward perfection, completing and enhancing one another. I have never witnessed such an event on stage, never dreamt of such a return of the monologue, such a force, simplicity, and beauty of the word, which transcends everything said and sung, which is actually only gesture, only stance and image and the opposite of "talking-about-something." The old man doesn't talk, he grows, and his monologue is the sound of his becoming greater. An infinite confirmation has taken hold in him. "The treasure that he couldn't lift, Death has raised." In Arnold's face there was only the reflection of ugliness. Death has torn away all the masks, opened all the drawers, and exposed everything. And Michael Kramer realizes that he wasn't wrong: it *was* there, it *is* there. He wasn't carrying an empty ark into the temple back then when he presented his newborn to eternity. He was holding infinite treasures aloft in his trembling arms, and Life didn't touch them, never unlocked the chest, either kept all the riches to itself or never found them. For Life is blind and frugal. But Death, like someone rich and powerful who knows the location of all gold, of all that is deepest and most hidden, has opened everything. "Death, this most charitable form of Life." This infinite righteousness, which lifts and protects, has recognized the person Life didn't grasp; the misshapen oddity whom everyone drove away he has received like a prince, this righteous Death. He is superior to Life just as Love is superior to him, and he is greater yet than Love, for even Love deserted the driven-off, the helpless one. Then it gradually dawns on the father that this is not a case of death, the death of a cherished only son, and a shameful death at that, given how all those see it who observe it from the outside and with conventional love; he feels it as something great, something that has befallen *him,* an experience that opens up his life's horizons and a grief that changes all the parameters of his feeling. It is as if God had revealed himself to him, so strong is his feeling of existence and truth and veracity at this moment of death. For there in the pillows the face of his boy lies opened like a book and he reads in it—reads word by word the confirmation that *it exists,* the thing that he no longer wants for himself, that he must know and accept now as present only for someone who will sooner or later arrive to take it in hand. What is time? Who would become impatient in the face of something infinite? What does it matter if such figures, mute ones unpracticed at betrayal, pass the sacred on to one another for a century longer, and if no one sees and experiences it: for ten centuries longer. Now, for a moment, in this dead countenance there stands displayed what *must exist.* And it *does* exist. Everything is as it should be; it *exists.* And we must continue on, strong, quiet, worthy precursors of the one who is on his way, who will not arrive in vain, the treasure seeker, the finder. Amen.

22 December 1900

Fragment: This life, which wants to be open and carefree and beautiful, involuntarily becomes a lie inside this twisted body, the way water takes on the color of the glass vessel in which it stands. But as soon as life has receded from this ill-fated son, he ceases to lie. On his cold, unmoving face there now stands a power, the existence of which one would have never guessed, had not a few brilliant sketches and studies betrayed it. But what he revealed was slight in comparison to what he was. From all the features of his dead countenance there now emerges, unafraid, his soul. And the father recognizes it: it is what he lifted high up back then with his trembling arms, without seeing it, believing—but now he sees it. And it is more exalted than he even dared suspect. It may not have grown at all in these twenty years, but it also wasn't touched by the pettiness and din and emptiness of this life, it *remained,* a soul waiting in patience and darkness. And *that it exists,* that is Michael Kramer's epiphany. He lives through a death, the loss of his only son, and the death is not *that,* not the loss: it is something that clarifies him, that makes the old man farseeing and full of wisdom and serene, a larger-than-life grief that changes all the measures and makes him incapable of ever again experiencing anything petty, insignificant, or fortuitous after something so triumphant, so immense. Whoever understands and honors Death correctly, grants Life greatness.

‖ NOTES ‖

(For figures who play especially important parts in Rilke's narration, short biographical sketches have been provided at the beginning of the notes to the specific diary in which they appear.)

THE FLORENCE DIARY

Lou Andreas-Salomé

Louise von Salomé (1861–1937) was born in St. Petersburg into a prominent family of Huguenot and German descent. Her father (1804–79) was a general in the czar's service and privileged to reside in the apartments of the General Staff across from the Winter Palace. Her family also maintained a mansion in Peterhof near the imperial summer residence. Although their only daughter lived mostly among immigrants and was brought up in the Reformed Protestant Church, she had a strong attachment to Russia. Her first important intellectual-emotional experience was the love of the (married) Dutch pastor Hendrik Gillot, a tutor to the czar's children, who gave her private lessons in philosophy, first named her Lou, and, at the age of forty-two, proposed marriage to her (she was seventeen). In the fall of 1880, accompanied by her mother, she went to Zurich to study philosophy and art history. Trips to various spas and to Rome followed, where she was introduced to the writer and early feminist Malwida von Meysenbug *(Memoirs of a Woman Idealist)* and to her circle of compatriots. Among them was the philosopher Paul Rée, a close friend of Nietzsche, who met her there in the spring of 1882. Both men were enthralled by her (Nietzsche proposed marriage almost immediately, Rée sometime later), and, after a brief ménage à trois, experienced successive fallings-out over what she saw as her independence and they as her promiscuity and unwillingness to commit. In 1886, she agreed to marry the Iranist Friedrich Carl Andreas (1846–1930) when, after the latest in a series of proposals (his) and demurrals (hers), he stabbed himself in the chest (barely missing his heart) before her eyes. They were married in June 1887, at which time Lou refused to sleep with him, an arrangement that held throughout their forty-three-year marriage. Her career as an author (at first of reviews, essays, and short fiction) began in 1890, when she had close contacts with the group of naturalist writers in Berlin. Extended sojourns followed in Paris and Switzerland (1894) and in St. Petersburg (with her friend Frieda von Bülow) and Vienna (1895), where she met Schnitzler, Hofmannsthal, and Beer-Hofmann, the most famous literary figures there. By the time she met Rilke in Munich she was well on her way to fame as an intellectually astute essayist and feminist critic as well as a significant voice in the fictional exploration of emotional conflicts.

Rilke's infatuation with her may have been sparked by his impressionable need for sympathetic reassurance. It was sustained, no doubt, by an unlikely erotic attraction, but also by the recognition of intellectual compatibility. There was an almost immediate understanding between two worldly God-seekers with an emotionally charged interest in theological questions. In the ensuing relationship Lou was able to rediscover her younger self in Rilke, even as she assumed the "teacher's" role of Gillot. And two sensitive and intelligent, though unequally experienced minds confronted important questions of art and life together and in the process enriched each other. Their closeness as lovers, discreetly guarded, lasted, in spite of Lou's marriage and their often contrary inclinations, until Rilke's decision in 1901 to marry Clara Westhoff. Though Lou dramatically broke with Rilke over this decision, the loss of the relationship was painful for her, and she began to suffer from cardiac irregularity, most acutely in 1905. During these years she had resumed an intimate relationship with her physician, Friedrich Pineles, whom she had first met and become sexually involved with in Vienna in 1895. He brought the needed stability back into her life and accompanied her on several therapeutic trips: to Venice in 1904, to Spain in 1905, through the Balkans to Turkey in 1908. Göttingen had become her permanent place of residence in 1903, when Andreas at last obtained an official appointment as lecturer for oriental languages at the university. It was at their house "Loufried," during a visit that lasted from 13 until 24 June 1905, that she and Rilke had their first reunion. This visit was followed by a trip they took together to see Lou's friend Helene Klingenberg (16–21 July) in Treseburg in the Harz Mountains. But neither their correspondence nor her diary mentions more than the mere fact of these encounters. The same holds true for their next meeting in May 1909 in Paris. Clara accompanied Rilke at that time, and Lou brought her travel companion Ellen Key. Rilke even had a copy of his new book (*New Poems: The Other Part*, 1908), inscribed simply "für Lou," delivered to her by (female) messenger. A second meeting in Göttingen in 1912 has left even fewer traces. It would seem that they did not truly resume their old closeness until Rilke's third visit to Göttingen (19–23 July 1914) and then during their frequent meetings in Munich, which continued until Rilke left for Switzerland on 11 June 1919, never to return to Germany.

By then Lou's interests had become concentrated on psychoanalysis, especially—almost obsessively—on the problems of narcissism. In this she was motivated in good part by the desire to understand Rilke's psyche better and help him with his problems. After first professional contacts—she attended, for example, the Congress of the International Psychoanalytic Society in Weimar in September 1911, accompanying her current lover, the Swedish neurologist Poul Bjerre—she moved to Vienna, where she lived from October 1912 until April 1913. She wrote to Freud, with whom she was to maintain a cordial working relationship based on mutual admiration. He invited her to participate in his Wednesday sessions and in his Saturday colloquia. During 1913, she joined Alfred Adler's discussion evenings. She also became friends with Anna Freud in 1921. In addition to her literary essays she published a number of perceptive psychoanalytical studies in *Imago* and other professional periodicals. But it was not until 1923 that she began her last career as a clinical analyst at a hospital in Königsberg. During these immediate postwar years her correspondence with Rilke became especially intense and intimate in a mature way, he writing of his poetic triumphs and of his declining health, she giving supportive advice and telling him discreetly how to live with his fears and uncertainties. Her last (known) letter to him is dated 12 December 1925, predating his last to her (13 December 1926) by a full year. But their written exchanges leave no doubt that, in the end and from a distance that was bridged by a spiritual proximity, they had become each other's closest intimates.

3   epigraphs: The two Emerson quotes are from his essays "Love" and "Circles"; the four unidentified excerpts are from untitled poems by Rilke that he later published in his *Mir zur Feier* (1899).

6   when, with kindred longing, I walked . . .: The allusion is to April 1897, when Rilke had returned to Munich (after a trip to Venice—his first Italian journey) but had not yet met Lou, who was living near his apartment at Blütenstraβe. See also page 32 and note.

7   Cascine: The Cascine is an elegant city park along the Arno on the northwestern periphery of Florence, famous for its nightly corso and promenade.

7   San Miniato: San Miniato al Monte, the former episcopal cathedral of Tuscany, lies on a hill overlooking Florence from the northeast. The dark green and gold of its mosaic glow brightly in the setting sun.

8   Endell: August Endell (1871–1925) was a leading Jugendstil architect and interior decorator in Munich who frequently visited Rilke and Lou Andreas-Salomé in Wolfratshausen.

9   Orcagna: Andrea di Cione, called Orcagna, a Florentine painter, sculptor, and architect, was active between 1343 and 1368. He designed the guardhouse Loggia dei Lanzi, construction of which began in 1376.

10   bright figures: Rilke stands facing the entrance to the Palazzo Vecchio near the northern corner of the Loggia dei Lanzi. As he steps forward and turns his eyes slightly to the right, he can see the line of portrait-busts of famous Florentines, which were installed beneath the arcades of the Uffizi courtyard in 1846.

13   Certosa of Val d'Ema: The Certosa of Val d'Ema is a former Carthusian monastery near the village of Galluzo a few miles south of Florence.

19   lecture on poetry: On 5 March 1898, Rilke gave a lecture titled "Moderne Lyrik" to the Deutsche Dilettantenverein, an academic association devoted to the promotion of

German culture in Prague. The key terms "confessions" *(Geständnisse)* and "revelations" *(Offenbarungen)* are used as vaguely in the lecture as they are in this diary. Rilke seems to have in mind something quite different from the raw self-disclosure that the idea of a "confessional" poetry is likely to evoke for a late-twentieth-century reader. According to the lecture, modern poetry is the work of a few isolated individuals who seek to fathom "the innermost solitudes of their being" and approach the "ultimate quiet sources of life" through an "unending dialogue with all things *[Dinge]*." Infusing the mysteries of *die Dinge* with an intense subjectivity, the artist brings forth beauty as the "rich language of his intimate confessions." Poetry especially, its questing implorations never to be assuaged, is an art of "revelations," personal and even very private, and of "unbounded confessions," which the poet seeks to express in a new form.

20   Burckhardt: Rilke refers here to Jacob Burckhardt (1818–97) and his "guide to the enjoyment of Italy's artworks," *Der Cicerone* (1855, 6th updated edition 1893).

21   Botticelli and Savonarola: In 1490, Girolamo Savonarola (1452–98) became prior of the Dominican monastery of San Marco in Florence, where Fra Giovanni Angelico da Fiesole had lived. He was a fervent reformer and iconoclast who castigated the Neoplatonism of Marsilio Ficino and the "pagan" worldliness of the circle around Lorenzo. His sermons attracted huge audiences, and his adherents, advocating a return to both municipal virtues and medieval (or what later in the diary Rilke terms "Gothic") traditions of religious severity, became a significant force in Florentine politics, especially after the expulsion of the Medici family in 1494. Botticelli was a convert to their cause; he is even rumored to have destroyed some of his works in a moment of Savonarolian zeal. But the reformers' opponents prevailed: after a spectacular trial instigated by Pope Alexander VI, Savonarola was hanged and burned at the stake in front of the Signoria on 22 May 1498. Vasari recounts how Botticelli went about trying to gather proof of the monk's innocence after his execution.

23   Medici villas: The Villa Medicea at Poggio a Caiano, some ten miles northeast of Florence, was built for Lorenzo by Giuliano da Sangallo between 1480 and 1485. The Villa Caréggi, three miles north of the city, was a medieval or "Gothic" castle when the Medici purchased it in 1417. In 1457, Cosimo il Vecchio commissioned Michelozzo to design its "Renaissance" expansion. During the time of Lorenzo it was this villa that hosted the Platonic Academy.

27   Kara Mustafa: Kara Mustafa, an Ottoman grand vizier, commanded a huge army in a campaign against Emperor Leopold I and laid siege to Vienna in the summer of 1683. He was defeated at the Kahlenberg by a combined German and Polish army (12 September) and lost another battle on his flight to Belgrade, where he was strangled by order of the Sultan on 25 December.

28   Marholm and Sudermann: Rilke groups Marholm and Sudermann together with Strindberg as three "notorious" dramatists of divergent purpose and unequal stature who share what many at that time considered a scandalously frivolous disrespect for bourgeois proprieties, both in their private lives and in their works. Laura Marholm

(1854–1905), born Laura Holm in Riga (Livonia, then a Russian *gouvernement*), was a popular dramatist *(Frau Marianne,* 1882) and journalist who championed the sexual liberation and social emancipation of women. Her writings on female psychology espoused a Nietzschean vitalism and individuality. During the 1880s she was close to the circle of naturalistic writers at Friedrichshagen near Berlin, where she became an acquaintance of Strindberg. Hermann Sudermann (1857–1928), an East Prussian writer of humble origins, was Germany's most widely performed and debated dramatist during the 1890s. His plays and novels depict the degradation of small-town life in Prussia during the period of rapid industrialization. The old-fashioned melodramatic forms in which he purveyed his naturalism made his social criticism highly popular among a usually antagonistic public and often provoked the scorn of the literary avant-garde.

28 "*im*-moral institution": Rilke alludes to an essay of 1794 by Friedrich Schiller (1759–1805), "Die Schaubühne als eine moralische Anstalt betrachtet" (The public theater considered as a moral institution), which advocates a bourgeois theater whose purpose would be to instill virtues and discourage vices.

29 dilettantish: Rilke probably has in mind Wagner's concept of a *Gesamtkunstwerk,* a "masterwork" that would fuse the individual arts of music, image, and word.

30 Lessing and "the transitional": Lessing's discussion of "das Transitorische" appears in section 3 of his *Laokoön oder Über die Grenzen der Malerei und Poesie* (Laocoon; or Concerning the boundaries of painting and poetry), written 1762–66.

31 Murat: Joachim Murat (1767–1815), one of Napoleon's most brilliant marshals and renowned as the greatest cavalryman of his age, was crowned King of Naples in 1808. After the emperor's defeat at Leipzig in October 1813, he signed a treasonous defense pact with Austria, which he broke when he learned of Napoleon's escape from Elba. Declining an offer of asylum at Trieste, Murat tried to recover his kingdom with only a few followers. But he was quickly captured, court-martialed, and executed at Pizzo (Calabria) on 15 October 1815.

32 fond of my Grasset, . . .: In February 1897 (i.e., two months prior to the time alluded to at the end of this diary's opening paragraph), Rilke took up residence in a boardinghouse on Blütenstraβe (literally: Street of Blooms) in Munich's bohemian quarter of Schwabing. At that time Lou was living at Pension Quistorp, locally referred to as the "Fürstenhäuser" (royal houses), in nearby Schellingstraβe. Rilke was reading Jacques Grasset, *L'antique Rome ou Description historique et pittoresque de tout ce qui concerne le peuple romain* (1796). Lou's novel *Ruth* (1895), a "tale" with many autobiographical elements, is the story of a sixteen-year-old orphan, Ruth Delorme, in St. Petersburg. Ruth is attempting to fulfill her "self-invented dream existence" by soliciting the love of her private tutor, Erik Matthieux, a married man with a partially paralyzed wife and an adolescent son, Jonas. She wants to achieve independence from her prominent and respectable guardians and become her adored teacher's "princely child": "To be permitted to love him meant: at last—at last the permission to be a child, to obey, to devote oneself, to give oneself away,—even if on one's knees." A worldly and less infatuated rival thinks of this as "poetry in conflict with life."

34 Benozzo Gozzoli: Benozzo Gozzoli (1420–97) painted the *Cavalcata dei Magi* frescoes in the chapel of the Palazzo Medici (later: Palazzo Riccardi) in 1459–60; his frescoes in Pisa's Camposanto (see pages 56–57), executed between 1468 and 1484, were partially destroyed in 1943.

34 Ferrara: The Council of Ferrara (1438–39) was part of the reform movement that had led to the convocation of the Reform Council of Basle (1431–49). In 1437 a quarrel had broken out over the appropriate venue for the discussion of a union between the Roman Church and Greek Orthodoxy. When Pope Eugene IV removed the council to Ferrara, his opponents in Basle declared him deposed and elected Amadeus VIII of Savoy to become his successor as Felix V.

35 the Medici: Lorenzo de' Medici, il Magnifico (1449–92), and his younger brother Giuliano (1453–78) succeeded their father Piero (1416–69), who was the son of Cosimo, il Vecchio (1389–1464), as rulers of Florence in 1469. Giuliano was stabbed to death at High Mass by assassins loyal to the rival Pazzi family, while Lorenzo escaped by fighting his way into the sacristy. Giulio (1478–1534), a natural son born after his father's murder, became Pope Clement VII.

39 a mother: Franziska Gräfin zu Reventlow (1871–1918), a writer and translator, came from a prominent family in Husum (Schleswig), where her father was a Prussian county administrator. She was disinherited in 1892 when she left her hometown for the bohemian life of Munich, where she initially wanted to become a painter. Rilke had been friends with her since his early days there; she mentions in an affectionate diary note of March 1897 that every morning during the difficult months of her pregnancy there was a poem from Rilke waiting for her in her mailbox. Her son Rolf was born on 1 September 1897; she never disclosed his father's identity, claiming she had wanted a child but not a husband. She and Rilke remained frequent correspondents. The letter from her may be a response to a poem Rilke wrote for her son on a postcard he mailed to her from Florence on 16 April 1898.

42 "Girls' Songs": Rilke's cycle of eighteen "Lieder der Mädchen," most of them written in Florence and Viareggio in the spring of 1898, were published in his *Mir zur Feier* (December 1899).

42 YOUR high hymn: The reference is to a poem by Rilke dedicated to Lou and titled "YOUR HYMN." It was probably meant to conclude *Dir zur Feier*, Rilke's book of love poems to Lou that he never published, largely due to Lou's objections to some of the poems' indelicacies.

46 Your letter: This letter does not appear in the published correspondence between Rilke and Lou Andreas-Salomé.

47 beach in east Prussia: Zoppot was a prosperous resort town near Danzig; in the 1890s it attracted some seven thousand visitors annually. See also page 74.

48 that summer: After graduating from the Graben-Gymnasium in Prague, and prior to enrolling at the university, Rilke vacationed at the Baltic resort of Misdroy during August 1895.

49 young Russian lady: Elena Michailovna Voronina (1870–1954), from St. Petersburg, was vacationing in Viareggio with her sister and father, a prominent botanist and member of the Imperial Academy of Sciences. She had traveled widely, was well read, and spoke several languages. Rilke's involvement with her was deeper than the diary entries suggest. He carried on an intimate correspondence with her after his departure and until they met again in May of 1899 in St. Petersburg (during his and Lou's first Russian trip), where he resumed his "courtship" of her. He broke off his visits to Elena when Lou showed annoyance at his absences from their scheduled social evenings, but he continued his correspondence with her after he returned to Berlin. Their relationship ended soon thereafter, when she informed him of her impending marriage (without, however, disclosing her new name, Kozicina). They met again by chance briefly in 1925 in Paris, where she lived as a destitute exile.

49 Wolfratshausen: Rilke, Lou, and Frieda von Bülow spent the summer of 1897 (from the middle of June until early September) in this rural village south of Munich near Lake Starnberg.

50 Dante's cenotaph: The cenotaph of Dante Alighieri consists of three larger-than-life-size figures and was placed in Santa Croce in 1829. It is the work of Stefano Ricci (1765–1837), a professor at the academy in Florence since 1802 who was influenced by Canova. A monumental statue of Dante by the Florentine sculptor Enrico Pazzi (1819–99) was unveiled on the Piazza S. Croce in 1865 as part of the public celebrations that commemorated the six hundredth anniversary of the poet's birth.

51 Pietra Santa: Pietra Santa is a town in the province of Lucca near the Ligurian coast and a few miles north of Viareggio.

52 that immortal triad: The triad *(Dreiklang)* is the fundamental principal of tonal music from the seventeenth to the nineteenth century. It is the accord, on either a major or a minor scale, of D (the root) and its third and fifth.

53 Giorgione and Lotto: *The Concert* was universally accepted as a Giorgione until Morelli attributed it to Titian in 1886. There is still disagreement over its authorship. The painting Rilke calls "the players" depicts a youth holding a sheet of paper, with a mature figure on his left pointing to it and a still older figure standing alone on his right. Lotto is only one of many artists to whom the painting has been attributed.

61 Lorenzo's poem: Burckhardt quotes these famous lines as the conclusion to chapter 5 ("Social Life and Festivals") of his *The Civilization of the Renaissance in Italy* (1860, 4th updated edition 1885), where they appear in the following form:

> Quanto è bella giovinezza,
> Che si fugge tuttavia!
> Chi vuol esser lieto, sia:
> Di doman non c'è certezza.

They introduce a song of Bacchus in the "Trionfo di Bacco ed Arianna" (written for the carnival of 1490) from Lorenzo's *Canti carnevaleschi*. Rilke translated this stanza and used it in "Der Bettler und das stolze Fräulein" (The beggar and the proud damsel), the penultimate of his *Geschichten vom Lieben Gott* (Tales of the good Lord) of 1900.

71   Lenbach: Franz Lenbach (1836–1904) was phenomenally successful as a portraitist of famous personages, including Pope Leo III, King Ludwig I of Bavaria, the emperor Wilhelm I, and Otto von Bismarck (in more than eighty versions). He favored a naturalistic style, with faces standing out against a neutral brown background. He frequently used photographs to achieve verisimilitude.

71   Böcklin: See the note to page 194, below.

THE SCHMARGENDORF DIARY

Clara Westhoff

Clara Westhoff (1878–1954) was at the beginning of a career in sculpture when Rilke met her in Worpswede in 1899. The daughter of a wealthy import merchant in Bremen, she had taken lessons—from October 1895 until March 1898—at a private art school for women (who were not admitted to the official academies) in Munich. There she met Vogeler at his studio in December 1897 and followed him to Worpswede in April 1898 as a student of Mackensen. She then apprenticed briefly in Leipzig with the sculptor Max Klinger, who had been impressed by her portrait bust of her grandmother, *Old Woman* (1898), when it was shown at the German Art Exhibition in Dresden. In December 1899 she moved to Paris where her friend Paula Becker joined her on New Year's Day, 1900. She studied at the private Académie Julian and under Rodin's tutelage for six months before returning to Worpswede. She and Rilke were married on 28 April 1901 in Bremen. Their daughter Ruth was born on 12 December of that year when they were living in Westerwede. Shortly after that they moved to Paris—Rilke on 26 August, Clara at the beginning of October.

Paula Becker

Paula Becker (1876–1907) was an accomplished painter who stood at the beginning of a remarkable though brief career when Rilke met her in Worpswede. Though her first contribution to an exhibit at the Bremer Kunsthalle in 1899 (two paintings and drawings) provoked derisive critiques, she was recognized soon after her death as the most original of the Worpswede artists, one whose modernist tendencies bear comparison with Gauguin.

She had moved to Bremen when her father, an official with the Prussian Railway Administration, was transferred there in 1888. At the age of eighteen she enrolled in a preparatory school for governesses and privately employed teachers, and graduated in September 1895. From April 1896 until 1898 she took lessons at a school for women artists in Berlin. She moved to Worpswede after a number of earlier visits on 7 September 1898, in order to study with Mackensen. On 31 December 1899, she moved to Paris and continued her training at the Académie Cola Rossi, a private studio in the Quartier Latin that was liberally supervised by the painter Philippo Colarossi. At the end of June 1900 she returned to Ostendorf, a small cluster of houses in the immediate vicinity of Worpswede, and became a regular participant in the Barkenhoff evenings. She and Otto Modersohn, a widowed older painter with a young daughter, were secretly engaged on 12 September 1900. Although she wrote him delicately ardent love letters, she also came to express doubts about their union—they married on 25 May the next year—and frequently corresponded with and visited Rilke in Berlin. Her death on 20 November 1907 from childbirth elicited from Rilke his longest and most anguished poem, "Requiem for a Friend."

Heinrich Vogeler

Heinrich Vogeler (1872–1942) was an artist whose etchings and book illustrations, many of them in a lavishly art nouveau style, made him famous for a few years at the turn of the century. He came from a prosperous family in Bremen, had studied at the art academy in Düsseldorf (1890–93), and traveled frequently: to Bruges, southern Italy, and Paris. He moved to Worpswede in 1894 as a student of Fritz Mackensen. There, in 1895, he bought an old farmstead with a large garden, which he expanded and refurbished to his own designs and christened "Barkenhoff." During an extended stay in Dresden he discovered a strong affinity for the paintings of Edvard Munch; in Florence he met Rilke and shared the latter's enthusiasm for Botticelli. In 1900 he returned to Worpswede from Munich, where he had collaborated with the *Insel* publishers A. W. von Heymel and R. A. Schröder, two major benefactors of the arts and crafts movement. In the spring of 1901 Vogeler married Martha Schröder (1879–1961). (See pp. 147–48, 169–70.) She was one of ten children of a teacher's widow in Worpswede. Vogeler worshipped her from the moment he met her in 1894—when he was twenty-two, she fifteen. In 1898 he arranged for her private education in the home of a wealthy acquaintance in Dresden. There she learned the craft of weaving, which she practiced professionally into her old age. The couple had three daughters, but their marriage was severely strained as early as 1910. They separated in 1920 and divorced in 1923, when Vogeler married Sonia Marchlevska, the daughter of one of Lenin's closest advisors. Vogeler had come to profess a utopian socialism, and in November of 1918 he was elected a member of the first Workers' and Soldiers' Council in Bremen. He established a commune at Barkenhoff in 1919 and, when it failed in 1923, donated the property to the Communist relief organization, Red Aid, which administered it until 1932 as a home for the children of fugitive political activists.

79   Schmargendorf: Schmargendorf was a small community and popular weekend vacation spot at the southwest periphery of Berlin, bordering on Grunewald Forest. The rural charm of this village contrasted with the more cosmopolitan appeal of the nearby resort towns Halensee and Dahlem. Rilke moved to Schmargendorf after his return from Florence in order to be near Lou, who lived there with her husband.

83   Lützow's Hussars: This largely ineffectual volunteer corps of some 2,800 infantry and nearly 500 cavalry troops (the "Black Band") under Baron von Lützow (1782–1834) acquired a legendary reputation for bravado after a desperate attack on Napoleonic units in February of 1813.

92   military novel: Rilke's plan to write a novel based on his experiences as a cadet in two military academies never progressed beyond the story of Gruber recorded here. It was published in only slightly revised form as "The Gymnastics Class" in Maximilian Harden's journal *Die Zukunft,* 10:18 (February 1902).

112 *The Book of the Good Lord . . .* and *The House:* The thirteen stories of Rilke's *Vom lieben Gott und Anderes* (Of the good Lord and other things) were published shortly before Christmas, 1900. The novella *Das Haus* (The house) appeared in the satirical monthly *Simplicissimus,* 5:5 (May 1900).

113 the drama: Rilke completed a "dramatic sketch" in two acts titled *Anfänger* (Beginners) at Easter, 1900. This playlet was published in 1902 as *Das tägliche Leben: Drama in zwei Akten,* after its premiere at the Residenz-Theater in Berlin on 20 December 1901. This performance, under the direction of Martin Zickel (1877–1932), was a complete failure and persuaded the Schauspielhaus in Hamburg to cancel rehearsals for a production there.

114 the song of the statue: This poem appeared as "Das Lied der Bildsäule" (The song of the statue) in the first edition of Rilke's *The Book of Images* (1902).

115 "Bridal Couple" and "Connections": "Bridal Couple" is possibly the title of a drama Rilke had begun in November 1899. Only a short fragment, the opening of act 1, exists. Nothing is known of "The Connections."

116 "Madness": Rilke included this poem in the second, augmented edition of *The Book of Images* (1906).

118 "Chanson Orpheline II": The section of this poem extending from "Nights are not made for the masses" through "and mean anybody—" was published as "Menschen bei Nacht" (Human beings at night) in the 1902 *Book of Images.*

121 *Poor Folk:* Rilke read Dostoyevsky's novel *Bednye lyudi* (Poor folk) of 1846 (first German translation as *Arme Leute,* 1887) at the end of 1899 in the original. He translated a "fragment" from it (the story of the student Pokrovskiye) "with great care" but could not secure its publication in the journal *Die Insel.* The manuscript of this version is now considered lost.

121 Nekrasssov and Biélinsky: The writer Nikolai A. Nekrassov (1821–78) and the critic Vissarion G. Biélinsky (1811–48) read *Poor Folk* in manuscript, as a work in progress, and were instrumental in preparing an atmosphere of eager anticipation of the work among the Russian intelligentsia.

121 Beer-Hofmann: The Viennese writer Richard Beer-Hofmann (1866–1945) had been at work since the summer of 1893 on a novel provisionally titled *Der Götterliebling* (The favorite of the gods), which was ultimately published in 1900 as *Der Tod Georgs.* Its second chapter has the protagonist Paul imagine orgiastic love-death rites celebrated during a spring festival in the temple of Astarte at Hierapolis, Syria. This vision is itself contained within a dream about his wife's slow dying. A short excerpt from this chapter, which Beer-Hofmann described as "a self-contained entity within the book," had been published in the exclusive art nouveau periodical *Pan* (for 15 November 1898) as "Fragment aus: *Der Tod Georgs*"; a longer excerpt appeared in the 4 November, 1899 issue of the Viennese weekly *Die Zeit* as *"Der Tod Georgs,* von Richard Beer-Hofmann, Fragment."

123 Lichtwark: Alfred Lichtwark (1852–1914), director of the Hamburg Kunsthalle, had been publishing the lectures held at his museum as pedagogical monographs since 1894. He was greatly interested in popularizing art appreciation and promoted scholarship on regional artists. His own study *Meister Francke, 1424* (published in 1899 in the series *Hamburger Künstler*), deals with a little-known altar painter from the early fifteenth century.

124 A poem at the *Edge of Night:* This poem appeared in the 1902 *Book of Images* as "Am Rande der Nacht" (At the edge of night).

125 "Whoever you are: . . .": This poem, under the title "Eingang" (Entrance), opens the 1902 *Book of Images.*

126 "The darkening . . .": This poem appears untitled in the 1902 *Book of Images.* In the 1906 edition it is titled "Aus einer Kindheit" (From a childhood).

129 Rubinstein: Anton Rubinstein (1829–94) was an internationally known concert pianist and composer.

130 "Again the woods smell sweet": This poem appears untitled in the 1902 *Book of Images.* In the 1906 edition it is titled "Aus einem April" (From an April).

133 Rodenbach: Georges Rodenbach's (1855–98) symbolist drama in four acts, *Le mirage* (published in Paris, 1901, but available the year before), draws on his famous "decadent" novel, *Bruges-la-Morte* (1892). It was first performed as *Trugbild* at the Deutsches Theater in Berlin on 15 September 1904.

133 "When you return . . .": The conclusion of this poem, beginning with "And thus we became dreamy violinists," appeared as a separate, untitled poem in the 1902 *Book of Images.* In the 1906 edition it became the concluding section of "The Son." (See page 207 and note.)

141 Stshukin Museum: Rilke saw the extraordinary collection of Western and Eastern paintings in the private gallery of the collector Sergei Stshukin in Moscow during May 1900. At this time he had moved into a small furnished room in the boarding house "Amerika" on the Vosdvishenka near the Kremlin Gate.

141 Worpswede: Worpswede was a poor farming community some fifteen miles northeast of Bremen in the Teufelsmoor ("Devil's Moor"). During the 1890s a small group of landscape painters settled there and, as the "Association of Worpswede Artists," frequently exhibited together, most notably at the Fifth International Art Exposition of 1895 in Munich's Royal Glass Palace. Their mentor was Fritz Mackensen (1866–1953), who lived there (except for one ten-year hiatus) from 1889 until his death. His friend Otto Modersohn (1865–1953), a fellow-student at the Art Academy in Karlsruhe, stayed for nine years before he moved in 1908 to nearby Fischerhude. Hans am Ende (1864–1918) joined them in 1889 after academic studies in Munich and Karlsruhe, and Fritz Overbeck (1869–1909) arrived in 1893 after four years of studies at the academy in Düsseldorf. He stayed until 1905. Rilke's monograph on the colony, *Worpswede* (1902), centers on the work of Vogeler, Mackensen, Overbeck,

Hans am Ende, and Modersohn, who agreed only reluctantly to be a subject of "art criticism." A sixth painter, Carl Vinnen, resolutely refused.

143 Hauptmann: Carl Hauptmann (1858–1921) was the older brother of the more famous dramatist Gerhart Hauptmann (see below, p. 261 and note). The son of a Silesian hotel owner, he studied philosophy and biological sciences under Haeckel and Eucken in Jena (1880–83), where he came under suspicion for his "subversive associations" and was once arrested on charges of being a socialist. After his marriage in 1884, he moved to Zurich and continued his education (1885–89). There he was influenced by R. Avenarius's "empiriocriticism" and became acquainted with a variety of social-utopian ideas. He wrote a brilliant dissertation (eventually published in 1893 as *Metaphysics in Modern Physiology*) and was expected to have a distinguished career as a philosopher of science (hence the diary's ambivalent *"Doctor"* Hauptmann). But he gave up science for literature when he moved to Berlin in 1889. Though he remained unsure of his talents, his stories and especially his plays, stolidly realistic and infused with the naturalism of the time, met with critical and popular acclaim. When Hauptmann visited Worpswede as a guest of Modersohn (he was only there for a week), he had begun to experiment with impressionist and symbolist techniques, still doubtful of his calling as a writer.

143 two sisters: The "two sisters" are Paula Becker and Clara Westhoff, not sisters at all but often romanticized as such in Rilke's imagination. This auspicious entry records Rilke's first encounter with the two women who were to loom so large in his emotional life during and immediately after his stay at Worpswede.

143 Holitscher: Arthur Holitscher (1869–1941), acquainted with Rilke since 1897, had left his native Budapest and the prospects of a career as a bank clerk for Paris, and then Munich, and a life in literature. He wrote novels, plays, essays, and, during the 1920s, a series of very successful travel books. Thomas Mann modeled the figure of Detlev Spinell in *Tristan* (1902) after him.

143 piano pieces: Strauss (1864–1949), Franz (1815–92), and Schubert (1797–1828) represent distinct phases of romantic lieder-composition.

143 "The Minstrel": "Der Spielmann" is an undated poem, probably written in the summer of 1898. Rilke included it under this title in *Die frühen Gedichte* (The early poems) of 1909, an expanded version of his *Mir zur Feier* (1899), where the poem appears simply as "Lied."

143 Nikolai Tolstoy: Count Nikolai Alekseyevich Tolstoy (1856–1918), who was distantly related to Lev Tolstoy, owned an estate in Novinki (northwest of Moscow on the upper Volga), where he was the landlord of the peasant-poet Spiridon Dimitreyevich Droshin (1848–1930) in the village of Nisovka. Rilke and Lou visited both in July 1900 during their second trip (9 May–22 August) through the Ukraine and Russia.

143 Hauptmann is extremely agitated. . . . : Paula Becker, in an entry in her diary (3 September 1900), casts Hauptmann and Rilke's opposition to him in a quite different light:

Dr. Carl Hauptmann is here for a week. He is a great, strong, grappling soul, someone who does not speak lightly. A great seriousness and a great striving after truth are evident in him. He gives me much to ponder. He read from his diary: "Things Contemplative and Lyrical." Harshly voiced German, weighty and inflexible, yet great and deep. Cast off your vanity and be human. Vanity erects walls between you and Nature. You can't get through to it. Art suffers accordingly. Grow deeper, live from the inside out, not from the outside in. And thus against Paris on my behalf.

In contrast to him Rainer Maria Rilke, a subtle lyrical talent, delicate and sensitive, with small, wonderfully poignant hands. He read us his poems, delicate and full of mysterious insight. Sweet and pale. The two men will never at heart understand each other. Realism and idealism perpetually at war.

144 "Over ocean waters . . .": The complete poem appears as "TO HUGO WOLF" in Hauptmann's *Aus meinem Tagebuch* (From my diary), published in 1900.

144 Kramskoy: Ivan Nikolayevich Kramskoy (1837–87) was primarily a portrait painter. Rilke greatly admired his two religious paintings, *Christ in the Wilderness* (1872) and the monumental *Derision of Christ,* which occupied the artist during the last years of his life and remained unfinished at his death. Rilke saw the painting in August 1900 when he visited the artist's son Anatoli to see the family's collection of his father's works. In the essay "Moderne russische Kunstbestrebungen" (Modern trends in Russian art), published 15 November 1902 in the Viennese weekly *Die Zeit,* but probably written at the end of 1901 in Westerwede, Rilke speaks of a painting by Kramskoy "called *Laughter."* It depicts, in Rilke's words, Christ surrounded by a derisive crowd that undulates with "great and small waves of that scornful laughter with which the rabble defends itself against those who are different and solitary."

145 Fidus: The Jugendstil artist Fidus, i.e., Hugo Höppener (1868–1948), was known for his drawings of ecstatic youths engaged in sun and nature worship.

148 Adiek: An experimental poultry farm on the small Oste river near Bremen, the property of Vogeler's brother Eduard.

149 Frau V. D.: Helene Voigt-Diederichs (1875–1961) was the wife of Eugen Diederichs, one of the German publishers of J. P. Jacobsen.

149 Peter Filippi: Possibly Pietro Filippi, an Italian stage designer and painter of theater sets who was active until the middle of the eighteenth century.

155 Frau Freitag: Perhaps one of the household helpers nicknamed via an allusion to Crusoe's man, Friday.

155 Frau Bock: The painter Marie Bock (1867–1956) lived in Worpswede between 1898 and 1902 as a student of Mackensen's before she left to study in Berlin.

155 *The White Princess: The White Princess* is a playlet in lyrical verse about erotic longings and the closeness of life and death. It developed from an idea or image Rilke probably

had conceived as early as 22 May 1898 in Viareggio, but a first version was not completed until the end of 1898 in Schmargendorf. Rilke mailed the manuscript on 13 July 1899 to the lavishly printed art nouveau journal *Pan,* where it was published on 15 July 1900 (vol. 5, no. 4). Plot elements of this "Scene by the Sea" find uncanny parallels throughout the diaries and in the relationships Rilke records there.

At the beginning of the play a young Renaissance princess, still a child when she was married ten years earlier and "as yet unredeemed," speaks of her loneliness to a soul mate, her younger sister Monna Laura. She imagines the clandestine arrival of a gentle dream lover who will come to her "from the soul of light." But a messenger brings news of the reality of an incurable plague that is devastating nearby Tuscan towns. As he comes to the end of his terrible report, the sun, in a display of its brightest splendor, begins to sink into the ocean. At this twilight moment the princess hears the oar stroke of an approaching skiff, but a silent *frate* in a black mask distracts her attention ever so briefly. And thus Love, perhaps no more than a visionary apparition, glides by unbeckoned, giving way to the unmoving presence of Death.

In the expanded version of 1904, which Rilke dedicated to Eleonora Duse (no doubt hoping she would play the central role), the two women resolve at the end to henceforth devote themselves to charitable work among their plague-stricken neighbors.

155 the painter's sister: Bianca Emilie ("Milly") Becker (1874–1949) was Paula's sister and a performer of classical music. She married the merchant Hans Roland in 1905.

155 songs of Mignon: In Goethe's novel *Wilhelm Meisters Lehrjahre* (Wilhelm Meister's years of apprenticeship) of 1795–96, the hermaphroditic Mignon sings four songs that subsequently inspired various composers, most prominent among them Schubert, Schumann, and Hugo Wolf. "So laßt mich scheinen, bis ich werde . . ." (Thus let me appear until I become . . .) appears in book 4, chapter 2, and was set to music by Schubert in 1821 (D 727) and 1826 (D 877, no. 3). The song Hauptman has repeated is Schubert's "An die Musik" of 1817 (D 547), based on a poem by Franz von Schober, "Du holde Kunst, in wieviel grauen Stunden . . ."

155 *Forest People:* Carl Hauptmann expanded his 1896 "drama in four acts," *Waldleute,* for its republication in 1900.

156 Dehmel: Richard Dehmel (1863–1920), a contemporary poet whom Rilke seemed to have greatly admired, published his poem "Mein Trinklied" in his *Ausgewählte Gedichte* (1900). The refrain "Dagloni, Dagleia" of the "Trinklied" from his collection *Aber die Liebe* (1893) was frequently parodied.

157 "Girls, those are poets . . .": This poem appeared untitled in the 1902 *Book of Images;* in the 1906 edition it was combined with "Others must travel long paths" (p. 204) to form a two-part poem with the title "Von den Mädchen" (Girls).

161 the Overbecks: Fritz and Hermine Overbeck were married in 1897.

161 Nadson and Garshin: The Russian poets Semyon Yakovlevich Nadson (1862–87) and Vsevolod Mikhailovich Garshin (1855–88).

161   a novella by Kleist: The work refered to is Heinrich von Kleist's (1777–1811) *The Beggar Woman of Locarno* of 1810.

164   Delacroix: Rilke apparently wrote down this aphorism from Delacroix's *Journals* from memory. He had read a longer version of it in a recent essay "Neoimpressionism" by Paul Signac (*Pan*, 4:1, 1898), who in turn had found it in Baudelaire's *Salon* of 1859.

167   half the size of this page: Modersohn's drawings were approximately 4 × 6 inches.

168   *Advent: Advent* is Rilke's third collection of poems, published in 1897.

169   "Annunciation" and the "Last Judgment": Both these poems appeared in the 1902 *Book of Images.*

169   Gerdes: Johannes Gerdes was an innkeeper in Worpswede.

171   Lev Levovich: Lev Levovich (1863–1947) was Tolstoy's eldest son.

171   Alexei Mikhailovich: Alexei Mikhailovich was the father of Peter the Great, and czar from 1645 to his death in 1676. Though he extended Russian control over eastern Poland and parts of the Ukraine, he resisted the incursion of European influence into Russian art and culture.

172   Ginsburg: Ilya Yakovlevich Ginsburg (1859–1939). Rilke saw his statuette of Tolstoy at the Radishchev Museum in Saratov in June 1900 during his return from Kiev to Yaroslavl.

172   Trubetskoy: Prince Pavel (or, Paolo) Petrovich Trubetskoy (1866–1938), an admirer of Rodin, had returned to Russia in 1897 after an extended stay in Italy (where he had had his own workshop in Milan since 1885) and opened a studio in Moscow. Rilke and Lou visited him there on 29 April 1899. His bronze statue "Tolstoy's Bust" (1899) went to the Russian Museum of St. Petersburg and was later bought by the Musée Luxembourg in Paris.

172   Secession Stage: The Theater of the Berlin Secession was a short-lived experiment that lasted less than two years (1899–1901). It opened officially on 15 September 1900 with a performance of Ibsen's *Love's Comedy* at the Neue Theater am Schiffbauerdamm before moving into its own house, the rebuilt former Quargs-Vaudeville Theater at the Alexanderplatz. Rilke tried unsuccessfully to arrange an exhibition of Russian art in its vestibule.

172   Lilies Studio: The "Lilienatelier" (named for a cloth wall-covering of heraldic lilies) was Paula Becker's studio in Ostendorf.

173   *Friedensfest:* Gerhart Hauptmann's naturalistic drama of domestic conflicts *Das Friedensfest. Eine Familienkatastrophe* (The Triumph of peace. A family's catastrophe) had its premiere on 1 June 1890 in a private performance of the *Free Stage* at the Ostendtheater in Berlin.

174   Fräulein B.: Again Milly Becker, Paula's sister.

174 "Thoma" poems: Rilke wrote three poems in honor of the sixtieth birthday of the painter Hans Thoma (1839–1924). Two of them, along with "To Music" and "In the Certosa," appeared in the first edition of *The Book of Images* (1902).

176 Loris: "Loris" was a nom de plume used by the Viennese poet and playwright Hugo von Hofmannsthal (1874–1929). His one-act drama *Der Abenteurer und die Sängerin oder die Geschenke des Lebens* (The adventurer and the singer, or the gifts of life) of 1899 is freely based on an episode from Casanova's memoirs: many years after their first encounter as lovers, the aging seducer, Baron Weidenstamm, returns to Venice and meets once more the singer Vittoria, who is now married and has a son by him, Cesarion, whom she claims is her brother. Their interplay develops variations on the themes of artistic freedom and social constancy, of pleasure and self-denial. Rilke had seen the first performance of the play on 18 March 1899 at the Deutsches Theater in Berlin in the company of Arthur Schnitzler.

178 Klinger: Max Klinger (1857–1920), famous for his ink drawings, etchings, and several monumental paintings with Christian motifs (e.g., *The Crucifixion,* 1890), had settled in Leipzig after studies in Paris and a sojourn in Rome. His symbolist paintings, most notably *Christ on Olympus* (1897, in Vienna), more and more gave way to sculptures, among them a polychromatic statue of Beethoven that combined onyx, bronze, and colored marble (1902), and a bust of Nietzsche (1904). Clara Westhoff worked in his studio for six weeks in August and September of 1899.

185 *Breite:* Rilke first became acquainted with Carl Hauptmann's drama *Ephraims Breite* (1900) in December of 1897, when he was among a group of literati who heard the author read from it at the house of the publisher Samuel Fischer in Berlin. (His description in the diary of his much later encounter with Hauptmann in Worpswede suggests that they had not been personally introduced.) The play premiered at the Lobe-Theater in Breslau (6 January 1900) before it opened at the Hamburg Schauspielhaus on 26 September 1900. Its protagonist, Breite, is the strong-willed daughter of a Silesian farmer, Gottlieb Ephraim. She is pregnant and fiercely in love with their foreman, Joseph Schindler, the illegitimate son of a tavern musician. She marries him against her father's wishes and against all social proprieties. Her new husband is unfaithful to her even on their wedding night and soon abandons her for the life of a "restless gypsy." This betrayal brings her to the brink of suicide, but as she is about to drown herself her sense of duty as a mother overcomes her despair. The "fallen woman" regains her honor by fervently devoting herself to her child, and she returns to her work on the farm with unbroken pride. Hauptmann characterized Breite (in a letter to Modersohn of 29 March 1900) as a "sovereign woman with monogamous feelings" whose "sense of honor as a mother wraps a cloak of pride and self-worth and dignity around her life as a woman."

THE WORPSWEDE DIARY

191 that winter: Rilke had journeyed to Hamburg with Vogeler in December 1898, and spent Christmas with the latter's family in Bremen. That Christmas was also the occasion of Rilke's first brief visit to Worpswede.

194   the banker Behrens: The banker Eduard L. Behrens (d. 1895), a wealthy patron of the
      arts who represented Belgian interests in Hamburg as consul general, had assembled
      one of the best private collections of recent art in Germany.

194   Böcklin: The Swiss Arnold Böcklin (1827–1901) was the most prominent symbolist
      painter in Germany at the turn of the century. He was a favorite artist of Paula Becker,
      who may have encouraged in Rilke an appreciation especially of his allegorical land-
      scapes and portraits. She saw in them both the influence of Botticelli and a strong sim-
      ilarity to the colors of the Worpswede moors, which she found to be "of the purest
      Böcklin mood." After Rilke's return to Schmargendorf, he frequently accompanied
      Paula on visits to Berlin galleries where they sought out Böcklin's works. On 11 Feb-
      ruary 1901, Rilke wrote a poem in three parts on Böcklin's painting *Frühlingslieder*
      (Springtime songs) of 1876, and dedicated it to Clara Westhoff, as he did a fragmen-
      tary poem (copied in a letter to her dated 5 March 1901) titled "Die *Pietà* von Arnold
      Böcklin."

195   Leistikow: Walter Leistikow (1865–1908), together with Max Liebermann, initiated
      the Berlin Secession in 1898. His favorite motifs were the woods and lakes of north-
      ern Germany.

196   "Prayer": This poem appeared under the title "Fortschritt" (Progress) in the 1902
      Book of Images.

196   Toorop: Jan Toorop (1858–1928) was a Dutch art nouveau painter.

196   Sichel: Nathanael Sichel (1843–1907), who had moved to Berlin in 1874, was noted
      for his "orientalist" portraits of young girls and women.

200   It was at that moment that I decided to stay . . .: A week after Rilke entered this state-
      ment in his diary he departed from Worpswede, not to return even for a visit until after
      his wedding in 1901.

204   "Others must travel long paths": This poem is untitled in the 1902 *Book of Images;* in
      the 1906 edition it is combined with "Girls, those are poets" (p. 157) to form a two-
      part poem titled "Von den Mädchen" (Girls).

204   Beer-Hofmann: For Beer-Hofmann, see the note to page 121.

205   Jacobsen: Jens Peter Jacobsen (1847–85), a Danish writer whose collected works were
      first published in German in 1888, was held in high regard around the turn of the cen-
      tury for his finely nuanced style. Jakob Wassermann recommended him to Rilke,
      who immediately felt a liberating artistic affinity and took him as a model for his own
      fictional prose. In a letter to Ellen Key from Rome, dated 2 April 1904, he mentions
      Jacobsen and Rodin as "the two inexhaustible masters" who both have a patiently con-
      centrated and penetrating way of observing nature and "the power to transform what
      they have seen into a reality that is a thousand times more intense. Both have made
      things, things with clear outlines everywhere and with innumerable overlapping in-
      tersections and profiles: this is how I feel their art and their influence." Rilke was es-
      pecially fond of *Fru Marie Grubbe* (1876; German ed. "with drawings by Heinrich
      Vogeler—Worpswede"), Jacobsen's first novel. He sent Paula Becker a copy of it as a

present on 18 October 1900 (i.e., two weeks after his unexplained departure from Worpswede). The story of Marie Grubbe (1643–1718), for which Jacobsen drew extensively on archival documents to evoke a distant historical ambience, is told as a sequence of "Interieurs from the Seventeenth Century"—so the book's subtitle—and recounts the heroine's rise to prominence at court and her search for happiness in love. *Niels Lyhne,* written between 1874 and 1880, is the story of a man without worldly ambitions who lives on his father's estate, Lonbarggard, until his death in the Dano-Prussian War of 1864. Rilke especially admired this novel for the way it blended psychological nuance, descriptions of nature, and a strong feeling for the historical past. The novella *Pesten i Bergamo* (1882) is centered around the appearance of flagellants among groups of carousers during an apocalyptic outbreak of the plague. *Fru Fönss* (1882) is the story of a forty-year-old widow from Copenhagen who travels to the south of France with her son and daughter. They disapprove of her marriage to a former lover with whom she moves to Spain. There she dies after five years, wavering between a desire for self-realization and a sense of duty to her children.

206 Fräulein Reyländer: Ottilie Reyländer (1882–1962) was a student of Mackensen's in Worpswede, where she stayed frequently between 1898 and her marriage in 1908, when she emigrated to Mexico. She later returned to Berlin.

206 "Are you still choosing?": At the time Rilke asks this oblique question of Paula, she and Otto Modersohn had been secretly engaged for two weeks.

207 "Song": This poem appeared in the 1902 *Book of Images* as "The Son." In the expanded 1906 edition, Rilke appended to it the excerpted lines from "When you return . . ." (See pp. 133–35 and note.)

210 "A young king from the North": This poem appeared untitled in the 1902 *Book of Images.* For the 1906 edition Rilke prefaced it with "Kings in legends . . ." (see note to page 225) and titled the composite poem "Charles the Twelfth of Sweden Rides in the Ukraine."

213 "You pale child . . .": In a letter to Paula Becker dated 5 November 1900—only a week before she announced her engagement to Modersohn—Rilke promises to send her a copy of this poem, commenting that "it does not really exist unless you have taken possession of it—especially this one that had its inception, so to speak, with you during these evening hours. . . ." The poem appeared in the 1902 *Book of Images* as "The Singer Sings before a Child of Nobles." In the fifth edition (1913), published seven years after Paula's death, Rilke formally dedicated the poem to her.

215 a Beethoven: Beethoven's arietta "In questa tomba oscura lasciami riposar" (In this sepulchral darkness let me rest) of 1807–8, text by Giuseppe Carpani, was written for Prince Franz von Lobkowitz.

216 "Sketch for a Last Judgment": Probably a preliminary version of "The Last Judgment," a poem that appeared in the 1902 edition of *The Book of Images.*

216 "Praise be to God on high . . .": "Gloria in excelsis Deo" (Glory to God in the highest) is the song of the angelic host (according to Luke 2:14) at the birth of Christ.

222   "Solemn Hour": The preceding two stanzas of the poem appear as follows in *The Book of Images:*

> Whoever weeps now anywhere out in the world,
> weeps without cause in the world,
> weeps for me.

> Whoever laughs now anywhere out in the world,
> laughs without cause in the world,
> laughs at me.

223   "In the faded forest": This poem appeared in the 1902 *Book of Images* under the title "Bangnis" (Apprehension).

224   "I know you're all listening": Rilke copied out this poem and sent it to Paula as a letter dated the same day as the diary entry.

225   "O how everything is far off": This poem appeared in the 1902 *Book of Images* under the title "Klage" (Lament).

225   "Kings in legends . . .": This poem appeared untitled in the 1902 *Book of Images*. For its place in the 1906 edition, see the note to page 210.

225   "I am there with you": Rilke copied out this poem in a letter to Paula dated 6 November 1900.

230   "On Receiving the Grapes . . .": Rilke copied out the first three stanzas of the poem in a letter to Clara Westhoff dated 8 November 1900, the day after the diary entry.

231   "Fragments from Broken-Off Days": This poem appeared in the 1902 *Book of Images* as "Fragmente aus verlorenen Tagen" (Fragments from lost days).

233   Sinding Concert: Christian August Sinding (1856–1941), a Norwegian composer influenced by Richard Wagner.

235   *The Death of Tintagiles:* Maurice Maeterlinck (1862–1949) published *La mort de Tintagiles* in a volume of three "petits drames pour marionettes" in 1894. It premiered at the Secession Theater in Berlin on 12 November 1900 under the direction of Martin Zickel.

237   "Blessing the Bride": Rilke sent this poem to Paula Becker as a letter dated 14 November 1900, in response to a letter from her declaring her "undying love" for Otto and announcing their engagement.

238   "Suddenly I know so much about fountains": This poem appeared in the 1902 *Book of Images* under the title "Von den Fontänen" (About fountains).

239   "I would like to sing someone to sleep": This poem appeared in the 1902 *Book of Images* under the title "Zum Einschlafen zu sagen" (To say to someone going to sleep).

240   "I have no paternal house": This poem appeared in the 1902 *Book of Images* under the title "Der Letzte" (The last of his line).

242   Lotte S.: Charlotte Scholtz; the poem was probably inscribed in her copy of *Mir zur Feier* (1899).

245   the poor girl who died in the South: The girl in question is Gretel Kottmeyer, a friend of Clara's from Bremen. The poem's speaker is imagined, as Rilke makes explicit in one of his letters to Clara, as Clara herself. "Requiem" appeared in the 1902 edition of *The Book of Images,* where it bore the inscription "For Gretel. Dedicated to Clara West-hoff." The dedication was removed in the 1906 edition.

251   Kropotkin: The memoirs of the anarchist Prince Peter Alexeyevich Kropotkin (1842–1921), *Memoiren eines Revolutionärs* (1900–1901).

252   the Boian: The legendary Russian folkpoet and bard, called "you nightingale of olden times" and "wise Boyan, grandson of Veles" in the opening lines of the twelfth-century epic poem *The Tale of Igor's Campaign.* Rilke composed a translation of this poem between 1902 and 1904 *(Das Igor-Lied. Eine Heldendichtung).* It was first published posthumously in 1949.

252   "Fragment": This poem appeared as "The Blind Woman" in the 1902 *Book of Images.*

258   Helene and Alma: Helene Klingenberg (1865–1943), née Klot von Heydenfeldt in Riga, was a close friend of Lou's in Berlin. Alma was Helene's sister.

259   Ivanov: Alexander Andreyevich Ivanov (1806–58) was a painter of Christian motifs (e.g., *Christ's Appearance before His People,* at the Rumyantsev Museum in Moscow). Rilke considered him the most important precursor of Kramskoy and the most authentic artist-prophet of Russia. He read Ivanov's diaries and letters in an edition prepared by Michail Petrovich Botkin and published simultaneously in Russian and German (St. Petersburg, 1880). Rilke also read a monograph on Ivanov by I. S. Orlovsky (i.e., Sophia Schill), published in St. Petersburg (1899).

259   Feighin: Jakov Alexandrovich Feighin (1859–1915), a theater critic and translator in Moscow, edited the journal *Kurier* (1897–1904).

259   Gertrud Eysoldt: Gertrud Eysoldt (1870–1955) was an actress at the Deutsche Theater in Berlin.

261   Gerhart Hauptmann: Gerhart Hauptmann (1862–1946), the younger brother of Carl, had trained for several years (1883–84 in Rome) as a sculptor and draftsman and had even taken lessons to become an actor. His career as a playwright began in 1889 with the scandal and sensational success of his first drama, *Before Sunrise,* which portrays the slide into degeneracy of a rich peasant family. Hauptmann was considered Germany's most versatile writer when Rilke met him. He was also becoming famous as a public personality, even a dignitary, in literary affairs, and acquiring the aura of quintessential artist and cultural icon.

261   Grete M.: Margarete Marschalk (1878–1957), whom Gerhart Hauptmann had met in 1889 and married after his divorce from Marie Thienemann in 1904. She gave birth to their son Benvenuto on 1 June 1900.

263 Josty's: A café with a large terrace at the Potsdamer Platz in the center of Berlin.

269 "Prayer": The first sixteen lines of this poem appeared as "Prayer" in the 1902 *Book of Images.*

270 *Michael Kramer:* Rilke and Lou attended the dress rehearsal of Hauptmann's "drama in four acts" *Michael Kramer* on 19 December 1900 at the Deutsche Theater, a performance that affected the poet deeply. Kramer is a painter, a solid craftsman of average ability but a revered teacher whose ethos and concept of the artist resonate with some of Rilke's own cherished convictions. Kramer has a daughter, who has accepted her averageness with businesslike resignation, and a deformed son, Arnold, who has succumbed to paranoid self-pity and has wasted his superior talent in bohemian debauchery. After a brawl with philistines in a tavern, he is found drowned, very likely a suicide. At the end of the play his coffin stands in the old man's studio near an unfinished painting of Christ that has occupied Kramer for seven years. His death mask hangs beside that of Beethoven—a reminder of his presumed proximity, in appearance and potential, to "the greatest of the great." Rilke quotes some of Kramer's words from memory and not quite accurately. In Hauptmann's published text, Kramer says of his son to a former student, Lachmann: "Was jetzt auf seinem Gesichte liegt, das alles, Lachmann, hat in ihm gelegen. Das fühlt' ich, das wußt' ich, das kannt' ich in ihm and konnte ihn doch nicht heben, den Schatz. Sehn Sie, nun hat ihn der Tod gehoben" [What now lies open on his face—all that, Lachmann, has been lying inside him. I felt, I *knew* it was inside him, und yet I couldn't raise it, this treasure. And look: now Death has raised it]. And: "Der Tod ist die mildeste Form des Lebens: der ewigen Liebe Meisterstück" [Death is the most charitable form of Life: eternal Love's masterpiece]. Rilke dedicated the first edition of *The Book of Images* to G. Hauptmann "with love and gratitude for *Michael Kramer.*"

INDEX OF WORKS BY RILKE IN THE DIARIES BY TITLE AND FIRST LINE

‖ GENERAL INDEX ‖